D1176309

"To move across strange contours of the earth's surface, to see stars never visible in familiar skies, to hear sounds that can only be heard in the high canyons of tropical rivers, to have time given by the Sun itself, and to discover the essential humanity of men who seem at first to be of a different species. . . . To realize a fraction more of the meaning of life on earth — that, in its absolute simplicity, is the point of it all."

Such is the spirit that moves the explorer Michael Swan, even as he asks himself whether the instinct to return to the primitive is not caged like a beast within each of us, even the most civilization-loving. We try to satisfy this urge with a picnic or a couple of nights in a pup tent. . . . But in this book the reader can go with Swan through the untamed jungle, penetrate the utterly wild country between the Orinoco and the Amazon, through the fabulous rain-forest, uncharted mountains and savannahs of the legendary Empire of Guiana — where the great Sir Walter Raleigh and later the steel-capped conquistadores hoped to find Manoa, the throne-city of El Dorado, the Golden King. . . .

Most people think of British Guiana as a strip along the coast, ten miles wide and two hundred miles long. Outside of a few prospectors, nobody goes into the interior. Even the natives "have never seen the jungle that lies a few miles from the Spanish conquest in which the chief smeared his body with turpentine and then rolled in gold dust — Swan describes the whole ceremony. The idea of original sin as a human fault, of a golden age preceding the sin, Swan found among the Caribs: the Carib Eden ended when the Caribs put Yurokon, the Bush Spirit's baby, into the pepper pot. Original sin here was cannibalism, in short.

Here is a great venture in exploration, full of danger and action — and information.

THE MARCHES OF EL DORADO

MICHAEL SWAN

*

THE MARCHES OF
EL DORADO

British Guiana, Brazil, Venezuela

*

> . . . yet unspoiled
> Guiana, whose great City Geryon's sons
> Call El Dorado   MILTON

> Guiana, whose rich seat are mines of gold,
> Whose forehead knocks against the roof of stars . . .
>   CHAPMAN

Beacon Press   Beacon Hill   Boston

PUBLISHED IN THE UNITED STATES BY THE BEACON PRESS IN 1958
PUBLISHED IN GREAT BRITAIN BY JONATHAN CAPE IN 1958

PRINTED IN GREAT BRITAIN

Contents

AUTHOR'S NOTE   11

The Two Worlds   15

PART ONE: The Forgotten Province   27

    The Forgotten Province   29
    The Anthropologist's Story   41
    The Barima   56
    The Falls of Towakaima   80
    Return   102

Interlude in Georgetown (1)   105

PART TWO: The Country of El Dorado   115

    Savannah   117
    The Country of the Makushis   139
    Wapishanas   160
    The Little World of Tiny McTurk   172

Interlude in Georgetown (2)   184

PART THREE: The Road to Roraima   187

    Up the Wide Mazaruni   189
    To the Mother of the Rivers   220
    The Way Back   254

Envoi   266

APPENDIX A: In Search of El Dorado   271

APPENDIX B: The Caribs   282

APPENDIX C: A Note on the Carib Language   292

APPENDIX D: Archaeology of British Guiana   295

APPENDIX E: The Schomburgks in British Guiana   297

APPENDIX F   298

BIBLIOGRAPHY   299

INDEX   301

Illustrations

1 A Venezuelan Indian met on the Savannahs, with fishing rods. *facing p.* 128

2 On the march through the forest of the upper Kamerang, on the way to the savannahs. 128

3 Akawaio woman expressing poisonous acid from a *matapi* full of scraped cassava. 129

4 Akawaio girl making a bead apron. The beads for the aprons are one of the most valuable currencies in the remoter Indian country. 129

5 The headman of a savannah village in Venezuela demonstrating the blowpipe. 144

6 Scene in an Indian hut. 144

7 William and Cecilia at the camp near the foot of the escarpment of Roraima. The ascending cornice is the route taken to climb the mural face. 145

8 At the foot of the mural face; the air is misty from the waterfalls coming from the top of the mountain. 145

9 Carib Indian boy fishing. 160

10 Indian girl, with a load of cassava roots in her *warishi* and holding a cutting of sugar-cane. 160

11 Just before sun-down most primitive Indians go down to the river to bathe. Modest to the last they cover themselves with their hands after removing their bead aprons, in the case of the women, or the red linen 'lap' in the case of the men. 160

12 The *benab* near the Towakaima Falls: the elder Marques in the centre, Robert to the right. 161

ILLUSTRATIONS

13 Indian boys at blowpipe contest.   161

14 Father Mather against the adobe walls of the St Ignatius
    Mission in the Rupununi savannahs.   176

15 Teddy Melville, second son of H. P. C. Melville, a Scot
    who settled in the Rupununi some sixty years ago and
    took an Indian wife.   176

16 Tiny McTurk.   176

17 Land-Rover in the southern savannahs of the Rupununi.   177

18 Tiny McTurk in the living-room of his ranch-house,
    repairing a gun. Note the various Indian trophies
    hanging on the wall to the left.   177

19 A seven-foot *arapaima* after landing by Tiny McTurk,
    with spear head still embedded in its back.   208

20 One of the most vicious varieties of *pirai* (or *piranha*),
    the cannibal fish found in the Amazon system of rivers.
    Its teeth can cut a piece of strong wire in one snap.   208

21 Taking a power-driven boat through white water.   208

22 Aerial photograph showing islanded nature of the
    Mazaruni and Potaro Rivers. The islands create great
    problems of current for the river-craft.   209

23 Hauling a boat over the top 'bump' of a patch of white
    water on the Essequibo River.   209

24 The Grumman amphibian landing on the Upper
    Mazaruni at Kamerang Mouth.   224

25 Akawaio Hallelujah Indians dancing to Hallelujah
    chants. The dancing is liable to continue throughout
    an entire night.   224

26 Removing bark as first stage in the making of a
    'woodskin' canoe. The bark must be removed at the
    season when the sap is rising.   225

27 Akawaio Hallelujah Indians at prayer at Imbaimadai, on Upper Mazaruni.   225

28 On the summit of Roraima, during a period free from mist: Austin in front, Peter behind.   256

29 The author approaching the mural face of Roraima.   256

30 The early morning view from the camp on Roraima across to its twin mountain, Kukenaam.   257

31 Arekuna Indian and his wife.   257

32 Arekuna Indians outside their open hut.   257

33 Arekuna Indian with his grandchildren.   272

34 Akawaio girl.   272

35 Austin caulking the woodskin he found at the Ataro landing.   272

36 The Kaieteur Falls, with the Upper Potaro River beyond.   273

Photographs nos. 3, 4, 6, 9, 13, 16, 20, 24, 25 and 26 are by David Attenborough; nos. 11, 17, 18, 19, 21, 22, 23, 27 and 36 are the property of the C.O.I.; the rest were taken by the author.

Maps

British Guiana   28

The Pakaraima area of British Guiana   188

Author's Note

THIS book is primarily an account of three journeys which I made, during the first half of 1955, into the Interior of British Guiana, our only colony on the continent of South America. On the third journey, to the plateau mountain of Roraima, I travelled across the Gran Sabaña of Venezuela and the high forests of Brazil. I had been invited to visit British Guiana by the Colonial Office, and I should like to express my gratitude to the Colonial Office and the Government of British Guiana for easing the difficulties of my travels through remote and difficult territory. On occasions these difficulties were solved by the use of a Grumman amphibian aeroplane. During my longest and most interesting journey, to Mount Roraima, I used the Grumman only for one short lap — because I wanted to have the sense of a slow overland journey by foot and canoe. But it is, I think, an affectation to despise the use of the aeroplane for travelling in remote territories. Besides giving a new dimension to travel it avoids the tedium of days on the estuaries of dull rivers and allows one to see far more of the country than would otherwise be possible.

In the interior of the colony the traveller must often rely on the hospitality of settlers, mining and timber camps, ranchers and Indian tribes. I would like to acknowledge with gratitude the kindness and hospitality which I received from Mr Coffy and Mr Smith of the manganese camp in the North-West, Mr and Mrs Charles Melville, Mr John Melville, Mrs Caesar Gorinsky, Mr and Mrs Ben Harte, Mr and Mrs Edward McTurk, Mr R. Turner, Mr and Mrs William Seggars and Mr Reggie Hill. Though they will never read these words, I must put on record my gratitude to my Indian guides and porters, Cyril and Rodrigues Marques, Austin and Peter Vierra, Antonio, Samson, William and Cecilia; and to the people of the Indian villages through which we passed, who always gave us so good a welcome.

I would like here to give a key to my use of names for the various races who live in British Guiana. I have called all Africans born in the colony 'Creoles', Indians whose origin is India proper, 'East Indians', and American aboriginals 'Indians' — avoiding the use of the cumbersome word 'Amerindian', which is in general use in British Guiana.

I have included two short descriptions of the coastal scene, a world entirely different from that of the Interior, in order to make some relation between the 'Sea Wall' and the 'Bush'. Little more than two per cent of the colony's population live outside the narrow strip of land which forms the coastal region.

Finally, I should like to thank Mr David Attenborough for allowing me to reproduce many of his remarkable photographs of the Guiana Interior. My own photographs of similar subjects could not bear comparison with his, and I have used my own photographs only in cases where better ones were unobtainable.

M. S.

For
MY MOTHER

The Two Worlds

NOTHING is foreign: parts relate to whole': it is a line from Pope's *Essay on Man*. When I am on the move, cheek by jowl with hens and pigs in some ancient Mexican bus, urging an unwilling mule through the inhospitable rain-forest, or admiring a recommendation of Baedeker in some sunny Italian town, I like to assure myself that nothing really *is* foreign, that all are but parts of one stupendous whole, as Pope puts it elsewhere. It is not a rational feeling, but the traveller who rationalizes is a lost man; he must let himself make those unlikely connections between very different things, and if he follows his nose long enough, obeys enough of the urges that beset him, he may, if he's lucky, see that parts have a way of relating to whole. I suppose most travellers are, like myself, obsessed by that 'otherness', that *'pothos'* which drove Alexander the Great to the extremes of the known world. There seemed to me, at one time, no greater otherness than the tropics of the New World. Fabulous jungles, strange animals without comparison in the Old World, Indian tribes with customs, lore and music that had their roots in cultures which had grown up in isolation till the Spanish conquerors and their followers began their own modifications; ancient ruins to be seen, even perhaps to be found, and life to be lived close to the earth, in contact with an untouched Nature. In Italy all Nature has been tampered with, the hills of Tuscany and Umbria form a landscape that is almost entirely humanized. Nature and Man supplement each other. Norman Douglas gave a warning to those who had fallen under the spell of the Mediterranean: never to forsake it in search of other worlds. 'The lovely islands of the Pacific', he wrote, 'have a past, but their past is not our past, and men who strike deep roots in such alien soil are like those who forsake their families and traditions to live among gipsies.' It is a solemn warning, but I cannot accept it. When a man has lived among gipsies he understands his own family and traditions all the better on his return. I loved this humanized landscape of Italy. I loved it enough to want to live in the wild areas of the world where Man, if he had been there, had drawn back from the scene, knowing that Nature was the master. I wanted to move through a country where civilization had not yet made a balance between man and his environment.

And now I write in Italy. In front of me is a seducing panorama of humanized valleys and hills, to which I shall raise my eyes from that other world, lying between the Orinoco and the Amazon, which is the subject of this book. It is a land veined with great rivers, a thousand lesser rivers and thousands more rivulets and creeks, a 'land of water' as its name, Guiana, signifies; where man has colonized only the flat coastal fringe, and planted his sugar and rice, leaving the vast tracts of the Interior to Nature and the Indian. Its features have been mapped, but the details of its geography are on no map, must be laboriously discovered by the traveller for himself as he pushes through the forest; foothills, escarpments, unknown or suspected cascades, falls three times the height of Niagara, creeks that bear gold or diamonds, great blocks of flat-topped sandstone, hills of solid iron or manganese — you may come across any of these by luck, or pass them by within a few hundred yards, with misfortune. I missed seeing one of the most beautiful falls in the world, discovered only in 1938, because the map I was using at the time didn't mark the fall. It lay barely half a mile from my route but the roar of the falling water, stifled by the walls of the gorge, seemed no more than the murmur of a fast-moving river, and I paid no attention to it. Geologists have mapped the broad pattern of its stones, but who knows what minerals lie in isolation, in places far from the river routes and the jungle trails where no man, not even the Indian, has ever penetrated? This is the country of El Dorado or, rather, where the myth-makers finally placed the country of the gilded king. Sir Walter Raleigh's romantic obsession may have been based on wild hopes and Indian tales, but the great rushes of the 1880s and 1890s, in north-west British Guiana and east of the Orinoco, proved his obsession no mere fancy. The colony dreamt of immense riches, of an endless reef of gold to rival the Rand, and no sooner had the dream been formed — and Great Britain on the verge of war with Venezuela to defend her Orinoco possessions —

than the gold was no more. El Dorado had been discovered and consumed.

The coastal fringe of Guiana which came into British possession from the Dutch in 1811 is the size of England and Wales and has the population of, say, Coventry. A sea muddied with the pink detritus of the rivers is kept from a coastland below the level of the sea itself by a sea-wall. Inland from the cultivated fringe the land rises slightly into a great desert swamp on which, throughout the year, the sun glistens between the perpetual clouds, a desert only relieved by patches of manicole and trulli palms. Beyond the swamps the forest, endless, compact, steaming after rain, its unseen creeks beneath the tree canopy draining into the rivers and rivulets. Here the forest may undulate but it never rises much above the level of the sea. Then, without warning it seems, the land rises fifteen hundred feet or more to form a vast shelf of sandstone, sometimes with grandiose gorges receiving the waters of the rivers at the higher level. It is at points along this shelf that the great falls occur — Kaieteur, Peaima, Princess Marina, Jane's, Art's, Maila, Nitshi. The land on the shelf itself begins flat as the land below, then turns into the foothills to the divided system of mountains which runs the length of the Guianas and without which it would not be a land of rivers. These mountains — flat-topped monsters of sandstone for the most part — emerge like islands or vast fortresses from the surrounding sea of jungle and savannah. They are the key to the geography of Guiana; in shape they are like no other mountains in the world, with their mural precipices and weirdly eroded summits from which the streams cascade to the land below, later joining forces with other streams to form the great rivers — the Essequibo, the Mazaruni, the Cuyuni, the Corentyne, the Berbice. It is these mountains that make the rain that makes the rivers, and make the clouds that sweep across Guiana throughout the year; warm winds laden with moisture from the Caribbean and the Atlantic move across the country unimpeded until they meet the land mass of the mountains. To avoid the mountains they must move higher where the cold air turns their moisture into rain, clouds and mist. Clouds are always clinging to the plateaux of the mountains, even when the surrounding sky is blue and clear, and even in the dry season the cascades from the summits flow continuously, though diminished. When the heavy rains come, the precipitation of the waters from so many sources can make the rivers rise thirty feet in a day.

Beyond these mountains to the south lies an area of British Guiana which belongs to another geographical region — the Rupununi savannahs, a small British section of the vast savannahs of Brazil. It is yet another world, intersected by the Kanuku Mountains, an uninhabited arm of hill, forest and river which Guiana proper thrusts out into the impoverished grassland. These savannahs will have their place in this book; the forest, the river, the mountain and the savannah, these will be its main protagonists; with man, white, copper and black, the lesser, labouring always against the enormous power of natural elements.

I think of a party I went to in Georgetown a day or two before I made my first trip into the Interior. The party was conceived with some wit; an '1855 bathing party', the invitation had said, with dress according. It is the constant complaint of the English in Georgetown that there is no bathing of any sort. 'There will be no bathing', said the invitation card, laconically. Subalterns of the Black Watch turned up wearing parallel striped bathing suits immaculately cut by local shirtmakers, with side-boards and red cheeks. Our host, the Governor's A.D.C., appeared as a superb reproduction of a *Punch* paterfamilias emerging from his machine at Brighton. The women, young government officials' wives or wives of the executives of the sugar firms, had spent long and ingenious hours with their dressmakers. Iced rum-punch flowed, the buffet was laden with spiced West Indian food which, at its best, rivals the food of any country, and the gramophone played sambas and mambos. A happy, splendidly absurd scene, and even more absurd when one realized that the artificially ample Victorian bather talking to the thin man wearing a converted rugger jersey was the head of the C.I.D., and that he was in earnest conversation with a sugar official about the imminent split in the People's Progressive Party; would Cheddi Jagan be able to retain power, was the communist domination of the party diminishing? Wherever people talked it was of this, or some other matter connected with the intricate politics of the colony. The frivolity of the scene was skin deep; almost everybody present was at the unceasing, frustrating but irresistible game of putting the colony right.

Hardly anyone in that room had been into the Interior. Most professed some interest in it and showed none; their lives were lived on the coastal fringe, bounded by their work, politics, the essential social round. Sensibly, whenever they took leave they flew up to the Caribbean to lounge on the glorious sands of Tobago or Grenada. For them British Guiana was two hundred miles long and ten miles wide; the Department of the Interior, run by eccentrics who 'liked that sort of life', ran the Interior and that was that. New arrivals in Georgetown who showed too much interest in the Interior as a place to travel in were made to realize that they were in some way guilty of an error in taste. I never knew whether this was born of a sense of dissatisfaction with the flat but not unbeautiful coastlands, or was rooted in the old economic necessity that the labour should be kept on the coast by not opening up the Interior. Certainly this suspicion of the Interior is not confined only to the whites. There is a special type of Creole who prospects for gold and diamonds for months at a time, but in general the coloured people of the coast have never even seen the jungle that lies a few miles from their homes, and think of it as a place infested with dangerous beasts and, particularly, the massakruman, the wild bushman, an animal of semi-human aspect.[1] An unfortunate result of this fear is the failure of Government's attempts to encourage the excess population of the coast to settle in the Interior and make agricultural land on the banks of the rivers. There is some attempt among the Creole intelligentsia to be conscious of the country beyond the coast, and Mr A. J. Seymour has written a fine poem on *The Legend of Kaieteur*. But in the main the intellectuals are more properly concerned with hammering out the question of the form their Guianese or West Indian culture should take, with producing a civilization based on that of Europe, yet not a sycophantic copy. Thus, unlike the English, they cannot yet afford the luxury of

---

[1] Charles Waterton had the massakruman in mind when he converted the head of a red howler monkey into a vaguely human head and, with all seriousness, passed it in Europe and in his *Wanderings* as a 'nondescript' found by him in the Guiana forest. When reviewing the *Wanderings* Sidney Smith denied the head's origin. 'It is', he wrote, 'clearly the head of a Master in Chancery — whom we have often seen backing in the House of Commons after he has delivered his message.' Many believed Waterton's claim but accused him of an act tantamount to murder.

inquiries into Indian folklore or a passionate feeling about the beauties of the Guiana forests.

I had learnt my lesson early and talked of the Interior only with people whom I knew to love it: a retired District Commissioner living in my hotel, or the erudite Director of the Museum. Since I had never actually travelled in the Interior of the colony they gave me advice, but looked on me as a greenhorn who must prove himself before being admitted to an easy intercourse on the subject. In the end I think I won my spurs in their eyes, but at this time they would smile a little when I casually referred to the books of Robert and Richard Schomburgk or the explorations of Barrington Brown; what did books mean when I had never trod the country itself?

In the early hours of the morning I left the party with a friend. Delicious cool breezes were blowing in from the sea, the chorus of the tree-frogs now the only sound, high-pitched like the interrupted song of some nocturnal bird, with the background of other species clicking like castanets, whirring like rapid wing-beats, cicada-like — and soon for me the unheard accompaniment to every night. The courting couples had ceased their passionate activity on the sea-wall, the moon was up, lighting the cloud masses. My companion suggested we should go to a certain bar — I must explain, incidentally, that we were now decently dressed — where we might find a character exotic enough to delight any writer. We found the bar in a fairly respectable quarter of the town. A group of Creoles were talking at a battered table, knocking back snaps of rum. 'All fools got d'eir own sense', one of the men was saying as we approached the bar, and the other replied: 'Yes, but him saucy, him got a major opinion of he'self.' From an inner room came the click of billiard balls.

'Is —— here tonight?' my companion asked the barman.

'Him here,' said the barman, with a broad grin, 'and him gone spent all o'ten dollar this night. In d'back room.'

We went into the back room. Sitting alone at a table in one corner was a smallish Englishman in his fifties, dark by nature but now with the brittle brown skin that comes from long exposure to the tropic sun. He was dressed in worn khaki drills, with a whitish open-necked shirt. He eyed us as we stood together drinking for some moments; then my companion, who knew him only by reputation, turned to him and invited him to have a drink.

I did not expect to hear the words that came in reply, nor the extremely cultured voice in which he spoke them.

'Yes,' he said, 'I'll bloody well take a drink from anybody who offers me one.'

We drew up two chairs and clapped for the barman. Although our guest had evidently drunk well that night he showed little sign of it. One knew that he was a man whose life would have taught him to carry his liquor to the end. He drank his rum and made no attempt to be sociable. We talked nothings to him for a while and then he said, quite politely and again in his unexpected accent: 'You know, if you expect me to talk about myself for one damn snap of rum you're mistaken. I'm sick to death of telling people my story. If you can get me a British passport *ça va bien*, or if you've got news of a good diamond location *ça va toujours bien*, but if you've just come to gape at me like a pair of bloody tourists — I tell you again, I don't talk for one snap of rum.'

We called for a bottle and for the next hour or so I tried to piece together a coherent picture of the life of this strange man, who seemed so entirely English and yet had no passport. Sometimes he spoke incoherently and with acrimony against certain relations of his. Poverty and years of misery had left their mark on his testimony, but it was not as bitter as it might have been. I checked his story with as many people as I could while in British Guiana, picking up his trail at various points in the Interior, in the North-West Province, at Bartica and the mining village of Arakaka. His name was known wherever I went, and each person who talked to me about him had a story to tell.

The first thing he told us, and the first thing I was always told about him, was that he was the illegitimate son of a peer of the first creation; and there can be no doubt that this is true. His mother went to Paris for his birth, and by French law he thus became a French citizen. His education was in England, but I gathered that he hadn't been sent to a public school; he lived with his grandmother — whether maternal or paternal I cannot say. As a very young man he went to live in France, where his grandmother supported him in some style, although when he spoke of his high-living visits to the Riviera I sensed a touch of fantasy. A quarrel with his family and his grandmother followed and, unprepared to earn his own living, he turned to petty thieving. This was a disappointment to me. I had expected him to describe some fantastic coup as a confidence trickster in the Carlton, Cannes, or tell us how he got away with the priceless jewels of a maharanee. But according to his story he never received a conviction for anything greater than petty larceny. These convictions were frequent, and finally, in the early 'thirties, he was convicted as an inveterate thief and sent to Devil's Island — or more properly, to the penal settlements of French Guiana. The voyage, as he described it, equalled in horror the dreaded middle passage of the slave-ships from the Ashanti coast to the islands of the Caribbean. Life in Cayenne was a life of semi-slave labour, sordid, brutal and corrupt, a life of almost futile reclamation of the forest-covered land for unwilling colonists. As he spoke I felt more than ever that France's reputation for being a good colonizer is not supported by fact. It was Napoleon III who matched the stupidity of his intervention in Mexico with the scheme to colonize French Guiana with convicts who, at the end of their sentence, were to be given land and forced to remain in the colony. —— was a convict there for more than fifteen years, learning every trick and practising the necessary corruptions. Then he managed to escape. He trekked for weeks through the forests into Dutch Guiana. Here he was still not safe. The Dutch, unlike the British, returned escaped prisoners to the French. When, as sometimes happened, convicts put in at Georgetown in a boat, they were not allowed to stay but were given a week's food and wished God-speed. On one occasion, I was told, a convict boat was blown on to the Venezuelan coast where, for some inexplicable reason, the convicts were all executed. —— made his way through Dutch Guiana until he reached the Corentyne, the wide river which divides Dutch from British Guiana. A boatman took him across by night, and he presented himself, an Englishman in need of refuge, at the manager's house of Plantation Skeldon. His troubles were not over; in Georgetown, when he applied for a passport so that he might return to England, they went into the case and found that he had no actual claim to British nationality. In fact, he pointed out reasonably, the authorities were using a legal point to keep him out of England. He added that his legitimate half-brother, now a man of rank and importance, had seen to it that he would never be able to return to England.

And so there he was, the citizen only of a country which would imprison him as soon as he set foot on its soil, the tolerated guest of a country which he considered by rights to be his own. The head of the Salvation Army in British Guiana had done much for him, the Archbishop had attempted to get a decent pittance for him from his family. He had prospected for diamonds and gold, been a store-keeper at Bartica, wandered from one good-natured house to the next, telling his story, receiving food and sympathy. One could not blame him for drinking. Any man who had lived such a life and with such a life still to lead needed all the artificial solaces that the world could offer.

We poured him another snap and were silent. To offer our sympathy seemed somehow absurd. I looked into his face and could recognize distinctly the inherited features of the great man whose son he claimed to be. Was it circumstance only that had led those paternal genes so far from any path his father could have imagined for them? Or was the capacity for misfortune contained in the genes themselves? We quietly gave him some money, stood up and said goodbye. I wonder, now, where he is. Drinking in that bar, work-ing in some river saw-mill, sponging off a soft-hearted missionary, or prospecting? I wish him a bonanza, a huge reef of gold, a hun-dred-carat gem stone. Then, perhaps, they might elect him a mem-ber of the Georgetown Club; a peer's son, rich, respected — with a passport, even.

Next morning I walked beneath the flamboyant trees on Main Street towards the museum. I was to have a last talk with its direc-tor before leaving for the North-West District, an area he knew well. I went up the spiral staircase to the museum offices, wondering what task I should find its director at. Would he be supervising the stuffing of a rare parrot or monkey, carving a model of Georgetown under the Dutch, reconstructing a Wai-Wai Indian's head-dress with some feathers from the Cock-of-the-Rock, at work editing his learned journal, *Timehri*, writing an article on Indian education, or merely making legends in fine calligraphy for his show-cases? I found him, in fact, making additions to his nine-hundred page bibliography of British Guiana.

His name is Vincent Roth, a powerfully built man in his seventies, with muscle-bound arms, grey hair *en brosse*, kind face, humorous eyes and a welcoming manner. In every British colony there is one man who makes it his business to be a repository of knowledge which would otherwise be lost; these men train themselves to be able to turn a hand to anything, conducting experiments on electric fish, rummaging in the muniments of Government House, and often becoming vociferous members of the Legislative Council. They love the colony in which they were born or to which they came as young men, and while they never lose their sense of being British, their roots in the home country have long since withered. Vincent Roth is one of these men and I look back with delight and regret on the long conversations we had together. He was born in Adelaide, his father an immigrant to Australia, a doctor of medicine and an ethnologist who worked among the aboriginals of Northern Queensland. At the beginning of the century Walter Roth came to British Guiana, and was appointed Commissioner, Magistrate, Medical Officer and Protector of Indians for the Pomeroon District. During his years there he produced a vast work on the arts and crafts of the Guiana Indians and a smaller work of great importance, *An Inquiry into the Animism and Folklore of the Guiana Indians*, a book to which I owe a great debt for any understanding I may have of the Indian mind. Vincent Roth has followed in his father's steps. My mind would stagger as I computed all the activities of his life. He has surveyed areas of the deep Interior, been Commissioner, Magistrate and Indian Protector, had once cut a rough military road through the jungle in the North-West at a time of boundary trouble with Venezuela; moreover, thirty great leatherbound private journals written in his beautiful hand are on the shelves of the local library. He has had every illness the forest can offer a white man, including three attacks of the terrible blackwater fever, and still looks as if he has another quarter century of life in him.

'Ah,' he said, turning to me from his desk. 'Sit down. Too early for a drink, or no?'

I said it wasn't and he went to a cupboard filled with gin bottles, each containing a differently coloured fluid, none of which was recognizable to me as a known drink.

'My liqueurs,' he explained. 'They're not bad. I cure gin with every fruit in the colony. So take your choice. Star-apple, guava, pawpaw, orange, peach — tinned peaches, I'm afraid — what's yours?'

We settled with glasses of star-apple liqueur, an excellent mellow brew, and I asked my questions. How many days was it from Arakaka by foot to the Barama River Caribs, would I get a boat easily at Morawhanna to take me up the Barima, were there vampire bats in the Barima-Barama area, were there any people now at Millionaire or Annie's Creek? Patiently he answered and wherever he could usefully elaborate on a point from special experience he would do so. He told me that the North-West was known as the Forgotten Province, that its coastal people were the most miserable and neglected in the colony. He gave me the fat manuscript of a report he and a committee had made on the conditions and prospects of the North-West. 'Some of it will shock you,' he warned me. 'But I can remember the time, back at the beginning of the century, when it was one of the happiest parts of the colony. There was gold then. And now there isn't, just a few miserable pickings but no real pay-dirt. But they've found manganese — who knows, manganese may do what gold in this country never could. Gold's a tricky, dangerous thing. Go in for gold and it's an obsession for life, but the people who've made money out of gold in this country you could count on the fingers of one hand. Did you ever hear of Axel Johnson? An eccentric American millionaire. Even he lost a packet. He had everything he wanted in the world except a gold-mine and he had to own a gold-mine, and some shysters sold him a so-called mine in the North-West.'

We talked on until it was breakfast time. Lunch, or 'breakfast', in the colony is at about eleven-thirty, a sensible time for the midday meal when work begins early to catch the cool of the morning. I went back to my hotel to breakfast off a plate of minute white prawns, 'chicken in the rough', eaten from a basket, using the fingers alone, and a salad of most of the fruits I had just seen pickled in Mr Roth's array of bottles. Then I went to make my final arrangements before boarding the boat that was to take me to the Forgotten Province.

PART ONE

The Forgotten Province

Make me thy lyre, even as the forest is:
What if my leaves are falling like its own?

SHELLEY

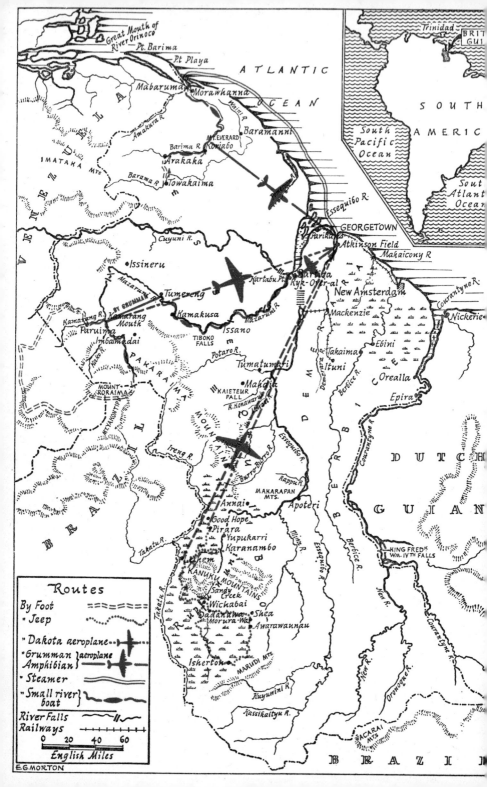

The Forgotten Province

THE sun's rays were sloping across the pink waters of the Demerara as I stood on the deck of the little coastal steamer, the *Tarpon*. Crates, bedsteads and a few small farming implements were being lowered into the hold, followed by a long wooden boat which looked as if it knew the treacherous waters of Guiana's rivers. A tall, fair-haired Englishman supervised its embarkation; suddenly the ratchets of the crane increased their speed and the boat crashed heavily on the deck, its wood seeming to snap in the process.

'Hell!' cried the fair-haired man, rushing forward to inspect the damage before turning to tell the craneman to be more careful. His inspection showed that the caulking of the boat had loosened and he gave instructions to his coloured assistant to get it seen to as soon as possible.

I wandered round the deck, listening to the half-intelligible conversation of the Creoles aboard as they made their last goodbyes to friends ashore, stepping over cases and bird cages and unidentifiable objects wrapped in newspaper. A few passengers sat on deck chairs talking to each other, and to one side, alone and oblivious to his surroundings, sat the Catholic Archbishop of British Guiana, on his way to inspect the coastal missions of the North-West. He spent the whole night in that comfortless chair, refusing a cabin, and whenever I saw him he was reading — not the missal which travelling priests usually mouth to themselves, but a detective story with a violent jacket.

Shortly before dusk we were moving across the estuary of the Demerara, as the little fishing smacks came in from the distant fishing grounds. The *Tarpon* pointed out to sea and in no time the coast,[1] lying below sea level, had disappeared except for a few high stands of manicole palm that thrust above the horizon. I went to the

---

[1] This part of the coast is known as the Arabian Coast. One explanation is that it is a corruption of the Arawak word for tiger-cat, 'Arowabiece'; the other, more probable, explanation is that it is a corruption from 'Caribbean'.

mess for a drink. The fair-haired man was there, and when I asked him about the damage to his boat he said that it was not serious but would hold up his work in the North-West. His name was Bleakly, and he told me he was a Government geologist on a survey of the coastal region from the Waini River in the North-West down to the estuary of the Pomeroon. Most of this coast, he said, was a shell-beach, and after years of neglect the colony was showing interest in the possibilities of the beach. Commercial interests hoped to produce lime from the shells so that the colony need no longer import its lime, but his assignment was to check on recent reports of the appearance of methane gas and pitchblende deposits, both in-dications of the presence of oil. He had little hope, he went on, of disproving the opinion of the great geological surveyor of British Guiana, Sir John Harrison, when he said there was no oil in this area. There was, however, every possibility of undersea oil off-shore from the boundary between the colony and Venezuela. A nice point arose here, he explained; the Waini River formed the boundary, but at the time of the boundary agreement in 1899 nothing had been said about the direction in which the boundary should extend out to sea. If it went one way the oil would be ours, if it went another the oil would be Venezuela's. We both foresaw another eruption of boundary trouble, similar to that which followed the discovery of gold.

A gnarled little Englishman in his sixties joined us for the simple meal supplied by the *Tarpon*. In the pleasant fashion of the colony he held out his hand and said 'Baker', and we held out ours and offered our surnames. Baker, like most men who live isolated lives, was the most talkative of men, and by the time we had reached the Nescafé he had told us the story of his life. For the first decade of the century he had been a motor mechanic in his home town in Suffolk. Then, in 1913, he was offered the job of head garageman to Booker's, the largest commercial concern in the colony. This taste of a new world had brought out his instinct to travel, and after serv-ing in the war he had travelled the southern continent, returning at last to Georgetown, Booker's and a wife. Until some five years ago he had lived in Georgetown; then his marriage had broken up and he had decided to put what little money he had into land. Twenty miles inland from the North-West coast, on the banks of the Koriabo

River, he had found an area of good soil, with open slopes suitable for coffee and a cool climate without the humidity of Georgetown. There were two hundred acres and he could have them at a pepper-corn price. It seemed as if at last he had found the terrestrial paradise he had been looking for all his life, a country that, as Raleigh said of the whole of Guiana, 'hath yet her Maydenhead'. He would start a new life. He built a house, took an Indian girl as his wife, adopted a small Indian boy, planted coffee, citrus fruits, coconut palms and avocado trees. At this point in his story I thought that we were about to hear the inevitable arraignment of the inefficiencies of government which is part of all such stories in British Guiana. He did, indeed, complain about the insuperable difficulties of marketing his produce and the lack of interest shown in it by govern-ment buyers in Georgetown; but his sorrow had a more tragic cause than the mere intractability of Man. Nature, who had worked so well for him during the first years, thrusting the trees from the soil and ripening the luscious fruit, had begun to desert him. The soil was pegasse, a crumbly soil whose richness, however well cared for, lasts for no more than five years. Already his coffee trees were dying and his fruit was withering in the bud. There was desperation, now, in his face as he talked, and after he had drunk a few snaps from a bottle of rum which Bleakly had produced he went still deeper into his story.

'I was a fool, I suppose,' he said. 'And living in a fool's paradise. I love working on the land and I've got to love my wife and kid. I thought I could make it. They warned me all right. Twenty years ago an Englishman had the same land, Major Morris, straight from U.K. He sweated his guts out — and the same thing happened to him. But I'm tougher than he was. They found him one day under a cocoa-mother tree with a charge of B.B. shot in his brains.'

My eyes lowered and for some moments none of us said a word, as we thought of the implications of this story. Then Bleakly picked up the bottle and filled our glasses. He and Baker both agreed that the only way to pass the night on this section of the coast was to drink through it. The great volume of water thrust out to sea by the Essequibo and the Pomeroon caused cross-currents which made sleep impossible. Already the boat was moving in every possible combination of pitch, roll and toss. Bleakly began to talk about his three months' survey of a suspected oil area in an unexplored part of Venezuela, which he had made two years before. The country was inhabited, he said, by Motilone Indians, who resented the invasion and waged incessant war on the oil men. Three of his Venezuelan Indians had been killed by arrows bearing a head six inches long. Others had been wounded by the same arrows, which had remained embedded in their flesh till they reached hospital in Caracas. Here a technique had been devised for their removal; a glass tube was eased into the wound, a little each day, and finally barb and tube were removed together. Troops had been sent in to protect those of the party who remained, but at night the main protection had been a series of reflectors placed round the camp, catching the light from arc lamps. The most psychological testing part of it all was, he said, that the Motilones were never seen, only their footprints. Eventually the oil company had employed an ethnologist to devise means of making friends with the Indians. At night he had placed bales of coloured cloth at various points on the river, hoping that they would be found and enjoyed. A day later all the bales had gone and he repeated the process until he felt that the source of this bounty might be received kindly by daylight. Bravely he went up the river with a canoe-load of cloth and, a bale under his arm, landed at one of the points where he had placed the cloth. No sooner was he on land than he was greeted by a shower of warning arrows, to each of which was tied a small piece of the coloured cloth. After a few further experiments the ethnologist retired defeated.

The night passed quickly with our talk and as the magnificent colony rum went through us we worked out the details of a fantasy. I told Bleakly I was determined to climb Mount Roraima, a flat-topped mountain of some nine thousand feet where Brazil, Venezuela and British Guiana meet, a mountain famous to the Indians of all the Guianas, who have named it 'The Ever Fertile Mother of the Rivers'. The mountain had haunted me since I had first read of it, just as it haunted Conan Doyle and inspired him to write *The Lost World*. I had seized on it as the goal of all my travels in the colony, and I found that it had come to have much the same meaning for Bleakly. But his ambition was greater than mine. He wanted to explore the entire chain of the Pakaraima Mountains, a cordillera dominated by Roraima. It had never been fully explored because no one had been able to devise a means of supplying an exploratory party with enough food for an adequate survey.[1] Disregarding these practical difficulties we spread our maps and let our pencils move among these inhospitable mountains, noticing portages for boats, seeking valley trails to avoid the more difficult mountains. 'I bet there're diamonds there,' Bleakly would say, tapping a point on the map. 'Who knows, this may be El Dorado after all. There's nobody who can say honestly that he knows it isn't. We know the kind of rock it is — geologically recent — but it's diamond country: and it's the same as with gold; diamonds are where you find them.'

Towards dawn, too fuddled to notice the violent movement of the boat, we went to our bunks and slept till woken by a brilliant sun piercing the porthole. At breakfast, neither of us feeling our best, we looked at each other and, remembering our night's fantasy, smiled. The Pakaraima trip, we knew, would come to nothing; but I was still determined to see the summit of Mount Roraima.

We went on the upper deck and stood in the sun. A rim of coast was visible to the left, and to the right the pink viscous water spread to a clear horizon. Some fifty yards in front of us I noticed half a dozen small delicate red points on the water which, as we drew closer, seemed like the sails of some diminutive craft. Fascinated I looked at them with Bleakly's glasses; they were like a beautifully caparisoned Lilliputian fleet, moving gracefully in the water, the sails seeming to be cupped by the wind. I realized that I was looking at a fleet of Portuguese Men of War (*Physalia*), but I did not then know what strange activities, activities that would have delighted Coleridge, were taking place beneath the lovely superstructure of the creatures. Below each were a dozen trailing tentacles bearing batteries of stinging cells, tentacles strong enough to entangle a fish that came too near. Once trapped, the fish tries to fight its way out and in doing so causes the tentacles to contract and draw the prey up so that it sticks to the glue-like lips of a series of squirming siphons. By the time the fish is dead it is enclosed in a bag composed of these prehensile mouths. In this bag the slow digestion

[1] In order to supply the ten members of the Boundary Commission of the 1930s, 400 miles from the coast, with enough food 300 men were continually going back and forth with supplies. For every 100 lb. of food dispatched, 15 lb. reached the Commission. The rest had to be eaten by the carriers on the journey.

takes place, the body disintegrates and fragments enter the various stomachs of the siphons. When gorged, this monstrous, beautiful creature discards what is left of the fish. And all the time above the water the fleet of tinted sails is moving in the sun and wind.

Towards midday the *Tarpon* changed course and the mangrove coast grew nearer. Gorlings, long-necked white birds, patterned the shell-beach, and we heard the screech of birds in the mangrove swamps. As we turned into the Mora Passage, past Waini Point, muscovy duck took off from the waters and an occasional scarlet ibis, or curri-curri,[1] flew for shelter in the impenetrable trees. There was no sign of man, the *Tarpon* was insurgent; this was indeed the 'Wilde Kust' of the early Dutch explorers, a no-man's-land between sea and terra firma, given a fictitious appearance of land by the thickness of the mangrove. To describe it Columbus might have used here, as well as at Cape Gracias a Dios, that expressive word, *honduras* — deepnesses.

We moved slowly in this narrow passage of water and gained speed only when we had entered the wider waters of the Waini[2] River. Now we saw people for the first time, a few Indian canoes were being paddled in the shallows by men in white shirts and trousers, while one lone canoe, paddled by a woman, began a hopeless race with the *Tarpon*, as if the woman could not bear to reach the stelling[3] after the boat itself, and miss half the fun. Then Morawhanna, the chief settlement of the North-West, came into sight — a strip of broken-down shacks running along the water's edge, most of them roofed with rusted corrugated iron. It was as miserable a place as one could have imagined, only relieved by the neat little government hospital and the police station on stilts, which stood apart on an area of grass. A fascinating array of faces was there to greet us on the stelling; some pure Negro, a few pure East Indian, two or three Portuguese (a saw-mill is owned by a Portuguese), but for the most part faces which revealed a long miscegenation between Negro and Indian, or 'bucks' as the Creoles call them. Cries

---

[1] The Creoles call it the 'Lazy Bird' because it never makes a nest for itself, taking forcible possession of the nests of the small white egret.

[2] Waini is an Arawak word for 'water', and is thus connected etymologically with 'Guiana' itself. On some old maps Waini appears as 'Guiania'.

[3] Jetty. Various Dutch words have been retained in the colony.

went out from boat to shore and were returned; Baker's Indian wife and their son were at the stelling with a small boat to meet him, and before I was ashore they were away up the Waini towards the Koriabo to reach his lost paradise before dusk.

Bleakly and I saw to the landing of our baggage and stores into a launch; across the river we could see a jeep waiting to take us the few miles into the forest-covered hills, where the government station, Mabaruma, lay. Mabaruma was founded a few decades ago by an imaginative Governor, who intended the inhabitants of fever-ridden Morawhanna to move up there and found a healthy little township on fertile soil. But it was not to be; the conservative inhabitants of the river bank loved their miserable swampland and the feeling of sociability which the river gave. They had come to think of their river as a lifeline, and the hills meant nothing to them. District Commissioners tried to force them to come to Mabaruma by refusing to lay water pipes, forbidding building, imposing a ban on a small refrigeration plant to preserve the fish until the *Tarpon*'s arrival. All was in vain; however derelict their village became, however bereft of the meanest commodities, they would not budge. The local Catholic priest remained with them, but he is a pastor with very few good words to say of his flock. For him they are a drunken, immoral crowd who live for their Saturday night's 'sporting' and who need a complete moral re-education to save them from damnation. He quotes a case of a father who handed his fourteen-year-old daughter over to a man who said he would marry her after six months if she satisfied him. An agreement, with a shilling stamp, was drawn up, but the man finally refused to marry her. Now, at twenty, the girl, unmarried, is the mother of four children. Education is so bad in the whole area that a man once said, quite wittily: 'Why, our children can't even help us to write a proper letter.' Certainly, as I wandered about the village, there were signs of utter demoralization at every turn, and it is a wonder that the people had the strength of character to resist the offered allurements of Mabaruma.

Our baggage was packed into the jeep and we climbed the lateritic hills along the winding track of red earth. At high points we could see range after range of verdant hills, far into Venezuela towards the vast deltas of the Orinoco. Silk-cotton trees pierced high above the canopy of the forest, and occasionally we would come to cultivated slopes from which all trees had been removed save the precious Ité palm (*Mauritia flexuosa*) — the Arbol de la Vida, or Tree of Life, as Father Gumilla, an early Spanish missionary, called it. This shining tree, with its great curve of leaves shaped like a fan, so preserves its water that even in times of drought its leaves are a lustrous green. Some Spanish chroniclers call it the royal palm of the plains, and whoever speaks of it does so with reverence for the bounty which it gives to those who must live on it. Its cone-shaped, scaly fruit has a taste as good as an apple, with firm yellow flesh. Its fronds are used to roof the native huts, the frond fibres form threads for hammock-making or rope, the pith of the tree can be scraped to make a flour for bread, the base of the leaf-stalk is cut into sandals; the tree-sap is collected and fermented into an excellent palm wine. And when the tree dies the Indians know that in its dead flesh a large beetle lays larvae which, toasted, are a great delicacy of the table. Sir Walter Raleigh was the first man to bring the Ité fruit to Europe, and he may also have brought flour made from the root. The Indians call this root Arù-arù and it is from this name that arrowroot is derived. The tree averages fifty feet in height, but in the Orinoco area trees of a hundred and twenty feet have been found. The Warraus, the coastal Indians of these parts, have a charming myth connected with the Ité palm, a myth which suggests a longing for Ités of such size and magnificence that all life can be sustained by them.

There was once a time, they say, when a mora tree was always found near an Ité. Monkeys would eat the fruit of the palm and take no notice of the mora — which made the mora jealous. The Ité, hearing of the mora's jealous behaviour, said he was going to leave, and uprooting himself moved inland. But the mora followed. As they moved together through the jungle the monkeys continued to eat the fruit of the Ité, but when they reached the swampland the Ité became submerged, and at last the monkeys came to feed off the topmost seeds of the mora, who, vanity now satisfied, dug in his roots once more and did not move. The Ité went on and on into the country of the Orinoco. It is for this reason that today you never see monkeys on the Ité, always in the upper canopy of the mora. The Warraus add that the Ités on the coast of Guiana are stragglers from this palm which strayed, and that only on the Orinoco will you find really magnificent Ités. The stragglers do not give enough wine, their pith is meagre, their fruit stringy.

These Indian tales invariably have the simplicity and meaningfulness of myth in its purest form. They are the products of a rudimentary literature, of minds that think and create imaginatively. They show, perhaps more than anything else, how mistaken it is to confuse the truly savage tribes of the deepest interior of the tropical forests of South America with the Guiana tribes, Caribs, Arawaks and Warraus, who, at the time of the arrival of the Spaniards, had formed some kind of culture, could produce excellent pots and artifacts which today give pleasure to see and handle. They had travelled among the islands of the Caribbean and, says Columbus, even gone in search of the Fountain of Perpetual Youth in Florida. Had the physical nature of their country been different, and had they discovered the maize-plant, they might have made for themselves a true civilization to equal that of the Mayas, the Incas and the Aztecs. Did adventurous travellers from this country, I wonder, ever reach the pyramids of Teotihuacán, make obeisance at the foot of the Great Inca or witness the rituals of Maya worship? And if they did, did they return to tell their stories beneath the Ité palm as they drank their cassava wine?

Trousered and skirted Warraus, mission Indians, stood at the roadside and with expressionless faces watched us pass. We came to a bend in the road which led up to the igneous rise on which Mabaruma stood. An avenue of tall rubber trees marked the road — the Avenue Philibert Pierre, named after an early settler on the hills. On either side of the avenue, set well away from the road, were wooden houses on stilts, a police station, a rest house, the District Commissioner's house, his garden gay with bougainvillaea and jessamine, and offices, a hospital, a house for the government forester, a shop and a rum parlour. The air was deliciously cool and it was quiet enough to hear the murmur of the breeze in the rubber trees. No place could have been more restful, but I could understand the loud, sociable people of Morawhanna wishing for none of it. One might as soon place a man from the Mile End Road on a Cumberland fell and expect him to be happy.

As we supervised the unloading of our baggage the Irish doctor,

Dr Talbot, small and leprechaun-like, came along to greet us with a warm handshake, a cheerful smile and an offer of a snap of rum. He had taken out over fifty teeth that afternoon, he said, and his arm was aching. 'Terrible teeth the Indians have,' he said; 'it's the lack of calcium in the soil. Otherwise, except for a spot of T.B., they aren't such an unhealthy lot, and they'd be a sight more healthy if they weren't frightened of coming to hospital. They've got it in their noddles that if you come to hospital they kill you there. But they're a decent lot of folk — the missions at Hossororo and down at Moruka have done a good job — I'm a Catholic, of course, myself, you understand. But you'll see tomorrow how polite they all are. You never pass an Indian without him raising his hat — they love hats. There, that's civilization for you, Indians raising their hats!'

I was interested when he spoke of the Indians of the Moruka reservation, and its mission at Santa Rosa. These Moruka 'Indians' have an unusual history. They are, in fact, what the Spaniards call mestizos, people of mixed blood. During the Venezuelan period of liberation, from 1821 to 1825, Spanish Venezuelans who feared persecution crossed the boundary into British Guiana and were given sanctuary. The highlands of Moruka were assigned to them and they took Warrau and Arawak wives, having for some reason come without their own wives. They settled well, grew coffee, cocoa, fruits and tobacco with efficiency, and were looked upon as an asset to the colony.[1] Today the vital Spanish blood which was brought to the Indians has weakened, Indian ways and habits have predominated sufficiently for there to be no really efficient form of agriculture. Yet Moruka Indians usually have minds which any European can recognize as being akin to his own — although this may be due partly to the fact that they are taught to speak excellent English at the mission schools. As I travelled in the colony I came to recognize a Moruka Indian instinctively. I met them as storekeepers in Indian villages on the Rupununi savannahs and at the Akawaio village of Kamarang; I met two boys in the Geological Department at Georgetown, earnestly studying maps of the mineral formation of the colony, deciding whether such and such an area was more likely to be quartz-mica-diorite than horneblende-granitite.

[1] Richard Schomburgk wrote of them when he visited the Moruka church: 'It was a fine stamp of men who were now rallied before the altar, and their outward appearance already led us to expect that they stood upon a higher plane of civilization than the natives around.'

Bleakly and I went back to the rest house, where an early dinner was being prepared for us by the Creole cook to whom we had given various tins and a bottle of Worcestershire sauce. As we passed through the main room we noticed that the table was laid for three, and when we returned from washing we found a tall grey-haired man in his fifties, sitting back in a Berbice chair,[1] with his legs up, a glass and half a bottle of Johnny Walker on a table at his side.

'My name's Wilson,' he said. 'Get yourself some glasses and have some whisky. Don't worry, we can finish the bottle tonight. I'm catching the *Tarpon* for Georgetown tomorrow. Made my supplies just last out.'

I asked him if he had been in Mabaruma long.

'God, no!' he said. 'Only a week, waiting for the *Tarpon*. I've been six months in the Orinoco delta doing field work. I think I've got some good stuff — I'm an anthropologist — hours of Indian singing, an absolutely filthy row, but then we anthropologists don't collect our stuff for aesthetic purposes. If we did there'd be precious little work done at all. I've been bush-whacking on field expeditions for so many years I'm apt to get cynical about it all.'

A strange, messy-looking dinner was brought in, dark with the Worcestershire sauce and better to the palate than it appeared to be. We ate hungrily and washed the food down with lime-juice and water. At the end of the meal we returned to our chairs and resumed the Johnny Walker. Wilson spoke with the delight of a man who had returned to a moderately civilized world after months in the wilds, and as men are likely to do at such times he seemed to reveal his whole character, to have no wish to keep something in reserve. He spoke with a roughness of manner and phraseology which at times I thought were assumed to cover a more sensitive nature, but if it were so the persona had become a genuine part of the man. His true nature was probably dominated by some super-ego. During the evening he told us a story about himself as a young man which did much to explain the origin of these two natures. The story follows in the next chapter. I have told it in the first person but, of course, I have not put down word for word what Wilson said. I

[1] A chair commonly found in British Guiana. It is constructed so that one may lean right back in it and rest one's legs on two long projections from the arms. It is one of the most uncomfortable chairs ever constructed.

have made various necessary changes, invented place names and attempted to give an artistic shape which the original lacked. It seemed to me to be an incident containing the essence of psychological tensions which can be produced when civilized people move of their own accord into the wild places of the world.

The Anthropologist's Story

WHAT I'm going to tell you happened more than thirty years ago but I don't think a month has gone by since without me thinking about it — giving me a jerk when I didn't expect it. It was one of those incidents psychiatrists call traumatic. I was a very young man setting out on my first field expedition, here in B.G., with a small grant from the Smithsonian Institute. I knew as much about field work — or life for that matter — as Government in those days knew about diamond smuggling from Brazil. At that time the Interior *was* the Interior — there wasn't any little Grumman amphibian to run you up to Imbarang in a few hours and keep you supplied with tinned peaches and Cooper's marmalade. You had to take every pound of stores and gear by boat and then portage it by foot for a hundred and twenty miles — and if you got to Imbarang yourself in a month you were lucky.

I loved every moment of that first trip. I'd lie in my tent-boat going up the Essequibo and purr to myself while I listened to the birds and the boatmen's shanties. I was looking forward like hell to getting down to work with a tribe of Caribs. In a few weeks, if all went well, I'd be chatting to them in their own language, they'd be telling me their myths and customs and I'd be making notes on methods of weaving and lists of sexual peculiarities. No, perhaps not that. Have you ever noticed it's almost always *women* anthropologists who manage to get the best information about sex? They get hold of stuff men wouldn't have a chance to get. I've often wondered how they do it . . . But in those days I wasn't a hardened old cynic. I was a bit of a prig, if the truth be known. I had beautiful notions about the Noble Savage — I'd even written a paper for a learned journal about him and Locke and Rousseau, and it seemed to me that about the best thing you could do in life was to go into a primitive society and learn its ways for the improvement and instruction

41

of what we impertinently called civilization. This, by the way, before I'd so much as seen Italy or Greece, and couldn't have told a Praxiteles from a Michelangelo. I thought animism was a much finer form of belief than Christianity, and when I heard about missionaries dressing Indians up in trousers and shirts I'd rage and fume. All the same, they were good innocent days.

As I said just now we had to do the last hundred and twenty miles on foot across the Kakerak Mountains, and it needed thirty Indians to carry my gear for a six months' stay. I'd been given a sketch-map of the area on the Coast, and after a week we reached a river that seemed to be the Kireng. The Commissioner for the Interior had told me I'd come across Mr and Mrs Blair two paddle-days up the Kireng, if the river were high and we weren't too slowed down by fallen trees, or tacoubas, as they call them. I'd learnt very little from him about the Blairs, because they'd made no trip to the Coast during the year or so he'd had his job, and he'd never met them. He knew that Blair himself had once worked on the Coast, and his wife had come out from U.K. three years before to teach at an Anglican school in Georgetown. When I'd asked him more questions he'd shrugged his shoulders and said, 'Oh, there's a few like them dotted about the Interior. Solitaries, individualists. If that makes them happy, I say, let them have their shanty and their few thousand square miles of virgin bloody jungle. Personally, give me the Coast, the club, a bottle of whisky and a game of snooker.' He was like every Commissioner for the Interior I've ever come across in the colonies — he absolutely hated the Interior. It's often puzzled me — like women anthropologists and sex.

Well, the river was low and we kept on having to unload to get the canoes over the tacoubas, and it wasn't till the afternoon of the fourth day that we rounded a river-point and saw a neat, well-built little house standing high up on a bluff overlooking the river, with a small savannah rolling away behind it to the forest. By the time we reached the landing place half a dozen little Indians with red loincloths had come out from nowhere to meet us. '*Buka tirak kra Blair?*' I said to one of them, proud of using one of my ten Carib phrases. The man answered with a splurge of agglutinatives, and I had to be content with smiling and pretending I'd understood.

At that moment a heavily built, bearded man of about fifty came quickly down the path. 'Blair,' he said, holding out his hand, and I said, 'Wilson.'

'Come up and have a drink,' he said, casually. 'And a meal in an hour or so. I shot a damn fat maam yesterday and the wife's roasting it with sweet cassava and tomatoes. You're in luck.'

I gave some instructions to my boys and followed Blair up the bank and into the house. It was a four-roomed bungalow raised on stilts, with a front veranda and a variety of homemade furniture; two coloured Brazilian hammocks were slung on the veranda, there were a few shelves of books and a pile of *Wide World* magazines in a corner. That interested me; Blair was living the Wide World life — why did he need to read about it? I went out on to the veranda while Blair went to see to the drinks. He came out with a bottle half filled with something the colour of paregoric.

'You're right,' he said, 'it looks muck. I suppose it is muck, but it's all there is and it's got a kick. We ran out of rum nine months ago. The Indians ferment this from cane-juice.'

'Ah,' I said, 'is that some sort of cane equivalent to cassava cassiri?' and then, remembering something I had read about cassiri, went on a little unenthusiastically, 'Is the fermentation begun by the old women masticating the cane?'

'You've been some time in these parts, eh?' he said. 'Actually, I distil this myself — and not by chewing. Don't worry. But mastication's beginning to die out with the Indians, even with cassiri, although the old people say the stuff's not as good as it used to be.'

I made a mental note to get information on these new methods.

Blair was very talkative — an excellent, simple and honest fellow. He asked me how the river was and told me he'd spent the dry season three years before in clearing the river of fallen trees. He gave me a short account of the recent weather and talked about his cow and goats; but never once did he show any curiosity about me. At first I thought he wasn't interested, but after a while I saw him looking me up and down and twigged that he was obeying some code that didn't allow you to ask what a man was doing when he was travelling in parts like this. I might be after gold or diamonds, running guns for a Venezuela revolution, or simply wanted by the police. It was better to let a man volunteer information. I told him I was an anthropologist come to study the Abako Caribs and write a thesis

about them. I had to admire the way he drowned his obvious
annoyance with a sort of rough amiability. I could see that *my*
Indians were, first of all, *his* Indians, and he didn't like the idea of an
outsider coming to rummage about in his property.

'You've got a hell of a large area to cover,' he said, 'and plenty of
hard going. You don't look very strong to me. And you'll find
they don't like telling you about their customs. They say "yes" to
everything.'

'There are ways of getting at the truth in spite of that,' I said.

'You won't find it easy,' he insisted. 'Where are you going to
make your headquarters?'

'Would you mind,' I began, 'if I had a place built on the river a
couple of hundred yards upstream? It's an ideal position on this bit
of savannah — and I was counting on seeing quite a lot of you and
picking your brains.'

I saw that my last remark had pleased and flattered him.

'Yes,' he said, 'I don't mind, and the wife won't. She might like a
spot of company for a change. I'll get some boys to get moving on
a hut tomorrow. You can mess with us at night if you like — we'll
work it out with the wife. She'll be back soon — she went down to a
fish-pond I built for her, for breeding lukanani. Then she was going
into the bush to leave some milk for an ocelot she found half dead
the other day.'

Ten minutes later we heard the long halloo which, Blair said, his
wife always gave as she neared home. I was surprised when she
appeared — I'd been expecting somebody quite different. She was
about thirty, tall and slim and really well made — khaki drill trousers
and a bush shirt set her off perfectly. She wasn't particularly pretty
and her skin had gone thin and sallow from too much sun. As soon
as she opened her mouth you could tell she was out of a rather
higher drawer than her husband, but she seemed too shy of me to
open her mouth much at all. She'd sit and look at Blair while he
talked about Indian ways and customs. Then she went off to see to
the dinner and we didn't see her again until she came out on the
veranda in a pretty linen dress and joined us in some more of the
atrocious cane-spirit. By now I'd managed to get Blair's confidence
completely — mainly by playing the innocent and flattering him with
questions. After a glass or two Nita — Mrs Blair — started talking

too. Her subject was animals. She told me she'd show me the little menagerie she'd collected. The Indians took her tracking birds and animals, even snakes. At ten o'clock they went to bed, and I got into one of the Brazilian hammocks on the veranda.

The next ten days were busy. My hut was finished in two days and I took thirty pages of notes on its construction. Blair brought along an intelligent Indian called Angus, who spoke some English and was prepared to teach me Carib. When I wasn't having lessons I was going up and down the river getting to know the Indians and being very liberal with beads, salt and sweets. The lessons went well — luckily I've always had a knack with primitive languages. I'd noticed that Blair had only a few Carib phrases, which he used constantly, and when more was needed he used Angus as interpreter. That was puzzling. It seemed to me impossible to get as near to the Indians as he obviously had without being able to talk directly with them. I got bits of information from Angus about Blair that made me see how it could be done. 'Mister Blair,' he would say, 'him very nice man, give we good things for balata and tonka beans, more better than other white mans. Mister Blair him do we good with medicine. No worms, take out bad teeth, and Mrs Blair she see our children no die. They very nice people.'

I was interested to find that Blair lived by trading balata — prices were good then; they tell me *ersatz* balata has wrecked the market now. I was such a prig in those days that I managed to persuade myself that Blair's having a commercial arrangement with the Indians rather took away from his devotion to them. It was a pretty rotten thing to think. I spent most evenings with the Blairs and gradually I pieced his story together. He'd been born in some Midlands industrial town, and from the age of six he'd wanted to go off to wild places. He'd had no education to speak of, and I think he'd only heard of one poet — Kipling. Kipling and the *Wide World*, that was all he ever read. When he was sixteen he worked his passage to Malaya and found a job on a rubber plantation. He'd saved money all his life with the idea of settling himself as his own master in some wild British colony.

'You know,' he said to me late one night when we were alone together and had drunk a good deal of my rum, 'I think I'm about the luckiest man I've ever known, and the happiest and contentedest.

I've got exactly what I wanted in this world, plus a wonderful little woman who loves me as much as I love her. By God, what would be the point of it all without Nita?'

Nita never said much when the three of us were together, but, like many shy people, when I went for a walk with her alone she'd talk all the time, very quickly and sometimes incoherently. She was an odd girl, a very odd girl. If you were unkind you might call her a little dotty. Her father was a prosperous Norfolk farmer, who had seen to it that she had a good education. Since she was a child animals had been her passion — animals and W. H. Hudson's South American romances. She would walk in the woods on the farm and imagine she was Rima in *Green Mansions*. A few years before she had leapt at the chance to come out to B.G. to teach, and she had met Blair at a sugar planter's party.

'Yes,' she said, in her earnest, slightly hysterical little voice, 'yes, we loved each other wholeheartedly from that very day, and next morning Geoffrey took me into his arms and asked me to come up into the forests and be his bride. And there's never been a regret from either of us. I don't mind if I stay in this lovely place for ever. I want to die with all its perfumes in my nostrils and all my dear little animals around me. You do understand, don't you? As an — er — anthropologist you understand the beauty of the life Geoffrey and I have chosen to lead. It is so exciting, so truly the way God intended us all to live, with our souls one and akin with Nature.'

I told her I understood perfectly.

'Living as we do,' she went on, 'teaches one to express one's being as it truly is, to be honest to one's spirit without having to obey the conventions that cage in the spirit of civilized man. You do agree? No spirit can exist if it is caged.'

'Oh, I agree entirely,' I said. I did, then, actually agree with her, but I couldn't help thinking it was a pity that a girl with a body as beautiful as hers had to express her spirit in words quite like these.

At the end of the first month or so I realized that Blair's attitude to me had changed. As my notebooks of tabulated information filled so I found it more and more difficult to keep up the pretence of ignorance that had flattered Blair to begin with. Whenever Nita, at meals, asked me how my work was going I couldn't resist the chance to tell them a score of things about Indian life that neither could know. Foolishly, I even once or twice put Blair right on a few points which he'd taken for granted — I did it because my training had made me hate a man to go on with his error. When I did this he'd grunt and say he wasn't at all sure I was right. His greatest resentment was over my being able to speak the language a little. Nita was quite different. When we were alone she'd get me to read to her translations I'd made of Carib songs and poems. But I could willingly have filled her with poison darts one evening when she said to Blair, 'Why don't we get Angus to give us some lessons in Carib, Geoffrey. You always said it was a language no white man could ever learn, and so I never bothered.'

'I had better things to do than learn Carib,' he answered gruffly. I imagined he had often made attempts to learn the language, and failed.

'I've *had* to pick up a few phrases for my work,' I put in. 'But it *is* an impossible language. I'm lucky, I'm one of those people with a knack for getting a language superficially. I'll never know it properly.'

In the weeks that followed I saw them less and less — Blair's surliness struck me as childish and irritating, and I had quite enough work to keep me busy at nights. But Nita would sometimes stroll over during the day to see if I were there and to get me to tell her what I'd learnt about the shamans, or the male puberty rituals. She'd listen quite silent and fascinated, and sometimes there'd be almost a flush on her sallow face.

One morning, when I was sitting outside my hut, I saw Blair's dug-out come round the point, piled with about five days' stores.

'Where are you off to?' I called as he neared.

'Somebody's balata's overdue at Impopai,' he answered. 'There must be something wrong up there, so I'm collecting it myself, or it won't get to the Coast for three months.'

I watched the boat disappear round the next point.

I was a little worried next day when a boy came over to my hut with a message from Nita asking me to dine with her that night. You see, I'd noticed for some time now that I'd been the recipient of a few of those looks of adoration which had once been reserved only for Blair. Nita was a congenital adorer, a chronic hero worshipper. I accepted the invitation because I didn't know how not to.

I turned up just after sundown. Nita had groomed herself more than usual — she even wore a little powder, and lipstick on those dry sun-cracked lips of hers. Now I've mentioned her body before, a beautiful body, and she wore a dress now that really did it justice. I've always been like the French in thinking that in lovemaking a good body is more important than a pretty face. We had dinner. I asked Nita why she hadn't gone to Impopai with Blair.

'I told Geoffrey my ocelot was ill and he'd die if I didn't stay and look after him.'

'Told him?' I asked. 'Do you mean it's not true?'

'No, it wasn't true. My ocelot is perfectly well.'

I blushed and got confused easily in those days, and now I did both. I didn't pursue the subject. It was better to let it lie. She was seizing a chance to let me know that she had lied to her husband so that we could be alone together. I knew so little about women; I was scared stiff — so much so that I drank far more rum during dinner than was wise in the circumstances. It was one of those glorious tropic nights you never forget. A huge silver moon nearly full, the Southern Cross glittering away, and all so light you could see the ridge of hills ten miles away. And it wasn't the mosquito season. Nita lay in one of the Brazilian hammocks and started reciting poetry.

Then she suddenly said, apropos of nothing, 'Oh James, you do like me, James, don't you?'

'You're a very, very charming girl,' I said. 'Of course I like you.'

'James,' she went on, 'bring your chair closer to me so that I may hold your hand while I say something to you from the depths of my heart.'

I moved my chair and she took my hand in a grip that was, to tell the truth, just a little horny. Then she started talking in her most exalted manner.

'James,' she began, 'I wanted to tell you tonight how much I admire all your hard honest toil with the Indians, all the selfless dedication of your life, the brilliance of your mind. When my spirit comes into contact with a spirit such as yours it feels itself so caged, so dissatisfied with what it is — it wishes to in some way partake of the other spirit. I wanted you to know that you have come to be a guiding light and inspiration to me. I felt I had to tell you — I should have been untrue to my spirit if I had kept it from you. Forgive me. Understand.'

I tried to laugh it off by saying, 'Oh, Nita, Nita, you're flattering me. This is my first field expedition — I've got doubts whether I'm much of an anthropologist at all. I wish I *were* dedicated. Geoffrey's worth ten of me.'

'Don't be frivolous, James,' she replied. 'Geoffrey is a rough, simple man who has never worked with anything but his hands. He has no intellect — '

'Lucky fellow,' I put in.

'Geoffrey,' she went on, 'has always lacked soul. At first I felt he had soul, and later I thought that he had other qualities that were worthy of love, even if he had no soul. Oh, but compared with you he seems like dross beside pure gold — how can I *not* see it? — how can I not find that my spirit calls to you? I am in love with you, James.'

Her other horny hand shot out and took mine. I felt a great rush of blood to my head, and the next moment I found myself lying with Nita in that bloody Brazilian hammock. I won't go into the rest of the details of that night except for a few general scientific observations such as it would be proper for an anthropologist to make. The first is that what a girl is like out of bed doesn't necessarily bear any relation to what she's like in bed. There was very little soul or spirit about Nita that night — she was all body. The second is that a man who is under the influence of drink and the sudden gratification of long frustrated sexual urges is more than likely to go a little mad.

In the early hours of that morning I found myself taking part in Nita's fine-drawn fantasies. She was going to get a divorce. We would spend our lives together studying the primitive societies of the world; we would become a famous husband-and-wife team. When Nita started on something she could be most persuasive.

I crept back to my hut before dawn and spent an awful day. I felt a complete cad. I remembered Blair's words, 'By God, what would be the point of it all without Nita?' I wondered whether his surliness to me had been caused in some way by Nita. My heart missed a beat when it occurred to me that he might be laying a trap, that he planned to return unexpectedly to find Nita and me *in flagrante delicto.* He was a big man — he'd probably give me the hiding of my life. My instinct was to pack and move on to some other territory. Then I thought of my work — if I left so much undone here my thesis would be pointless, I'd never get my doctorate. I *had* to stay and unravel the ritual patterns of the spring solstice.

Nita came over to my hut at midday.

'James,' she said, 'you can take me with you on your visit to the village this afternoon. I will help you. You must teach me. And afterwards we shall walk together in the forest and I shall tell you the songs of the birds.'

Up to now I've been telling this story rather frivolously, ungallantly making game of poor Nita, with her Rima complex. That's only a way of salving my conscience. There wasn't anything frivolous about it at the time, and what followed was only too serious. It taught me a great deal about human nature, and about myself. It made me discover my own ruling weakness. It's no exaggeration to say that I've spent the rest of my life since that time getting control over that weakness. It meant almost a conscious remaking of myself. I've never been the same man since that time.

For the next three days I forgot all about my Indians. I gave in. Nita obsessed me with lust. Then one morning Blair's boat turned the point — without him; only Angus, who climbed up the bank and handed me a note from Blair which said that there was some trouble in Impopai and he'd run out of cartridges. Would I give Angus a box of B.B. and send him back straightaway? Angus was evasive when I questioned him. He said Kenaima was in the village. Kenaima was the Carib evil spirit, a spirit that enters a man and makes him kill. Indians won't talk about Kenaima and this seemed an opportunity not to be missed. I packed some gear into the boat and we paddled up to Blair's landing, where I explained what had happened to Nita.

'I'm coming with you,' she called back, and a few minutes later she was with us in the boat.

It was a long weary journey between the high walls of trees on either side, with only the occasional swoosh of a cayman and the flash of a scarlet ibis to relieve the boredom. That night we found a disused hut and Nita and I slung our hammocks there, holding hands in the twilight. We made good time and reached Impopai next day, where the whole village came to meet us, armed with blowpipes and bows. We found Blair in the large open-sided Strangers' hut.

'Christ!' he said when he saw us. 'You!' Then he got up and took Nita in his arms.

Angus cooked a meal, and while we ate Blair told us what had happened.

'When I got here,' he said, 'I found they hadn't got a pound of balata for me among the lot of them. The whole place has been in chaos for weeks. Three men and a woman have copped it from the Kenaima, and nobody will go into the forest. They say Kenaima must have come to earth and entered the body of somebody in Amoko — that's a village ten miles away. The piaiman here's been blowing curses on to things and sending them by night to Amoko — by magic. But they say it's a very strong Kenaima and they don't think blowing will do any good. Now there's no doubt about the murders. There must be some crazy man at Amoko who's coming into the forest and doing them. And if this village is to get any peace and I'm going to get any balata we've got to stop the killings.'

'You were going to Amoko?' I asked.

'Yes, with Angus.'

'You know the solstice is in a couple of days,' I said. 'This is quite clearly part of the preparations for a wild solstitial ritual. I've read about it in Schomburgk. They've probably been drinking cassiri for days and chewing coco leaf. They'll be almost mad. I strongly advise you not to go till after the solstice.'

Blair looked me up and down and, smiling, said, 'I know, son. You're probably quite right. That's why I wanted plenty of cartridges. In case they're rough.'

I said nothing. I knew he was enjoying a slight triumph.

'You can't go alone!' Nita cried.

Recovering myself I said, quickly, 'Of course not. I'm coming with you.'

'And I'll come too,' Nita said.

There was some argument, but in the end it was decided we all three should go. We started out at dawn next morning. It was a bad trail through the forest and the going was slow. I felt, still, that we shouldn't have come — I still think it was unwise, in the circumstances. All the same I was excited by the possibility of seeing Indians in a state of ritual frenzy. The gentlest of savages had to have periods of releasing their atavistic energies. But white men stood the chance of being riddled with poison darts at such times.

The trail got worse — roots and mud and creeks all the way, and then rain. Nita didn't complain once. As we got near the village I felt I was taking part in one of those bogus South American jungle books — that there really were little men in the tree-tops with blowpipes.

Eventually the trail brought us to a small savannah, surrounded on all sides by the forest, and Blair said, 'The village is about ten minutes away.' Turning to me in a faintly insolent way, he added, 'What do you think our plan should be now, Wilson? You know how these people's minds work better than I do.'

I had very little idea what we should do. It was something I'd been thinking about all morning without result.

'I — I — ' I began, and then eventually, 'I should warn you again, Blair, they may be dangerous.'

'Yes, we know that,' he answered. 'You told us so last night.' Then he began to needle me mercilessly. 'Now's the time I wish I could speak their language,' he said. 'If I did I'd go in unarmed with Angus following with the gun, and I'd call for the headman and tell him if he didn't get rid of the Kenaima, Impopai was going to send over one so strong he'd kill off the whole village. Do you think that's an idea?'

I could feel Nita's eyes boring into me.

'What about,' I said lamely, 'what about our shooting a few cart-ridges in the air — they might come out into the savannah. It might be better to meet them in the open.'

'What good would that do?' Nita said. 'The shots would scare them. We want to talk to them calmly.'

I was beginning to curse the whole foolish expedition. Neither Nita nor Blair had the knowledge to conceive the danger we were in; and we were in danger — I say that now after a lifetime's experience. Their determined ignorance might cost us all our lives. I felt I could do nothing. I was utterly powerless.

'I think Nita's right,' Blair said. 'Your idea wouldn't work. There's only one thing. I can make myself understood after a fashion. I'll go in.'

There was an absolute silence for some moments. I was the only member of the party qualified to go in. I knew that. Nita looked from Blair to me and back, with an expression almost of tortured ecstasy on her face.

'Look here, Blair,' I said finally, 'you talked me into this expedition last night. I know more about this sort of thing than you do. I tell you again it's madness to go into the village. Take my word, for God's sake.'

'Then you vote for turning back? I don't. I think we've got to get rid of this Kenaima. What do you say, Nita?'

'I say that either you or James should go into the village.'

'Good — I have your permission,' Blair said.

'Yes,' she replied in an ecstatic whisper. 'Yes.'

The next half hour was the worst I've ever spent in my life. Nita watched Blair walk across the savannah and go into the forest. There was no fear for him on her face, only an expression of adoring love. She was imagining down to the last detail the scene in the village. Her husband was the hero of whatever should happen. Even if he were riddled with a shower of poisoned arrows she would have been satisfied in some strange way. She said nothing for twenty minutes. At last she turned to me and looked me up and down, an expression of absolute disgust on her face. Then she spoke—calmly, but with that almost hysterical exaltation of hers.

'If he dies,' she said, 'I shall love him for what he's done. I shan't regret it for a moment. When you live in wild places this is part of the living. You take it, and if you die you die. There's no room for cowards in the forest. And you are a coward. A coward! You don't deserve to live in the forest. What's all your learning worth if you can't do the things you've got to do?'

And then she started to cry. I didn't try to justify myself. My mind was heavy and confused. I didn't have the strength to remain faithful to the stand I'd taken. What I did next made any justification impossible. Without a word I strode off towards the village, to help Blair. There was no logic in what I did. And then, in a moment, this pathetic attempt at redemption was transformed into something quite ludicrous.

Blair and Angus emerged from the forest. They were not alone. They were surrounded by a gaily chattering group of Indians.

None of them had blowpipes or bows, and Blair was smiling as he came towards us, crying out, 'Unpack the salt, Nita, I've promised them all we have. They're a jolly nice lot.'

I walked back with them. The humiliation was agonizing. I wanted to rush off into the forest and never see Blair or Nita again. But ignominiously I had to go with them into the village and try to eat the excellent pepper-pot which the headman offered us. After the meal I tried to muster the remnants of my professional zeal to ask a few questions about the Kenaima. Yes, they told me, there had been a Kenaima in the village, but he had passed on towards the mountains some days before.

We stayed the night in the village, and I let Blair and Nita have the Strangers' hut alone. I knew she would want to be alone with her regained idol. He was her man again in every sense. I was a miserable creature who had disillusioned her. Blair was more civil to me than he had been for a long time. Now that he had triumphed so decisively he had no need to be antagonistic. But Nita never spoke one word to me, ignoring me completely the whole of the journey back.

I knew I could never stay on at Imbarang. The ignominy was complete. I would have to leave so much undone. I should have to go to some new territory and see if I could complete my notes on male puberty rituals there. I told Blair I must move on, and he was extremely kind and helpful over everything.

★   ★   ★

Wilson drained his whisky glass and looked at us, anxious to tell from our faces what we felt about his confession. Myself, I could understand his actions entirely, and sympathized with him. And yet at the same time I could admire the foolishness of Blair.

Wilson gave a resounding laugh, the sort of laugh which, one felt, he could never have given when he was a young man. 'Looking back on it all now,' he said, 'I wonder if I wasn't bloody lucky. Perhaps my unconscious mind had been working to get me out of that ridiculous affair with Nita. Sometimes in the middle of the night, when I'm out in the field, I thank God I was able to return her to Blair intact — or almost. God, if I hadn't done what I did I might have been saddled with Nita for life! She was a determined girl.'

The Barima

THE summit of the hill of Hossororo, five miles from Mabaruma, is the highest land in the area, sweeping in steep heavy
folds eastwards down to the Barima river, and diminishing to
the west, in a series of valleys, as if some ancient cataclysm had drawn
the land together, like hands crumpling a sheet of paper. Heavy
clouds rolled seawards, their shadows passing over the dark vegetation of the forests. There was silence everywhere except for the
distant call of the tiger-bittern, the most prevalent bird on the
coastal fringe here and so named because the Indians say its call is
like the purr of the jaguar. Then, as I began the steep walk down
towards the river, a change of breeze brought the high notes of
children chanting: 'One and one are two, two and two are four, four
and four are eight', a sound so familiar and yet here so musical that
one might have improvised a tune from it. Five minutes later I was
approaching the open-sided schoolhouse where the Indian children
sat with their white-habited teacher. Their heads turned towards
me as I passed on down the hill.

Sister Teresa, the head mistress of the school, is a remarkable,
vital woman, who was given an O.B.E. for her work at the Santa
Rosa mission. There is no doubt about the success of the Catholic
missions in the North-West — not only have they brought Christianity to Warraus and Arawaks who a mere half-century ago were
animists, but they have brought the ideas of civilization with
them. An Indian in these parts would be ashamed to wear the
bead apron or the red cotton lap of his parents; he cleans his
teeth and brilliantines his hair, saves his money for shirts brought by
Georgetown traders. The Government approves, since it is the
policy of the colony to integrate the aboriginal in all areas of mixed
population — even, presumably, if this finally means the creation of
the miserable Morawhanna type throughout the North-West. Yet
wherever one goes one hears that the natural energies of these people

are leaving them; children learn to chant the multiplication table rather than how to choose a purpleheart whose bark is ripe for a woodskin canoe; they learn to read the Lord's Prayer but are losing the exact art of shooting sunfish with bow and arrow. Generations are growing up with a smattering of education, the old forms of life are dying — and so little is being put in its place. No wonder they suffer from lassitude, bemused in their limbs, content to lie in their hammocks rather than go hunting in the forests. Another discouraging aspect of this etiolated community is the almost complete disappearance of the native handicrafts. Archaeological work at the various middens of the North-West has unearthed the best pottery of British Guiana, and the basket-work of a generation ago, with its geometrical symbolic decoration, is of great beauty. The basket-work of the mission Indians is vulgar and without distinction of any kind, designed and executed to the orders of the nuns, and made from thin round withies, not the flat coloured strips which were cut from the stalk of the calathea.[1] Not many years ago there was a thriving trade in these Indian *pegals* in Georgetown, but now it is only possible to find them by going to Indian areas of the colony to which civilized decadence has not spread.

By the river at the foot of the hill lay the house I was looking for, the trade-store and saw-mill of Mr Solomon. Breathing the bitter fumes of sawn crabwood I made my way to the shop door and went in. Bales of calico rested beneath sides of bacon, boxes of B.B. shot shared shelves with glutinous sweets, baked beans, hairclips and gumboots. In the next room a man who lay asleep in a hammock gradually became aware of me and emerged smiling to ask what he could do for me.

It was Mr Solomon himself, a Chinese of great charm who had come to the North-West many years before to set up his shop and to augment his takings by trading in the local woods. I had been told that he could help me in a thousand ways. He invited me to go upstairs into a room overlooking the river, where we could talk and have tea. He talked delightfully about the various monomaniacs who still believed there were reefs of gold to be found in the North-West, about the manganese discoveries and the proposed railway.

---

[1] *Calathea butea* and *Calathea juncea*, plants which can grow straight and leafless, as high as eighteen feet.

He said that there was gold everywhere, but so thinly spread as to be unworkable. He told me of his own prospecting days when he had so often found wonderful slabs of gold quartz which suddenly would come to an end a few feet below the ground.

'There's a fine old fellow who comes in to tea every day,' Mr Solomon said. 'He's eighty-six and comes from Manchester. We call him Old Brown. He doesn't have a penny in the world, so I give him a little shack at the back there and he does a few odd jobs for me. He's an inventor.'

Ten minutes later Old Brown came into the room. He had the heavily white-bearded head of an Old Testament prophet, with light blue eyes that twinkled from behind steel-rimmed spectacles. In his clear, faintly Mancunian accent he said how delighted he was to see me and took my hand in a vigorous grip. We sat down at the table and Mr Solomon's daughter brought in the tea — a specially strong pot for Mr Brown. He turned out to be one of the most charming old gentlemen I have ever met, and when by a strange coincidence we discovered that we had both travelled in the Usumacinta valley of southern Mexico his face lit up as he realized that he could talk his head off to me. He was a construction engineer and had gone to Mexico in 1896. After each job he had spent his earnings in travelling, usually walking hundreds of miles through harsh country. He had worked on railways in the Amazon and walked through the Guatemala forest in search of Maya ruins. The gold shout in the North-West had brought him to these parts in the first decade of the century and he had had his pickings. With an amazing memory for detail he described the various gold-bearing creeks near Arakaka. 'Ah,' he said, 'when I first came here I knew it was the country for me, and I've never got tired of it for a day since. I went back to Manchester twenty years ago after I'd done well out of making rattan chairs for Mr Solomon, but do you know I was ready to leave next day and come back. The tropics get hold of you. Once you've lived in the tropics you'll never be happy anywhere else. I'm a T.T.T. — a Typical Tropical Tramp.'

I asked him about his inventions and he told me that he was working on a device for aircraft that would prevent crashes on take-off and landing. He used Mr Solomon's lathe, and had made a collection of odd bits of aluminium for his work. He'd been making a very intricate part that afternoon, he said, and hoped to have the complete model ready in a month or two. When Mr Solomon and I began to make arrangements for my journey up the Barima he said he must get back to his work, and we could soon hear the scrape of his file across the surface of the aluminium.

Mr Solomon said he could supply me with a boat, but he had no idea whether the boat would be able to get to Arakaka. There had been little rain the last week or two and the rivers were low. This meant that tacoubas would be exposed and the boat impeded. But I could try. A few hours' rain would be enough to bring the river a foot or two higher. I agreed to be at the Ariaka landing next morning at five o'clock, where I would find the boat and an Indian boatman.

When I left Mr Solomon's I went to say goodbye to Old Brown, whom I found in the cool sloping sunlight, vigorously smoothing a superbly made piece of precision machinery. 'Wish I were going up-river with you,' were his last words to me. 'After the mangrove you get to some fine forest. Beautiful big moras, and lovely crab-woods.' A few yards away stood the broken-down wooden shack where he lived. It was difficult to imagine that it was the home where this supremely happy man would end his days. I walked on up the hill and turned to wave goodbye at the point where a fold of the slope obscured most of the river from my view.

It was dark and cold as we loaded my gear into the police jeep that was to take me to the Ariaka landing. By torchlight I checked that all was there; the boxes containing rice and tinned pumper-nickel, corned beef and stewed steak, hammock and mosquito net, olive oil and, almost more precious than all, my tins of herbs, bought in Soho to give some adventitious flavour to the food I would be eating. The bush[1] on either side of the track was strangely illumin-ated in the headlights, and twice dark animals — perhaps labbas[2] — flashed across our path, for the animal life of the forests is nocturnal. We zigzagged down a slope whose bush had been burnt away for maize planting, and then came to the little Ariaka stelling.

[1] With understatement the British, in their tropical colonies, call even the most impenetrable and splendid forest merely bush. Under no circumstances does a true bushman ever use the word jungle; it would be like an aficionado talking of a toreador, or Miss Nancy Mitford referring to a mantelpiece.

[2] *Coelogenys paca*, a rodent-like animal, about two feet long.

The boat was there, with Roger, the Indian boy — tinkering with its engine, his bronze face strangely lit by the hurricane lamp. I shone a torch on to the water, to find that its rays could not pierce the thick blanket of mist that lay over the river, and added its mystery to the scene. My boxes were piled into the boat, I said good-bye to the policeman, and five minutes later we were feeling our way gently along the Barima; Roger seemed to know by instinct each point and curve of the river as we pierced the mist — mist that had now worked its way to my skin, where it rested, cold and clammy. First light came, the sky paled and then it was grey dawn with the trees on either side of us flat and silhouetted, visibility still no more than a hundred yards. Then I felt the touch of the sun, and as it rose dimly above the hills the mist seemed to evaporate in a moment. Within five minutes the path of the river had lost its mystery, the mangrove had become a hedge of individual trees, the dark water sparkled on its surface and we could see the black ducklar pelicans a quarter of a mile away, at first motionless on the trees and then silently dropping into the water in pursuit of a fish. Long after they had become conscious of us they would continue their diving, and only when we were almost abreast with them would they rise shrieking into the air and flutter up-river. I asked Roger why they allowed us to get so far within gunshot and he said that they had no fear of being shot — their flesh was too fishy for good eating.

I could now see what kind of craft I was travelling in. It was a tent-boat built according to a design suitable for Guiana's rivers. Thirty feet long, with a shallow draught for low waters and a screw that could be raised at will to avoid tacoubas or obtrusive rocks. It was open except for a middle section with a roof supported on four posts. Tarpaulins were rolled on all four sides of the roof, ready to be lowered when it rained. I reclined like some pasha beneath his *baldacchino* and gave in to the endless fascination of the mangrove. The river being low the trees did not rise as trunks from the water; instead each long rearing trunk broadened towards its base and then splayed out into four or more legs — straight, not twisted like olives — so that each tree seemed like some grey pre-historic monster whose giraffe-like neck ended in a canopy of leaves. And between the arches of these powerful roots you could see the dark interior of the swamp, where the images were endlessly repeated. How perfectly these predatory legs express the nature of the mangrove, a species which through slow centuries advances across the stretches of the river, or even from coast towards the sea, its heavy seed dropping from the treetop into the mud where, if it is not swept away by the tide, it shoots out its tentacles and makes the almost liquid mud a little firmer. Or, where seeds cannot hold, the tree shoots out branches which, in great curves like flying buttresses, pierce down into the mud and give further support to the parent tree. No man can live in these huge areas of mangrove, and when I spent half an hour pulling my way among the trees in a woodskin I could imagine no more mysterious or inhospitable place. Yet this predatoriness is an attempt by Nature to gain fruitful land from the sea and rivers. Roots strengthen the mud, leaves fall and strengthen it again, until where there had been water there is earth and other trees can grow to choke the mangrove. A hundred and seventy years ago the coastlands of British Guiana were mangrove swamps; the Dutch turned them from swamps into fertile sugar plantations and kept the sea at bay with a wall. If there had been no mangrove there would have been no soil to drain and plant.

As the day went by and the mangrove gave way to earthen banks we passed the occasional huts of river Indians, and saw them paddling in their woodskins, always hugging the river banks; they were sometimes bare to the waist, displaying their huge copper-coloured shoulders that had been developed by day-long paddling and by carrying heavy loads on their backs. They were Warraus and Arawaks, in so far as they were not a miscegenation of all the tribes that had lived in these long-disputed parts. In the years before the arrival of the Spaniards, they united to fight the invading Caribs, and although they were at one time physically distinguishable there is little point today in making a distinction. It was the sight of their tree-houses at a time of inundation which made Alonso de Ojeda (who saw them in the Orinoco delta) name their country Venezuela, or little Venice, and Raleigh supports him when he writes, in *The Discoverie of Guiana*, that the Warraus 'are a very goodlie people and verie valiant, and have the most manlie speech and most deliberate that ever I heard of what nation soever. In the summer they have houses on the ground as in other places: In the winter [i.e. rainy season] they dwell upon the Trees, where they build very artificial towns and villages'.[1] The Arawaks[2] were a fairer, handsomer people than the Warraus, and were employed by the Dutch to recapture escaped slaves. In the Schomburgks' time (1840-44) the Warraus had degenerated enough for them to be despised by other tribes for their dirtiness and negligence. 'They are industrious,' says Robert Schomburgk,[3] 'but most negligent in their persons and villages.' Perhaps there is some tribal defect which recent 'civilizing' has augmented.

Caribs, Arawaks and Warraus all believed, and no doubt still believe, that Man was created in the heavens and then placed on the Orinoco delta. The Warrau myth of the first man who came to earth is typical of the simple beauty and humour of Indian mythology. According to them the Warraus once lived in the sky and knew no animals other than birds. Their great hunter, Okonorote, one day shot a rare bird with his arrow, but when he went to pick it up he found a hole in the ground, and looking through it he saw the plains below and all the animals of the earth. He made a rope, lowered himself to the plains, shot a deer and found its flesh good to eat. He went back to the skies and told the rest of the tribe what he had seen, and all decided to visit earth with him. The last to leave was a fat woman whose body stuck in the hole, where she remained, making it impossible for the tribe to return home again. This unfortunate woman's name was Okonakura, now the Warrau name for the Sun.

Once the Indians came to earth they learnt the art of boat building so that they might move about these aqueous coastlands. They made remarkable sea voyages in their little boats, colonizing the islands of the Caribbean and keeping lines of communication with the Orinoco delta and Guiana. They would even make trading voyages from Guiana with a boatload of bread for islands two hundred miles away. When Raleigh made his first attempt to reach the golden city of Manoa, where El Dorado ruled, he had with him 'for Pilote an Indian of *Barema*, a river to the south of *Orenoque . . .*

---

[1] Both the Schomburgks dispute this last description, and Raleigh's vagueness suggests that his information was second hand. He may have recalled Amerigo Vespucci's two letters to the Gonfaloniere of Florence, giving a description of huts built on piles in the rivers. These were those seen by Vespucci's captain, Alonso de Ojeda.

[2] The name derives from *Aruwa*: jaguar.

[3] *Journal of the Royal Geographical Society*, vol. XII, 18 and 2, p. 175.

whose *Canoas* we had formerlie taken as he was going from the said *Barema*, laden with Cassui bread to sell at Marquerita'. He was not, in fact, a very good pilot, and but for Providence Raleigh might have been completely lost among the maze of rivulets on the delta, a maze that made the Spanish sailors say:

Quien se va a Orinoco
Si no se muere, se volver a loco.[1]

By tradition the Warraus and Arawaks were the prey of the warlike Caribs, but Raleigh heard otherwise — and his information, apart from his credulity over El Dorado and Amazon women, was surprisingly accurate. 'They were woont,' he writes, 'to make warre upon all nations, and especially on the *Canibals*, [i.e. Caribs] so as none durst without a good strength trade by these rivers, but of late they are at peace with their neighbours, all holding the *Spaniards* for a common enimie.' Raleigh laid the foundations of British friendship with the Indians by exemplary behaviour and by forbidding his men to make love to Indian girls — although, as he charmingly puts it, 'we saw many hundreds, and had many in our power, and those very young, and excellently favored which came among vs without deceit, starke naked. Nothing got us more loue among them than this usage . . .' Without Indian help he would never have been able to make his way to the mainstream of the Orinoco and the village of Morequito, the nearest he was ever to come to the land where he imagined the fabulous Empire of Guiana to lie. I am tempted to quote pages from his marvellous book, but for the moment I have digressed enough. . . .

In the heat of the afternoon, when the midday squalls of rain were over, I slept, now bored by the unchanging mangrove and the screeching ducklars, which were almost the only birds I had seen that day. I woke towards four o'clock to find another world. The low mangrove had given way to tall trees, rooted on firm earthen banks, and a quarter of a mile away was a small bush-covered hill. My map told me we had reached Mount Everard, the point on the Barima where the geology of the land changes, where the broad,

[1] He who goes to the Orinoco and doesn't die, will come back mad.

unimpeded water narrows, flowing between striated rocks. Here the tacoubas, rapids and hidden rocks begin.

There is a sawmill at Mount Everard, owned by an East Indian, and we tied up at the mill stelling to find out the condition of the river. A Creole sawyer told us it was 'bad, man, bad', and I could see from Roger's face that he was not looking forward to the rest of the journey. He suggested we spent the night at Mount Everard in the hope that more rain would fall in the night and raise the water level. It was early and I was anxious to get as far as we could that day, so I said we would go on. Roger told me a little shamefacedly that if we did we would have to take an Indian pilot and bowman with us, as he himself didn't know this stretch of the river. The Creole obligingly went off to find a bowman, and soon we were slowly on our way again. Victor, the bowman, stood at the bows looking into the dark amber water, discoloured with decayed vegetation. A large paddle was in his hands, and as a rock came into our path he would swing us to one side with a deft movement of the paddle. Thus we zigzagged from point to point, the hull sometimes grating unpleasantly on stone or fallen tree. The standing trees, crabwood and cedar, now towered higher still, their canopies a dark dead green, with no sign of lianas or epiphytes. The soil they lived on formed a shallow coating to the stratified rocks now exposed by the drop in the river level. Where the mangrove had been insecure because of the liquidity of its soil these fine trees seemed to send out grasping roots to maintain an equilibrium. But as they grew taller the strength of the roots at last would give out and the tree would topple over into the river. Every two years so many trees have fallen that the river becomes almost impassable, and the long task is begun of hacking the trees loose from their moorings on the bank. The river was now due, I gathered, for one of these purgations.

Towards dusk we rounded a point to find a tent-boat moored at a landing below a bluff on which stood a small wooden hut. A Creole was sitting in the bows preparing fishing lines, and he waved to me cheerfully.

I told Roger to stop the engine and asked the Creole if there was room for us to camp at this landing.

'Dog bust my liver there sure is, man,' he called back. 'You can have d'hut all to yoursel'. I'll be spending d'night a fishing, d'buck girl she has hersel' and d'baby under d'tent and my bowman he slings his hammock there by d'engine. Help yoursel' man.' We tied up and I climbed the soggy bank to the one-roomed hut on stilts. It was strongly made in European style. The room was empty save for a leaflet showing a girl reclining on a Dunlopillo mattress; 'The Inside Secret for Better Sleep', said the legend. Near it, burnt on the wood, I read '02997379 Pte. Dunn, Black Watch'. I learnt later that the hut had been built by a platoon of the Black Watch which had been sent up the Barima on a bush scheme.

I slung my hammock after a number of unsuccessful attempts to tie the special hammock knot which ensures one against unpleasant awakenings. Among white people who travel rough in the rain-forests of South America hammock lore is an endless and enchanting topic of conversation. Different kinds of kraua hammock rope, made by the Indians, are compared, the advantages of net hammocks made from Ité palm fibres weighed against those made in heavy weave from wild cotton; fancy coloured hammocks made in Brazil are universally condemned by those in the *afición*, and almost any Wapishana hammock preferred to those of other tribes. One man will tell you he had a Wapishana travelling hammock so fine that you could draw its whole length through the aperture made by the thumb and index finger. Another will tell you about the finest hammock he ever saw in his life, which an Indian wouldn't sell to him even for two hundred fish-hooks and a pound of gunshot. *Hamaca* is a Carib word and both the article and word were introduced to Europe by the *conquistadores*. The one I now hung was a very poor specimen, made in a Georgetown factory, heavy and graceless. But when I reached the Wapishana country on the Rupununi savannahs I managed to find one of superb workmanship.

Before taking to my hammock I went for a short walk along an Indian trail which led inland from the river. The path was slimy and overgrown but to one side I saw a stone emerging from the growth. It seemed not to be naturally there, though its form was natural enough. I pushed the undergrowth away with my stick, but no inscription showed through the pale green patina of mosses. When I got back to the boat to see how Roger was getting on with our meal I asked the Creole if he knew anything about the stone. 'Sure,' he replied. 'That stone it marks d'body of an Englishman.

He went swimming from dis landing, oh long long ago, an' an electric eel he got him.'

We ate, darkness fell and I took a hurricane lamp up to my hut, fell gratefully into my hammock and began to read my nightly chapter of *Our Mutual Friend*. As darkness became more absolute the sounds of the forest intensified. Of all the nights I spent in the Guiana forests I never knew one to approach this in its extraordinary variety of sound. By day the forests are silent except for the birds — and often these are silent — but at night a score of species of frog orchestrate and a thousand varieties of insect whirr like louder and more imaginative cicadas; one frog syncopates like castanets, another chills with a sound like a baby crying, another imitates to perfection the distant sound of an outboard engine, another bleats, another is a flight of heavily winged birds, but not one deigns to descend to the simple Aristophanic brekekekex. Then I would hear the Indian game bird, maam (*Tinamus major*), who comes out from his ground nest to add his melancholy call. And closest to me of all were the strange hard-backed insects and moths who clustered round my lamp or hurled themselves with imbecile force against my netting. I was glad of these sounds; they meant that life was here. I knew what Ruskin meant when he wrote of scenes 'ringing with voices of vivid existence, for no air is sweet that is silent'. From the river during the day the forest had seemed so dead, and the river itself a graveyard for the corpses of trees.

I slept soundly and it seemed as if hardly a few hours had passed before I awoke with a start to the roar of a tube train passing by the hut — but no, such a sound would have been familiar if unexpected; this was like no sound I have ever heard — a ghost tube train, perhaps, in some form of mechanical agony. The roar rose to a climax of sound and agony and then made its diminuendo. It was the dawn chorus of a family of red howler monkeys, whose roar carries a dozen miles through the forest and is the most remarkable sound to be heard there. The red howler (*Mycetes seniculus*) is a morose little animal, weighing twenty-five pounds or so. The vast volume of sound which issues from the male is caused by an enlarged bone cavity in its throat, which acts as a kind of megaphone. Some Indians believe that if you drink water from this bone you can cure any ailment of the throat.

We had decided the night before that Roger should return to Hossororo and I should continue in the '*bateau*' in the charge of Henry
Brown, the Creole. The boat was hugger-mugger with baggage
and bundles when we started off, the mist dissolved with the early
sun. There was a strong smell of fish, for Henry had caught a dozen
large flat fish which lay salted on the roof, waiting to be toasted by
the sun. It was still cold enough for me to wear a sweater, for the
river itself would lie in the shadow of the trees till the sun was high.

Henry, as captain of the boat, left the steering to an Indian and
the guiding to his Indian bowman. Although he had made the river
trip to Arakaka hundreds of times this was a part of the river which
he knew must be navigated by men who had lived there all their
lives. So we sat together on the roof and talked. Henry was about
forty and a fine type of Creole; immensely loquacious and know-
ledgeable, with a power of image-filled language which delighted me
all the time; he had that energy and determination which years of
paternalistic government have made so rare in the British Guiana
Negro. Henry was not a man to whittle his life away in Georgetown
lamenting that life was poor, and waiting for an all-provident
government to improve it. He had prospected for gold at various
times, but now for eight years he had been general foreman to an
Englishman named Major Lewis, who had succumbed irretrievably
to gold fever. He looked after Major Lewis's machinery, had himself
built the excellent *bateau* we were in, and invented a retractable keel
for passing over tacoubas. He adored his master; his talk was often
a recital of Major Lewis's dicta: 'Major Lewis says if a fellow don't
have enough to eat in B.G. it's because he's lazy — and it's true', or
'Major Lewis he says that if he start eatin' local food at his age he'll
die', or 'Major Lewis says Arakaka way is full of gold still and we
got to go on and on till we finds it'.

Major Lewis, I gathered, was in Canada raising funds for a new,
large-scale assault on this elusive pay dirt. From Henry and from
other people whom I was to meet during the next few days I learnt
a little of his story. When he retired from the Army in 1937 he put
all his money into a quest for gold in the Arakaka area. He had
dredged the river with heavy machinery, and found gold there, but
never in paying quantities. He had prospected every possible area
of the upper Barima, and then by good fortune had taken a concession

on a large ridge of land lying ten miles south of Arakaka. Some years later a government geologist named Matthews proved that the ridge was composed of manganese ore, and the Union Carbide Company of U.S.A. immediately asked for the concession. Major Lewis offered to sell his rights for £40,000, making as part of his condition of sale that he should become manager of the exploitation company. Eventually he sold his concession for £20,000 without the managership. He was now a man in his middle sixties; at this point in the story I would have imagined him retiring to a pleasant hotel on some Caribbean paradise like Tobago, passing the rest of his life fishing for barracuda and reminiscing at sunset with a rum swizzle in his hand. But no, his nature was too romantic; the little fortune was the chance to prove that he was right in believing El Dorado was not worked out. He has put his money into yet another gold-prospecting company, and Henry dreams of the hatfuls of ore that the mud of the Barima will one day give up.

While he talked Henry's eyes missed nothing on the river bank. Once, in the middle of a story, he suddenly raised his gun to his shoulder and fired, and a fine iguana fell into the river from an overhanging branch. An Indian retrieved the little dragon with its three feet of whiplike tail, and Henry said it would make a banquet for him and his wife that night — with a slice or two for each of his eight children. In countries where iguanas are eaten it is usual to defend the custom by saying the flesh is more delicious than chicken, but Henry was too honest for deception. 'Yes, it's like chicken, man,' he told me, 'but give me chicken any day of d'week in preference. Major Lewis he may be right when he say it ain't right to eat any animals that are green.' Another time he told the steersman to take the *bateau* inshore and, leaning over, he pulled from a branch a black snail-like crustacean the size of a cricket ball. I remembered Raleigh's story of the oysters that had grown on trees and wondered if this was what he had been thinking of. In fact it was not, but its habits are similar. When the river is low the female snail slowly climbs the trees by means of a suction vacuum opening, which Henry showed me. Its eggs are laid on the branches where they gradually develop. The Arawaks call it *cracata*, the Caribs *curuape*, and both think its flesh a great delicacy. Its juice is heated and used as a cure for earache. Henry's reunion dinner with his wife was now complete; curuape for hors d'œuvre, excellent salted gillbacker[1] for the fish course, and roast iguana for the entrée. Dessert would be no problem.

A king vulture passed overhead, its red hood and neck quite plain in the sun, a huge and lovely bird, flying to a forest banquet with heavy flapping of wings, alone and sovereign. Henry told me that all other vultures withdraw from the carrion when the king arrives and wait for him to gorge his fill before presuming to eat another morsel. He had seen the lesser creatures lower their heads and walk backwards from the feast. I was, I'm ashamed to say, at the time a little suspicious of what Henry told me, but Schomburgk's descriptions of these scenes, which always fascinated him, arc even more bizarre than Henry's. He says that after the ordinary vultures have withdrawn the king stands looking at the feast with his head and neck drawn deep into his wings; for some minutes he contemplates, encouraging his salivary flow, and then moves into the attack. His appetite is so great that often he is incapable of flight after the meal. Schomburgk's passage on the habits of the bird was fantastic enough for the naturalist Von Tschudi to disbelieve it completely, but he wrote, in fact, without exaggeration. I found later that most Indian chiefs wear a king-vulture feather as a sign of their position.

There were showers during the day, but most of the time we could sit on the roof and enjoy the unfierce sun. It is impossible to sit in the sun on the Coast, but normally the sun is bearable in the Interior, and in general temperatures are lower. I imagine this is because protective moisture rises all day from the rain forests. There was no need to sleep today; unlike the mangrove the forests here had variety and the eye could be satisfied continuously; clouds of yellow or blue morphos butterflies would rise and flutter across the river, kingfishers were everywhere with their exaggerated proboscies, and occasionally I would see a bird whose name I have forgotten, a bird with a body which might form the prototype for some superb aeroplane of the future. Two or three times during the day we passed rafts of logs tied up to the bank and the hammocks of Indians slung in the bush near by. The Indians were waiting for a

---

[1] The glue made from the gillbacker is probably the toughest glue in the world. Henry swore to me that he uses it in preference to nails.

rise in the river level, when they would steer their little rafts down to the sawmill at Mount Everard. These Warrau woodsmen have no weapon against the forest other than an axe. Unable to penetrate the forest they are creaming off the marketable trees along the river, and before long the only trees left will lie too far from the river to be manhandled. As it is, the wood merchants of George-town complain that the lengths of wood are far too short. This is because the Indians must hack up a fine cedar trunk into lengths which he can man-handle into the water. One day, as in the case of gold in this area, only machinery will be able to do the work.

We arrived at Arakaka during the late afternoon chorus of a family of red howlers. This scattering of a dozen or so shacks stood on a beautifully situated bluff thirty feet above the Barima, with a view northwards above the jungle. A handful of Creoles came down to meet the boat and helped me unload my boxes.

During the gold shout early in the century Arakaka was a flourishing little township with a hotel, and shops which served the cluster of near-by mining centres — Crocodile, Millionaire, Golden City, Determination, Five Stars, Old World, Annie's Creek. The Barima was kept so free of tacoubas that a small steamer could go up-river to Arakaka itself. Ten thousand gold and diamond prospectors then worked the area, and the saloons of Arakaka did splendid business. Now there are only Major Lewis and a handful of prospectors, one little room which serves as a rum parlour, a shop which grubstakes the prospectors and buys their gold, a rest-house cum court-house for the visits of the District Commis-sioner, a lock-up, a police post and a few battered shacks. The keeper of the rest-house came down to meet me, an old Negro with a Coptic cast of face, a straggly little beard and skinny body.

'Me is Chin, sah,' he said in his slow sweet voice as his hand went out to shake mine, 'me guess yo' most certainly would appreciate a good hot, strong cup tea, eh? Me go straight now down to me Mammy and get that very thing fo' yo' now, sah.'

He moved slowly off towards a shack some fifty yards away. I was surprised to hear so ancient a man refer to his Mammy and when I questioned him later he said that she was his foster mother, which did little to satisfy my curiosity. In fact she was his 'reputed wife', as mistresses are called in British Guiana. A Creole once described such a relationship to me as a state of 'faithful concubinage'. Old Chin had returned with the tea daintily laid on a tray — the teapot and cup were of thin porcelain, probably left over from Arakaka's better days. While I drank the tea Chin talked to me. Being of the old school his language had not been modified by education. For me, no doubt, he did not speak in the full Creole dialect, which is almost incomprehensible, but his language had the simplicity of grammar and the love of high-sounding phrases which are such a delight to hear. He had prospected all his life, all over the colony, and now he was out to grass as the rest-house keeper here at Arakaka. One of his stories specially impressed me, and as I wrote it down very soon after hearing it, I think I have preserved many of his phrases intact.

'Permit me mak yo' understand, sah,' he began, 'dat what me about to inform yo' of ain't such things as liard fellas tell. Back in d' great year of 1912 oh dere was a time fo' all all o' we Arakaka side here. An' it was a time, me say, when him wid d'shut mouth nevva catch fly. All a man got to do is open he mouth. Permit I an explanation. Dat year d'river him went down and down and down and still d'rain nevva come, and down dere, me tell yo', sah, dere comes a day when by d'glory o' d'Lord not one dam drop o' water lies in d'river bed. An' one fella him starts adiggin' of d'river bed and in he battel him find good good pay dirt. So all o' we begins adiggin' in d'river, shoulder to shoulder, thousan's of we waiting against d'arrival of d'rain once mo'. An' at night us go down to d'river wid bush-lanterns o' spirit in a bottle wid a wick and a fella c'd look down to d'river from here and see no single t'ing but all o' we lit up by d'bush lanterns already referred to. All us monkeys sure knows on what limb to climb and soon even a two cents man c'd change his half bit gold. Fo' six whole an' glorious weeks it was d'same, sah, me is tellin' yo': 1302 ounces of d'finest gold in six weeks, sah. An' den d'rain him come an' in one night d'river rise twenty — thirty feet and all dat good gold is lost again to we. Me waits all I life since, sah, fo' dat miracle to occur but once again, but me fully supposes dat me goes to d'cradle of Heaven above without seein' amore dat miraculous occurrence.'

Chin's story was no exaggeration. When I began looking into

the fascinating history of the Guiana gold-rush I found that this was the most famous story of the period. There was an irony of which Chin was no doubt ignorant. In 1902 a dredger had been brought to Arakaka and had worked on the same spot as the diggers, producing a mere one hundred and thirty ounces in nine months before being abandoned. Why should ten times as much gold have been dug by hand in six weeks a decade later? The answer is, I am assured, that the gold is alluvial and river-borne. Somewhere, in its course from the Mountains of Emeria, the Barima picks up its particles of gold. And the Mountains of Emeria are part of a cordillera on whose western side Sir Walter Raleigh believed El Dorado to lie and in whose foothills he 'sawe all the hils with stones of the cullor of gold and silver'. The river-borne gold is still in the North-West, but so thinly spread in water and alluvial soil that only such men as Major Lewis still think it can be made to pay.

Looking back on the history of the gold-rush one is forced to sympathize with F. T. Palgrave's rather irritating remark, made when he was in the colony, that 'the first man who brings in the news of remunerative gold-fields ought to have from the colony a rope for his reward, and if it silences his voice before he has time to make his discovery public so much the better'. During the seventeenth and eighteenth centuries the careful Dutch, who then owned the colony, took little notice of the El Dorado myth, quietly planting their sugar on the riverain lands of the Essequibo, Demerara and Berbice. They presumably thought, with Lord Bacon, that 'the hope of mines is very uncertain, and useth to make the planters lazie in other things'. A Dutch prospector did, in fact, find gold traces in 1719, but decided the find was not workable. The less phlegmatic Spaniards north of the Orinoco revived their interest in El Dorado in 1775, when an expedition set off for the cordilleras, from which only one man returned to tell the tale. The first true gold shout in British Guiana came in 1857 when the colony had been a British possession for forty-six years. This was on the Cuyuni, a large tributary of the Mazaruni, whose head-waters flow south from the Mountains of Emeria, whereas those of the Barima flow north. The 1857 shout came to nothing, and for thirty-four years prospecting was sporadic: 1884, for instance, was a good year, with

250 ounces registered. Then, in 1891, came the great Upper Mazaruni shout, followed in a few years by the Barima shout. In 1891, 101,297 ounces were registered, and in 1923 only 6000 ounces. A 42½ lb. nugget was found in the shallow workings of the Upper Mazaruni.

In reading copies of the colony's magazine *Timehri* for this period it is impossible not to notice the general feeling of euphoria produced by the gold discoveries. British Guiana was a poor colony. Sugar was passing through one of its hardest periods. Standards of living among the Coast Creoles and East Indians were low. Everybody, from the humblest cane cutter to the Governor, imagined that gold would transform the colony into a rich and powerful land. El Dorado was found. In defending Raleigh against the defamation of David Hume, the staid historian of the colony, James Rodway, said of Raleigh's account of El Dorado that 'every sentence glows with truth and accuracy'. There was talk of a vast auriferous belt across the country. The village of Bartica Grove, at the conjunction of the Mazaruni and the Essequibo, was imagined as a potential entrepôt city for the mining areas of the Interior, and was accordingly redesigned in city style. The Chief Sheriff of the colony, Henry Kirke, wrote: 'Bartica with its unfinished houses, its phantom avenues, rowdy diggers and ladies of the demi-semi-monde may be said to be *in transitu*, but soon, we hope to blossom forth in the full sheen of its perfected existence.'

An interesting issue to the gold shouts was that they brought Britain near to war with Venezuela over the boundary question. In 1895 Venezuela tardily decided that the Dutch had squatted on Spanish territory and that the true border should be formed by the Essequibo — an arrangement that would conveniently have given the entire gold area to Venezuela. A dishonest American named W. L. Scruggs was employed by the Venezuelan Government to gain the ear of President Cleveland and whisper the magic words 'Monroe Doctrine'. Cleveland sided with Venezuela and said that the United States would resist any wilful aggression in this area by Britain. Eventually an arbitration commission was appointed and the historians of Europe gathered a wealth of information[1] on the early colonization north and south of the Orinoco. All agreed that

[1] Their findings may be seen at the British Museum.

the Venezuelan claims were fictitious, and apart from two small concessions, the boundary remained as it had been defined by Sir Robert Schomburgk in the 1840s. A British newspaper wrote of the concessions, 'We have lost nothing that would not have been dear at a £5 note.' One of these concessions, the land at the mouth of the Barima, would, in fact, be of great value to us today. The manganese from Matthews' Ridge must be loaded on to ships at Barima mouth, and Venezuela naturally has the yea and nay in the matter.

Matthews' Ridge lies some ten miles inland from Arakaka, and a rough jeep track traverses the corrugations of forest-covered ridges which compose most of the fine landscape of this region. There was a half-way camp, known as Five-Mile, and a messenger had been sent on my arrival to ask for a jeep to come down to collect me. When Old Chin had gone back to his foster mammy I sat on the rotting veranda of the rest-house and read, waiting for the jeep. From the rum parlour came the murmurous conversation of a few prospectors, and one or two members of what Sheriff Kirke called the demi-semi-monde were sitting laughing on a grass verge. Above these sounds I had heard for some time a long moan uttered at regular intervals — the moan not so much of a man in pain as in misery. When Chin returned once again I asked him about the moaning.

'Oh him, sah, him is a Highlander in d'lock-up awaitin' d' District Commissioner at d'end of next mont'.'

My eyes opened wide. Was some brawny Scot from the Black Watch moaning away in that unwindowed lock-up without benefit of habeas corpus? What had he done to be arrested in this god-forsaken place? After questioning Chin I realized that I had mistaken 'H'islander' for 'Highlander'; it referred to anyone who came from the islands of the Caribbean. The aspiration is general and unfailing. Chin's modesty with me made him deny knowledge of what this H'islander had done, but at the rum parlour I learnt that he had raped a four-year-old girl, the daughter of one of the villagers. The father had threatened to murder him and he was in the lock-up as much for his own protection as for the enforcement of the law. For rape of this kind, I gathered, he would get a stiff gaol sentence, but, in general, rape in these parts was not taken too seriously. There had been the case of a Creole employee of the manganese company who had been arrested for raping an old woman. While waiting for the D.C. to hold court he had been allowed bail on a £12 surety, the money being taken from his weekly salary by the Company. When finally he came up for trial the D.C. fined him £3, which meant that the court returned him £9. When the money was handed to him he burst into delighted laughter, crying, 'Dog bust me liver, is me a fool widout he own sense? Me goes and rapes dat ol' woman d'ere and, ho, me gets a full thirty-eight dollas fo' d'deed. Dat is d'fairness of d'law hisself.' Delighted, he took the old woman and her husband off to the rum parlour where the thirty-eight dollars were spent in sporting.

The manganese company employs Creole labour for heavy road-making work, and Carib labour for cutting lines through the forest for further prospection. The Creoles are not allowed to have any women in their camps, so Arakaka supplies their sexual needs. Each man shares a 'keeper' with two other men, and they visit Arakaka once or twice in the week to see her. The system works well enough, though in such a situation animosities are inevitable. The Creoles will certainly sleep with Indian women, and the purity of Carib blood will be reduced yet again.

Night fell, a dark moonless night, and still the jeep hadn't arrived. Hours went by and then I heard the distant hum of an engine. Slowly it approached and we carried my boxes by torchlight through the low bush to the beginning of the track. We found, not a jeep, but a ten-ton truck. The delay had been caused by an accident in which it had stuck in a drainage ditch. The driver had sent for a bulldozer to extricate his truck. It was a slow, weird journey along that narrow muddy track, rutted two feet deep with tyre marks, with the headlights bizarrely illuminating the vegetation of the high forest. At one point I could make out a magnificent towering purpleheart, standing alone in a piece of cleared land. Beneath this tree, half a century ago, a prospector had murdered his two companions for the gold. The murderer was hanged; tradition has it that the purpleheart was his gallows, but I doubt whether the District Commissioner in those days would have had so romantically grisly an imagination.

At last we came to a cluster of three corrugated aluminium huts, each with a cheerful electric light outside, and from one hut a dark and stocky man appeared to greet me. His name was Coffy, the camp manager, and he ushered me into his hut. The aluminium walls shone brightly in the light of the naked bulb, haloed by hundreds of insects. A fine jaguar skin decorated one wall, a six-foot bow and a blowpipe another. Two bush-shirted men rose from their Dunlopillo-cushioned armchairs as I entered and introduced themselves. One, a plumpish, jovial man in his early fifties was the office manager, the other an American botanist who had been sent by Union Carbide to make a systematic study of the ecology of the area in order to trace the relationship between plant life and manganese. He had just finished his work and was going down-river next day to Mount Everard. Here he had a rendezvous with the B.G. Airways Grumman amphibian which would fly him direct to Georgetown. After a few hours in Georgetown he was catching a Pan-American aeroplane direct to New York. He sat drinking his whisky, and described the dinner he would have at Suchow's in just three nights from now.

The whisky flowed and the talk never ceased — talk about jaguars, Caribs, Kenaima and the True Caribs on the Barima's twin river, the Barama,[1] above the Towakaima falls. We talked of gold, diamonds and snakes, the trees of the forest and the huge precipitations of the clouds, of poison arrows, manatees and manganese. And there was the story of the over-efficient Creole who had painted the camp's outside lavatory seat with black paint and forgotten to inform anyone, with unpleasant results. During the conversation Coffy made one of his wise remarks about life in equatorial forests. 'Any fool can be uncomfortable in the bush,' he said. 'You've got to be clever and a rare stickler for comfort, otherwise it's — awful.'

I slept well that night in an improvised bed, lulled to sleep by the insistent sound of hardbacks hurling themselves against the resonant aluminium.

We breakfasted early next morning in a hut raised on stilts which formed the camp mess. It was completely open on one side, the other three walls being formed of flattened pieces of tree-bark.

[1] Both rivers derive their names from the Carib word *bereme*, meaning ant-bear.

Smith, the office manager, went down the road to the office hut to give the labourers their pay — in the form of chits negotiable at the camp store. I spent the morning with Coffy, hearing the story of the camp, and making plans for my trip to the Barama in search of the tribe of True Caribs. He had heard of them; the Indians employed by the Company were comparatively sophisticated and civilized, but they had often told him of the Barama tribe who had cut themselves off from civilization centuries ago and had preserved all their ancient customs. The Schomburgks had never visited them. The District Commissioner had never penetrated to the reaches of the river where they lived, and the only law they knew was tribal. We studied the untrustworthy maps of the area, and the only trail which went in the general direction of where I imagined the tribe to be ended on the Barama some way below the Towakaima falls. This would mean going above the falls and paddling up-river till we came to the villages. It meant travelling two sides of a triangle, but this seemed unavoidable. Coffy said he could spare me two Indian carriers — to let me have more would have slowed down the cutting of an important line. To avoid an eventual anticlimax, I should say at this point that I never reached the lost tribe, although the journey in search of it proved to be exciting and worthwhile.

In the afternoon Coffy drove me in his jeep to the camp at Matthews' Ridge. It was an appalling road, for stretches at a time a mass of viscous mud which was difficult to cross even with four-wheel drive. I then realized what had lain behind Smith's remark that though he had been at the camp six months he had only once met Jay, the geologist at Matthews' Ridge. Nobody would make that trip in the jeep unless he had to. The consolation for the constant jolting was a series of superb, always changing views from the top of each ridge. Finally we saw Matthews' Ridge, defiant and fortress-like on the skyline. It had still its 'maydenhead'; not a scar on its tree-covered slopes, not a sign that man had been preparing for over four years to tear the face of its earth for precious ore. First a railway had to be surveyed and constructed through the difficult terrain, so that the ore could be taken to a point on the river where ocean-going ships could penetrate; powerful machinery had to be constructed on the spot to convert the unrefined ore;

contracts with the Government had to be ratified, a dozen projects to be completed before the first ore was extracted. If, in ten years' time, the first boatload of ore is sent northwards all will have gone well.

Jay came out from his assaying laboratory to greet us, and ordered bottles of beer. We talked for an hour during a furious rainstorm and then walked over to his aluminium hut. It was beautifully set on the cleared lower slopes of the ridge itself, with a background of tropical vegetation and banana plants. His wife came running out to meet him with a parakeet on her shoulder, a pretty young English girl in a gay summer dress, whom he had married a few months before in Georgetown. She brought in a plate of thin cucumber sandwiches and a pot of tea, and talked gaily to us about the deliciousness of life at the Ridge, and how whenever she was in Georgetown she couldn't wait to get back to the camp. There was no insincerity in what she said; she was clearly a profoundly happy girl.

On the journey back Coffy said that we would stop at one of the Creole camps on the roadside and ask what news there was of the wild bushman, the massakruman. There had recently been many complaints from the Creole workers that the massakruman had been active, and I was promised a fine spate of language and practical folklore. We pulled up at a camp, where the workers were now washing away the sweat of the day before cooking their evening heap of rice and meat. Coffy called one man over and asked him, very seriously, if the massakruman had been to the camp the night before.

'Baas,' said the man, 'that debl fella him come las' night and all d'nights, him never leave we alone, him saucy like a jigger wid we. Las' night him come as is his usual custom and him knocks wid an axe o' wid a club on each tree as him passes, in a manner of announcin' hi' approachin' arrival. Oh, an' how quick him go from place to place, here an' there and ev'rywhere. But we's safe, baas, dat deb'l won't do we no harm cos we is in a group here an' he no like a cluster of persons. But if jus' one o' we went out alone he'd kill d'fellow. An' dere's on'y one way to kill d'debl an' dat is to put a silver coin in yo' cartridge an' shoot he. Yes, sah, a silver coin will fully accomplish all dat is required. An' dere ain't no need even to shoot cos d'massakruman he know dere is silver in d'gun an' he go and never come back no more.'

I asked him if he had ever seen the massakruman and he said, 'Sah, no man in dis camp has seen he, but we all heard he. But him like a big big hairy ape wid d'strength o' ten men and d'intelligence of a living person, sah.'

CARIB POT FROM THE NORTH-WEST DISTRICT

CARIB BASKET WORK

The Falls of Towakaima

THERE was a great deal for me to do at the Five-Mile camp; although each of my two droghers[1] could carry about 100 lb., such essentials as hammocks, lantern, paraffin, blankets, ammunition and trading goods made it impossible to take much food. I had to weigh the value of a light tarpaulin against four tins of corned beef. Finally the two loads were put aside ready for the morning and the rest returned to their boxes.

At seven o'clock to the minute the Indians appeared round the point of the road. They were small men — Rodrigues Marques, and his nephew, Cyril, who was about twenty-five. They wore shirts and khaki trousers, but no shoes. Rodrigues had a Spanish style moustache which went well with his name, and Cyril had the fine dark down on his face which showed that he was not a pure-blooded Indian. They spoke Carib, called themselves Caribs and had lived the life of Caribs, but somewhere in their family tree a European ancestor would be found. Later Rodrigues told me that long ago a Spaniard had come to the village where his people had lived, and that one of his forefathers had been that Spaniard. He explained this with the few words of English which he and Cyril had picked up from the Creoles — an English which reflected Creolese in its grammar.

Each had brought his carrying basket, his *warishi*, with a few personal belongings at the bottom. I looked closely at the workman-ship of the warishis; one can tell from a glance at his warishi how decadent an Indian has become, or how far he has preserved the simple crafts of his people. These were beautifully made, firm and well bound, the flat split stems of the iturite reed woven to form a geometrical pattern, representing in the most abstract form a snake

[1] Derived from the name for Dutch sailing boats which tramped the Caribbean in former times.

opening his mouth to swallow a scorpion. The headbands and arm-straps are made from the pliant inner flesh of a young tree. They last for perhaps a week of continuous travel before they have to be replaced.

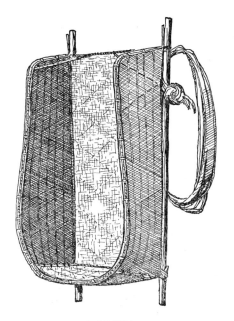

A WARISHI

Cyril and Rod, as I decided to call him, packed my baggage into the warishis, covered it with sections of plantain leaf and laced the whole securely with thin lianas. Then, without a word, they hoisted their burdens on their backs and strode off through the long grass towards the forest. I shook hands with Coffy and was off down the slope towards the creek where my excellent breakfast fish had been caught. The forest began abruptly beyond the creek, but the trail we were taking was not what I had expected. Years ago it had been a simple Indian trail, wide enough only for travelling in Indian file, but during the border disagreement with Venezuela it had been hurriedly widened and given the grandiose name of Military Road, a name it still humorously bears on the maps. When the possibility of war with Venezuela had passed, the road was

given back to Nature, and I had expected to find it overgrown with
the worst obstacle of the forest, secondary vegetation, and a crop
of new trees. But trees and vegetation do not grow easily at the
sunless ground level of the forest; the thousands of green saplings
which make passage so difficult between the grown trees remain
saplings perhaps for years until a parent tree falls, allowing the sun
and air to come to them so that the fittest may start its swift climb
to the canopy above.

And so today the trail was like a dark Sussex ride in autumn after
heavy rain — though no horse could have stood for long the corrugations of the tangled roots that lay beneath the mud, and the
endless sodden leaves that were about to disintegrate into muddy
humus; for leaves are falling every minute of the day and night in
the rain forests. Twice a year each individual tree sheds its leaves,
but the new green leaves are full-blown before the last of the old
leaves have fallen. In colour the leaves reverse the order of nature
as we know it in Europe. Once, when I flew over the forest at the
end of a period of rain, I was delighted to see the sodden autumnal
appearance of the tree canopies — the most delicate yellows and pale
bronzes, instead of the black-greenness of a week before. Though
the colours were springlike in their gaiety I presumed that the old
leaves had faded. In fact, in a week the old green leaves had fallen
and the young bronze and yellow leaves had replaced them.

I felt a strange excitement as I walked the trail. I was back in the
deep forests again after three years. For as long as I can remember
woods and forests have satisfied an indefinable yearning in me.
When I was five I spent some time in a fever hospital near East-
bourne, where part of the grounds were heavily wooded with
ancient trees which had survived that callous destruction of the
Sussex Weald. The nurses would never let us go into the green
mysterious gloom, which, they said, was full of snakes and nasty
things; and I would stand in fear and fascination at the edge of the
wood, wondering what kind of life was to be found there. Then
there was the beautiful and forbidden Shelley Wood near my
school, where on free summer afternoons I would sit reading on
last autumn's leaves in a pool of sunlight and imagine that Shelley
himself had once come to this spot. That was my summer wood.
In autumn there were exciting muddy runs to be made through

Marlpost Wood, with its streams and bridle-paths and low-branched trees. It was, I remember, on a hot summer Sunday in this wood that, with a friend, I came into a clearing where a high stone tomb stood alone, surrounded by iron palings. It was the tomb of a man neither of us had then heard of: Wilfred Scawen Blunt. And what tingling pleasure the inscription gave us as we read that on his Arabian travels he had taken with him barrels of water from the near-by stream. In those days I had cared only for the atmosphere of the woods. I had no idea what trees I walked amongst or what birds sang in their branches. The nearest I ever came to being a naturalist was to go searching for edible fungi with an Inselbuch as my guide. The woods drew me by an attraction which today I still don't understand. Perhaps it was the first untried expression of a need to know the primitive natural components of our world and life, without which a man walks, unknowingly, in a kind of darkness. Thoreau speaks for me when he says, 'I went to the woods because I wished to live deliberately, to front only the essential facts of life, and see if I could not learn what it had to teach, and not, when I came to die, discover that I had not lived.' The woods taught him to 'simplify, simplify'. I think they have taught me to see the marvellous complication of European civilization with a greater clarity, and to value it all the more.

All that day as we walked, crossing creeks and cutting our way through the saplings to avoid areas of secondary vegetation, I feasted my eyes as well as I was able, for in the forest it is always wise to keep your eyes fixed on the ground immediately in front of you. I knew that it was foolish to look up and sense that 'terrible doubt of appearances' which the forest, more than any other scene, can give; but I would look about me till I tripped on a root or over a fallen tree. It was these trees I liked least, not merely because they were obstructions, but because they are the favourite sleeping places of snakes during the day. A wise man never steps over a trunk, for that would make his leg a close target for the awakened snake; he steps up on to the log and then down, taking a full pace to do so. The effort is correspondingly great and it is the mark of a forest greenhorn to be wise in this manner. We saw few snakes that day and I myself only one — a beautiful coral snake which sluggishly moved off across the sodden leaves without so much as turning its poison fangs in my direction. The snakes are there, but unless one has an Indian's eyes one does not see them — and those that one sees are only those too sluggish to retreat as the vibrations of approaching feet give warning. There is only one snake in the forests which does not feel fear in the presence of man, which will attack from a hundred yards and kill with certainty if his fangs go home: the bushmaster.

The dangers of the forest are largely mythical; the legend of the green hell dies hard; what dangers there are — jaguars, snakes and the ferocious giant ant-eater — are nothing compared with the fatigue brought on by twisted roots and mud, or the lacerations of the razor-grass in areas of secondary growth; the ache in the back as you walk through tunnels in this vegetation; the perpetual saturation of one's body and clothes with a cool sweat, in air that is humid but not hot; the sudden deluges of rain against which there is no protection, nothing to be done but walk on with shirt and trousers heavy and clinging, thinking of the sunny clearing where you may camp and change into dry clothes. The physical dangers are forgotten; they themselves build in a man's mind a psychological resistance to them. Absolute necessity can arouse one marvellously; within an hour I was beginning to forget my dread of snakes, and I found myself walking across a slender, slippery tree-trunk bridge with a creek tumbling over rocks ten or twenty feet below. We crossed thirty such bridges that morning, bridges which the Indians trotted across with their prehensile toes clinging to the moss and bark, but which I crossed with infinite deliberation, the insteps of my boots finding out the curve of the tree, knowing that I must not fall. Sometimes Cyril or Rod would take pity on me and come back to take my hand.

We made good time that morning, averaging about two miles an hour. Rod walked in front and Cyril behind me. Sometimes they would point to a spot on the leaves that seemed no different from the rest, and tell me a herd of peccary, the bush hog, had been through during the night. We saw no animal that day or on the days that followed, since the only way to see animals during the day is to search for their tracks and follow them to the lairs where they lie sleeping, waiting for night to come and the hunting to begin. At one point Rod turned to me, and in a calm voice with an inflection which suggested he was asking my permission said, 'Me shoot tiger, sir.' My heart jumped and I looked round for the animal he seemed to have spotted so casually. He smiled the remote Indian smile when he realized what I had thought and explained that we had come to the place where two weeks before he had shot a jaguar.[1] Knowing that the Indians only shoot jaguars who have become troublesome I asked him why he had killed it. 'Him kill I good good hunting dog, sir,' he replied.

At midday, with the sunlight refracting feebly on the planes of the leaves far above us, we sat down to rest and to eat some raisins and chocolate. I sat on one of the great pelvis-like buttresses of a mora tree, whose trunk towered up smooth, straight and branchless for two hundred feet, before bursting like some petrified firework into the mysterious canopy, a world too distant for us to see, or to hear the activities of its inhabitants. A creek rushed past us on its way to the Barima and I drank and drank its cold delicious water.

Rested, and without the preoccupations of roots and obstructions, I began to look at the forest with all my senses at the ready. Our dark world below was like some subterranean country that had never known the benefit of the sun. Columns of mora, cedar, silverballi, crabwood and savannadalli, unadorned with branch or leaf, stretched themselves taut with the effort to reach the sun. At ground level, between them, there was no vegetation, only the slim and patient saplings; a few lianas were drooping at the middle levels — for lianas, like the trees they attach themselves to, exist to escape the pallid, lifeless lower world. Even the trunks of the trees are like monolithic aerial roots whose existence is only justified when they have reached the upper world. Below there are no insects in the air, no flowers except in the oases of sunlight, no orchids or epiphytes, few birds other than the ground-nesting maam and powis. From above I could hear the screech of macaw and trogon, the quick nervous cry of the pai-paio, and once more looked up longingly into the canopy. That is the frustration of the tropical forest; what life and colour one would see if one walked all day in the upper world, the unending tree-roof, where the burgeoned trees mass like vegetable clouds, hosts to orchids and vines, fritillaries

[1] Indians and Creoles always call jaguars 'tigers'. The word jaguar itself is a French corruption of the name *yaouar*, used by the Indians of the Oyapock River in French Guiana.

and the great morphos butterflies who rarely come to earth, and sail like birds in the canopy; where marabunta wasps raid the flowers and small insects move unknowingly into the beautiful, innocuous-seeming petals of the pitcher flowers, to be trapped and slowly devoured by sinister osmotic action; where sloths move dreamily along the branches, their bodies hanging upside down; where ant-eaters from the forest floor come in search of food; where the families of howler monkeys dismally await their urge to roar. But most of all I should like to walk in that canopy to see the birds; for it is here, in the sun, that the coloured birds live — toucans, parrots, macaws, trogons, the glorious varieties of humming birds, with their feathers gleaming and fading phosphorescently as the light falls from different angles, the colonies of bunya birds and the snow-white bellbirds.

But all was a world of the imagination; no man has ever lived in the forest canopy or visited it long enough to know its secrets; it is a world immune even to the scientific predatoriness of man, who can climb to the summits of great mountains, but can never climb through the vegetation of the tree-roof and see that moment when, it is supposed, the queen ant, who has flown up to the sun from the forest floor, makes coitus with her suitor and falls — not flies — back to her nest in a fallen tree-trunk.

I lowered my eyes after these minutes of colourful fancy; I would see no trogons here below, with their scarlet chests, only the dun-coloured maams and powis or an occasional ant-bird. No orchids, tillandsias or cattleyas, nor even the strange insects that provide food for the birds. Here there were no flies, no wasps, no insects of any kind. This world, with its still air and silence, is man's stratum of the forest.[1] It was only here that I would be able to see into the life of things.

After we had eaten, we moved up the escarpment. Rain merci-fully held off for the rest of the day, and there were fewer creeks,

---

[1] It was that fine writer and greatest of all geographers, Alexander von Humboldt, who described the rain forests of South America as 'forest piled on forest'. Even the canopy is stratified, and many fully grown trees never reach the upper canopy. It is at these intermediate levels that the ant-eaters forage. On the forest floor climatic conditions vary very little, with not more than five degrees' variation in twenty-four hours. In the canopy the variation is twenty degrees. Rain does not evaporate on the floor, so that conditions are always wet; in the canopy the rain evaporates at such a rate that from above steam appears to be rising from it. On the floor, air moves at an average rate of a mile a day, while the air in the canopy averages ten miles a day.

although the areas of sunlit space — and consequent vegetation — increased. Always, as we pushed through the undergrowth, we would see the same scarlet flower, the somuto, petals tightly rolled before opening and, like so many flowers of the tropics, obscene. I realized later why there were so many open spaces: this flat part of the forest had once been a favourite area for Indian cultivation. The Indians had made their little garden places by cutting down the trees and burning the stumps and vegetation. In the resulting humus they would bury their sticks of cassava and leave them untended until the time of harvest. In spite of the usual speed of growth in the tropics it takes nearly a year for the cassava roots to mature; various sections of the field are planted at different times, so that some roots reach maturity in each month of the year. And then the land after some years would tire, or the Indians themselves would wander northwards, and the garden places would be left to Nature, the saplings would rise and the undergrowth proliferate.

At four o'clock, after we had walked some twenty miles, Cyril said to me, 'We come Pedro's garden place, sir, camp there.' I was relieved. I had imagined we might have to sling our hammocks between trees in the forest. There was, Cyril added, a benab — or hut — at the garden place. We turned off the main trail into a narrow path, and a few minutes later we were in an area of cleared bush about a hundred yards square. There were grass and cassava plots and a magnificent plantain tree, whose great leaves flapped in the breeze and were glossy enough to reflect the beams of the sun. The sky was blue and clear, the sun — after our day in pale filtered light — a thing to worship. In the middle of the clearing stood the benab, a hut open on all sides, in which we found Pedro's simple property — he was away cutting lines for the manganese company. There were his black calabashes, his low wooden seat, his matapi[1] for expressing the poison acids from the cassava, his stone-studded instrument for scraping the cassava root into flour, his manairi for sifting the flour, and his sandura — his drum of bush-hog skin — to pass the lonely hours of the evening and to scare away the evil

---

[1] On the Oyapock, French Guiana, matapi is the Indian word for the camoudi snake. The cassava matapi is a long snakelike basket which is filled with flour, and then by leverage so stretched that the hydrocyanic acid is removed. This acid is processed into a black treacle-like substance called casareep, which has the property of preserving meat. Casareep is kept permanently in the 'pepper-pot' and meat is added as required.

spirits of the forest, and marauding animals. The place was ours to do as we wished with, the plantains were ours to cut; that is the Indian communism of the forest and no man disputes it. If he goes down to his landing and finds somebody has taken his woodskin he shows no anger, but goes in search of another man's woodskin. The more remote from civilization a tribe is, the more the sense of personal property is lacking; thieving is meaningless and dishonesty must take other forms.

I changed into dry clothes and put my soaking drills on to a tree stump to dry in the sun. Rod looked at me and without saying a word walked off into the bush, returning with a length of bush rope, strong and pliable as cord. A few minutes later my clothes were hanging drably from the line. It was now Cyril's turn to go into the bush, but he was going in search of a powis (the crested curassow), a maam, or a duraquara (the Guiana partridge). Evening was approaching and the partridges would be awake. I heard soon the distant rolled sound of the partridge's cry — 'dur-r-r-a-quar-r-ra' — but I knew that it was Cyril, one of the best hunters of the district, enticing the female to reply and lead him to her. The reply came; there seemed no difference whatever in the sound, and when some minutes later a shot rang through the forest we knew that Cyril had not missed his mark. Ammunition is so scarce in the forests that an Indian will only shoot when he is certain of his prey. He stalks it till he is so close that he cannot miss. Again we heard the beautiful, pellucid call. Indians are superb mimics of the voices of animals, birds — and men. They can mislead even the jaguar: an Indian luring an acouri with its call was once jumped on and killed by a jaguar who thought he had found his favourite meat. They bring the yarrau fish towards them with a low seducing whistle; they reproduce the mating call of the tapir by blowing into the enclosed palms of their hands; they attract certain fishes to the air by splashing the surface of the river in such a way as to suggest the falling of ripened seeds. I noticed that if I ever taught an Indian a new English word he would reproduce not merely the right sound but an unintentionally satirical echo of my own particular way of saying the word. A few years ago an Englishman came across an Indian in the bush, dressed in nothing but a red linen lap, or loin cloth, who approached him with outstretched hand, saying in a perfect parody of an educated Englishman's accent, 'I say, how absolutely delightful to meet you.' He then relapsed into his own language, for the phrase he had spoken was all the English he knew. Years before, he had accompanied an expedition led by an Englishman who had greeted fellow Englishmen in the Interior in this manner.

Cyril came back with his partridge and began to pluck and draw it while Rod built a fire. I was lying in my hammock. During the day, walking in file, there had been little chance for us to know each other, although I had been impressed by both men's wish to be good hosts to me in their forest. They had shown no emotion all day; this detachment did not mean that they were indifferent; I knew that I was being studied, sized up. Probably as they talked together they were discussing me and coming to some kind of judgment. Wary of this I had tried all day to win their confidence in me as a bushman. This wasn't mere vanity; if Indians disapprove of the character of the man they are conducting through the forest that man may wake one morning to find he is alone, and that he doesn't stand a chance of following the scarcely marked trails. Apart from this self-preserving motive I was hoping I might be able to make some kind of rough contact with the Carib mind. I had engraved on my mind the fine words of Richard Schomburgk which I had read some weeks before, and which are worth recording here because they contain so much wisdom about civilized man's relations with primitive man:

Treat . . . an Indian as a friend, so as to let him feel through intercourse with you that he is of the same flesh and blood that he honours and respects in yourself. Do not budge a single hair's breadth from the truth; do not be guilty of any weakness he may be inclined to commit; be circumspect in everything you do; do not repulse his friendly advances, however hard it may prove, with severity or false pride; share his innocent pleasures; let him see that you sympathize with his troubles and his sorrows, and truly you will get on better with these folk than with the outwardly brilliant companionship of Europe. Morality and virtue need not be brought from civilized Europe — Indians have a far more tender regard for them than we have.

Schomburgk spoke for his time; civilization may have had its malign effect on the virtue of some Indians, but in general I think his words need little modification today.

I ate my heaped plate of rice and tinned steak while the Indians sat down to a partridge stew, for which I had given them some curry powder. They dipped the whitish fragments of a cassava flat-bread into the sauce and enjoyed the new taste. This bread, like all the cassava bread I was to eat, had the consistency of crisp asbestos and was as savourless. It is without taste even to the Indians, who make it edible by dipping it in the pepper-pot or a smaller pot of spiced and peppered sauce. It has a high starch content, and such large quantities are eaten that the Indian's body is usually covered with svelte layers of fat which conceal the development of his muscles. The culture of the Indians of the tropical forests of South America is a cassava culture, just as that of Central America and Mexico is a maize culture. The Mayas owed their civilization to the discovery of maize, and I have often wondered what the history of the equatorial forest Indians would have been if they had discovered maize rather than the inferior cassava. The Maya lowland culture flowered in a terrain no more welcoming than the Guiana forests; with maize the Caribs, Warraus and Arawaks might have stabilized and united, afforded the luxury of a cultural élite, built great stone cities and carved fine idols and altars. Or was there inborn genius in the Mayas which would have triumphed over the disability of cassava, a genius which did not exist in their distant cousins of Guiana?

In the last light of the evening I lay gently swinging in my hammock, while the rain fell a foot or two from me. I then saw the simple ingenuity of the benab; its floor was raised a few inches from the surrounding ground, and the manicole palm-leaf roof overhung like an eave, so that the water fell clear of the floor and drained away in a neat rivulet. I looked up at the sloping roof and admired the geometrical laying of the leaves, which formed a simple pattern of great beauty. I noticed that the hut was constructed from many different kinds of wood — and then began my long questioning of the Marques. They were patient; they told me the central uprights which supported each gable end were always made from the strong slender trunk of the kouta tree, that kakarali must be used for the horizontal sideposts, and the cross-beams at the gable ends must be made of the strongest wood of the forest, krokai, on which to tie the scale lines of the hammock. I lighted the lantern and watched Cyril, sitting by the dying fire, laboriously scratching letters with a stick on the hard earth. Slowly he scratched out the unformed letters of his first name. It was all he could write, and always in the evening when he was pensive after food he would sit with his stick and make his mark. I asked him if he had ever been to the mission school, and he said no. 'But me is Christian, sir,' he said. It is always fascinating to know what Christianity means to primitive people who have been converted by its evangelists, and I asked Cyril about his early life and his conversion. He had been born and brought up, he said, in the village of Siniaparu on the Barama, and during his childhood he remembered seeing only a few white men, traders who had come to Siniaparu, given the children names (John Thomas, I gathered, was a common name) and moved on. 'When me still small,' Cyril went on, 'me go Arakaka side and white man he give I name Cyril and talk Christ. Me first hear Christ there.' The missionary had talked to him and other children for three days about Christ and the Christian God; then he had baptized them, and passed on up the river, leaving his seeds to flower. Cyril, however, had no conception whatever about the meaning of Christianity, or indeed that Christ himself was anything but a white man who promised much. When I asked him what he felt about his religion I received the simple but effective reply: 'Nothing.' 'But you *are* a Christian?' I insisted. 'Oh yeees, me is Christian,' he said, with the long sighing sound that punctuates all Carib speech.

I must have been a pest to them that evening; while they longed, in Indian fashion, to discuss each tiny incident of the day in the low agglutinative murmur which is the Carib language, here was I asking question after question and producing laughable sounds in imitation of the Carib words which they taught me. They concealed all signs of irritation, however, and repeated words and verb conjugations endlessly until I could transliterate them with some accuracy. The most significant thing about the language was the complete absence of English neologisms; all post-Conquest words were of Spanish origin, which suggested that in the past the Spanish influence from the Orinoco colonies had spread south into this part of British Guiana. When, much later, I was with the Akawaio[1] Indians who live in the high country of the Pakaraimas I found the Spanish neologisms existed but were much more infrequent. For instance, the Barama Caribs call a hat a *sumbederdu* (*sombrero*), while the Akawaios call it an *avok*. Both, however, call a gun an *arakabusa*, from arquebus.[2] Other Spanish neologisms among the Caribs are: *perro* = dog, *sapatos* = shoes, *sapato laoawundich* = socks, *plata* = money, *aranka* = orange (Sp. *naranja*). My questions made, I think, one small contribution to etymology, when I stumbled on the derivation of the word manatee, a derivation which appears in no literature on the subject which I have seen. The manatee is an aquatic mammal with a fishlike tail (it was the origin of the mermaid legend) and suckles its young from udders. I was asking the Marques what their word for milk was, and when they replied '*pakamanatil*' I asked what 'breast' was. '*Manatil*', they said. (See Appendix B.)

At last, as the night sounds of the forest intensified, I ceased my questioning and lost myself for half an hour in the crazy world of Dickens, while the Marques settled to their conversation — low, monotonous, full of sighs and yet punctuated with sudden starts of laughter as they presumably recollected some amusing happening of the day; the way I walked across the tree-trunk bridges, or the time Cyril caught his foot in a root. My sight weakened by the feeble light, I lay in my hammock feeling so exalted that in spite of the exertions of the day sleep would not come. I tried to imagine the scenes that were taking place at that moment in the civilization I had left; and I remembered what I could of Rilke's words that I had read long ago and which now seemed once again so appropriate:

> In order to write a single verse, one must see cities, and men and things; one must get to know animals and the flight of birds, and the gestures that the small flowers make when they open out to the morning. One must be able to return in thought to roads in unknown regions, to unexpected encounters, and to partings that had long been foreseen; to days of childhood

---

[1] Akawaios are of Carib stock, speaking a Carib dialect.

[2] According to Alfonso Vinci in *Samatari* (Bari 1956), the Scirisciana, south of the Orinoco and a tribe under Spanish influence, call a gun a *bombamade*.

that are still indistinct . . . and to mornings by the sea, to the sea itself, to oceans, to nights of travel that rushed along loftily and flew with all the stars.

There for me is the truth of travel, to cram the mind to bursting with the sights of the world so that the memory need never starve. The flower will wither but the seed will prosper. I shall never believe, with Proust, that travel is a romantic vanity, or that a writer can view the universe with the eyes of a hundred others unless he has glimpsed something of its vastness with his own. 'Le seul véritable voyage,' says Proust, '. . . ne serait pas d'aller vers de nouveaux paysages, mais d'avoir d'autres yeux, de voir l'univers avec les yeux d'un autre, de cent autres, de voir les cent univers que chacun d'eux est.' Yes, that is the greatest journey of all, but it is the imaginative journey that only genius is allowed to make.

We breakfasted in the first light and were away into the forest long before the sun had risen above the treeline, but we knew that above the canopy the sky was heavy with rain clouds, since the filtered sunlight would seem, almost, to be switched on and off as the clouds occulted the rays. The trail worsened; the land was saw-edged, a series of ascents and descents, the descents by their steepness becoming almost as tiring as the ascents. At one point, on a very steep rise, I peered through the forest at two huge and strange objects that blended in colour with the tree-trunks. I left the trail to examine them; one was an iron drum, some ten feet long, embedded deep in the humus; the other a round cauldron with gaping mouth like the head of some robot mastodon. All the visible surfaces were corroded with rust and I felt that time and the action of the water would one day reduce these abandoned monsters to dust. Abandoned they were, since 1934. They had been on their way to play their part in Axel Johnson's gold-mines at Crocodile and Old World. Against all advice they and other machinery had been brought up the Barama and landed at the village of Mazawini. No survey had been made of the terrain, a tractor merely pushed off along the trail, dragging the machinery behind it, its fuel the forest timber. After fifteen miles of slow advance and frequent breakdowns they had reached this point on the escarpment. The tractor was too weak to continue with its load.

The machinery was abandoned in the forest, and the gold-mine closed. The cauldron and the drum stand as perfect monuments to the optimism and the courage of Guiana's gold prospectors; and, perhaps, to the lost savings of ingenuous investors.

Rain came soon; not the furious showers of the day before, but a continuous downpour through which at times it was difficult to see. Our pace was slowed down, and I plodded on, trying to fill my mind with thoughts to make the hours go by, singing little songs to myself, repeating stray lines of poetry, anything to find some mental release from this dark subaqueous world, and from the exhaustion which gradually grew on me as we marched. I did not dare to ask how far we were from the Barama and the Towakaima falls, in case I should be told that we could not after all get there that day. Then, in the late afternoon, I noticed a change in the vegetation which suggested we were approaching a river, and soon I heard the distant roar of falling water. We increased our pace, and as we gained the crown of a barranca I realized it would be the last for that day — in the distance I could see the end of the trail, and a sliver of the river as it passed the gap in the corridor of trees. A few minutes later we were at the river landing; the sound of the fall was still distant, but the water was white and swift. We looked about for a woodskin at the landing to take us down-river to an inhabited place, but there was none. We shouted in the hope that someone would be fishing round the point, but when this was done we realized that we would have to make our way through the forest to the village, that we would have to leave the comparative comfort of a trail. It was a hard hour that followed, spent with our backs bent, winding through the vegetation, using 'cutlasses' frequently. At one point we came across the largest, most magnificent colony of bamboos I have ever seen, the poles eight inches in diameter and curving gracefully up for fifty or sixty feet. As we crunched across ground covered with fallen poles I looked up to see if I might by chance have come at one of those twenty-year intervals when the bamboo comes into flower. But the great poles were blossomless; I learnt from the Marques that it is possible to live a lifetime in the forest and never see the bamboo in flower.

We came to a track which, after ten minutes, led us to a clearing on a bluff overlooking the river. I could have cried out with delight as I stood once more in the hot sun and looked across to the empty benab. I imagined then that I had been through the worst the forest could give, and now that there would be food and rest I was glad to have done so; I did not know how endlessly the forest changes or that I was to know it in far darker moods.

I went down to the river, and, standing naked on a fallen tree trunk, washed away the day's sweat while birds sang and the slim body of a sunfish flashed for a moment on the surface of the dark water. While I stood drying in the sun a woodskin with three men rounded the river point. I hailed them and beckoned them to approach, and as they did so I tied my towel round my middle, remembering the extreme Indian modesty in such matters. Although the water was smooth it still ran swiftly with the force gained at the falls and it took some time for the woodskin to reach the landing. The paddlers were two pure Indian boys and an older man with some Negro blood, a small simian body and a sunken face suggesting some chronic illness. All were dressed in shirts and trousers that hung in tatters on their bodies. None spoke any English, and I signed to them to come up to the clearing, where Cyril interpreted for me. I wanted to know how far up the Barama, topside of the falls, there were villages, and whether they would take us up the river in their corial.[1] Expressionlessly the man, whose name was Robert, told Cyril that the people who lived topside of the falls were far, far away up near the Baramita, in the higher country. 'Did he know the river above the falls', I asked. No, he said, no one ever went above the falls, there was nothing there, though he had heard the river was dangerous. He knew every stone and current in the reaches of the river up to the falls, had known them since he was a child, but no one knew the ways of the river topside. To test his sincerity I produced cartridges, fish-hooks and bright cloth and said that if he himself couldn't take us I would give him some of each if he could find someone who would. His eyes goggled at what I showed him, but still he repeated that it was impossible. I gave him some cartridges and asked him to call for us in the morning and take us to his place.

When they had gone the Marques, too, told me that it was impossible to go topside, but I decided to leave the decision till the

---

[1] The largest sized Indian boat.

morning. If a way could be found to reach the Carib tribe I would find it then. Meanwhile I lay in my hammock, while the Marques prepared our food.

That night the insect and frog noises were as varied and as loud as they had been when I had slept on the bank of the Barima — the same castanetting of the tree-frogs and the orchestral scraping of crickets. I had so come to accept the frog's imitativeness of sound that I thought little of it when a fresh sound, a long purring growl, joined the rest; but when it increased in volume I began to feel uneasy. 'What is that?' I said, and Rod replied with complete calm from the depths of his hammock, 'Him tiger, sir.' 'Good God!' I cried, exploding, 'get your gun, get your gun!' 'They no hurt we, sir,' said Cyril, soothingly. 'Me leave tiger, tiger leave me.' His unconcern gave me confidence. 'Don't they ever attack men?' I asked. 'Tiger him go for man when in couple, sir.' 'How do you know there aren't a couple out there now?' I persisted. 'Only one, sir,' he said with a smile in his voice. 'He may go for his mate,' I said. With infinite patience he answered, 'No sir, tiger, him alone, sir, he no come for we.' And with this assurance I went off into a dreamless sleep. I might not have done so had I known that the jaguar's lack of interest in man is by no means proved, or if I had read the missionary, W. H. Brett, on the subject: 'Although the jaguar rarely attacks man, it is well known that he will do so if very hungry or favoured by darkness.' There are two types of jaguar in Guiana but many varieties, ranging from the rat-tiger, which is the size of a domestic cat, to the black jaguar, which can be nine feet long and is the boldest of the tribe. Richard Schomburgk wrote that he had 'been furnished with several accounts of the jaguar attacking people of its own accord' and Robert Schomburgk awoke one night to find a large black jaguar rubbing its back against the underpart of his hammock. At first he took it for his dog and gave it a sharp slap on the rump, which so astonished the animal that it took a flying leap through the canvas wall of the tent, like a well-trained circus performer going through the paper hoop. Richard Schomburgk gives credence to the mythical Warracabra jaguar which is supposed to hunt in ferocious packs and to imitate the shrill call of the trumpet-bird. The Indians say that they live in the highlands and only come to the lower country when food is scarce. Certain areas of the forest are avoided because they are the hunting grounds of Warracabra jaguars, and the myth is taken seriously, although no such animal exists. It is an invention which suggests that the Indian knows the potential danger of the jaguar, that there is good reason for the Arawak counsel of prudence, *Hamaro Kamungka turuwati* — 'everything has jaguar'. Jaguars are the most common first ancestor for the many tribes who claim an animal pedigree — and the original name of the Carib tribe — *Carinye* — means 'arising from a jaguar'.

Jaguars appear constantly, and anthropomorphically, in the Indian stories, but not always as villains — there is clearly respect for the great ancestor, as well as fear. There is a Carib story remarkable as an example of the ethics of the forest, in which even the animals may share. An Indian one day found the body of a tapir and, although he knew that a jaguar had killed it recently, he took it, smoked the meat and brought his wife to eat it with him. The wife saw that her husband had not killed the tapir himself, and expecting a visit from the jaguar built herself a high platform to sleep on, while her husband slung his hammock by the fire. The jaguar came and the woman called to her husband to take care, but even water and a burning ember held close to him would not wake him. By now the jaguar was close and she climbed to her platform out of reach, while she watched her husband being killed by the jaguar, who ate his flesh instead of the tapir's. For four days the jaguar feasted on the body while the woman watched, accepting the morality of the tiger's revenge.

Another story, told by the Warraus, again explains why the tiger kills Indians. One day, they say, Tobe-horoanna, the black tiger, caught a young man and put him in his pot. 'Don't be frightened,' he told him, 'I'm not going to eat you. You shall live.' Tobe-horoanna's brother and sister came home and when they saw the young man they asked whether he had been given anything to eat. 'No,' said Tobe-horoanna. 'Then give him a bush-hog,' they said, 'but if he doesn't eat it all we shall have to eat him.' The young man tried to eat all, but he couldn't and the tigers gave him a bowl of cassiri, which he drank, only to vomit it up the next moment. Tobe-horoanna and his brother thought there was something wrong with his mouth and so they held him down and pulled his jaws wide and poured down more cassiri. But the sister told them to stop; she

G

liked the young man and wanted to live with him. So they set him free and told him to prove he could support their sister as his wife by going into the forest to hunt. When he came back with a good bag Tobe-horoanna said he could have his sister, who eventually bore him twin sons. One day, when they were growing up, their father took them into the forest where they frightened him with their growls like thunder, but when he mentioned it to his wife she said that all tigers growled like that when travelling in the forest. Soon he began to feel homesick and went to see his mother and sister for a holiday. They were delighted to see him and asked if he had a wife. When he said yes, they told him he must bring his wife and children to see them. Very soon he did this, but when they arrived they found his mother had been drinking cassiri and her tongue was wagging. She looked at his wife and said, 'That is no proper wife — why, she is not even a woman. Don't you see she is a tigress and one day she will jump on you and destroy you. Shame on you for bringing her here.' And in fury she and her daughter set on him and killed both him and his wife who was defending him. Only the twin boys escaped and they returned to tell Tobe-horoanna what had happened, and he, very angry, went off and killed the mother, the daughter and all the guests who had been drinking cassiri with them.

Robert, the Indian, arrived while we were having breakfast and looked so hungrily at our food that I gave him some pumpernickel and jam. It is unusual for Indians ever to go hungry and I wondered at the almost ravenous way he ate. I had not realized then that the Barama Indians below the Towakaima falls were a people weakened by consumption and by undesirable miscegenation, that their will to improvement is almost non-existent. What I saw of their miserable settlements that morning made me wish that all the Indians of the Barama had preserved their customs and racial purity by fleeing to the country beyond the falls.

Robert lived with his wife and family a mile down-river. His wife lay so listless in her hammock that at my approach she turned away from me and took no further notice of our arrival. Skeletal curs, with fur burnt from rolling in embers to destroy parasites, barked round us; small filthy children burst into tears and ran

from us. The benabs were badly made with palm leaves laid inex-
pertly on the roofs. Only a pair of green parakeets relieved the sense
of sloth and hopelessness produced by the place. These wretched
people had been civilized to a certain point by contacts with white
men, who had then abandoned them, like the rusting machinery in
the forest. The rags they wore symbolized only too well the half-
world they lived in. How strange it is that missionaries should see
something sinful in nakedness. This is the constant cry of travellers,
but it can never, alas, be said too often.

There was less sign of sloth at another place we visited, a few
points down-river. The huddle of huts stood in an acre of forest
that had been cut and burnt, three rafts of crabwood trunks floated
at the landing. The women sat in their hammocks feeding their
children — I noticed one who shared her full breasts between a
new-born baby and a boy of four. It is usual for the children not
to be weaned until the birth of the next child. A man sat making
arrows from the flower stalks of wild sugar cane; they were fish
arrows, with a detachable head so that the shaft would not be
broken by the struggles of the fish. Another man sat tapping a
big sandura drum, another lay motionless in his hammock. Some
distance away, sitting on a tree-stump, a boy sat with something
on his lap which he was studying intently, as if he were reading.
An Indian reading is a rare enough sight and I approached him.
He was cleaner than the rest, with combed hair and a clean white
shirt; and there, indeed, on his lap was a grubby little book. I asked
him what he was reading, and he held up the book for me to see; it
was called *Elementary English*. He had evidently not yet learnt
much from the book, but slowly I gathered that he had been to the
mission school at Hossororo, and would like to be there still, but
that his help was needed to cut the crabwood and make the cassava
clearings. He was the first of a series of young Indians whom I
was to meet in all parts of the Interior who had genuine aspirations
to improve themselves, to find their places in the great white
civilization. Invariably they were unhappy people, cursed by
sensitivity and a half understood sense of superiority to others of
their tribe. Fifty years ago they might have been the mythmakers,
the poets, of their people, or found an outlet for their imaginations
in the mysteries of shamanism. I told this boy that if he wanted to

go to the mission school he should tell his father that he must find other help for the garden place and the tree-felling, and get into his woodskin and go back to Hossororo. I often, now, wonder whether he took my advice, or whether he battled with moods and tenses for a few more weeks before giving up his dreams of a better life.

Our visits paid, beads and fish-hooks handed out, I asked Robert to take us up to the falls. It was a long pull in the corial against heavy currents. Going down-river the Indians had used their cruising rhythm — a deep forceful pull followed by a gentle dig at the surface of the water and a click of the paddle on the gunwhale. Now they used their most powerful stroke and chanted the rhythm as they went, deep hard pulls in rapid succession. There were two stretches of rapids to get through, with water breaking white everywhere on vicious rocks. I realized, as we wound expertly between the rocks, that to navigate these rivers beyond the tidal points — where falls and rapids begin — means an intimate knowledge not merely of every impeding stone but of the different currents produced according to the height of the water. Robert had not been merely intransigent the day before when he had refused to go above the falls. Even though I had every confidence in his navigation I I can't say that I was relaxed as we fought our way up the rapids. At times the force of water was so great that the combined efforts of four men paddling with all their force was only sufficient to keep the corial immovable; it seemed that at any moment the flood would have its way and we would hurtle back. Then we would inch our way past the barrier and finally into gentler water, where the Indians would break into the recovery rhythm. They wore no shirts in the corial and I could see the enormous development of chests, shoulders and arms which has been produced by centuries of paddling and burden-carrying. In comparison the lower part of an Indian's body is quite undeveloped, the legs are often skinny. The average height of an Indian is about five feet five inches, but his weight must be out of proportion to his height; to be tall is no advantage in the forest, so all physical development has gone into broad shoulders and barrel chests.

We landed half a mile below the falls and walked through the forest, the roar of the water gradually increasing. At last we reached the river bank again, and a hundred yards away the great waves of white water tumbled over an irregular mass of black rocks. It was no neat sheet of falling water, and for that reason seemed all the more vicious. We jumped from one smooth surface of basaltic rock to the next, until we could get no closer to the falls. Beyond them lay the country and the tribe I wanted to see, but by now my optimism of the day before was leaving me. Once more I asked the Indians if there were any way we might go up-river, and wearily, expressionlessly, they shook their heads. Were there paths through the forest? I asked. Yes, they said, there were probably old trails, but they would not know where they led. I did not press the point. I thought of our dwindling stock of food. If I had insisted I think the Marques would have agreed, reluctantly, to go above the falls, but once our food was finished half our time would be spent in hunting. 'Ah well,' I said to myself, 'perhaps it's better to have a dream of a lost tribe than actually to find one. Perhaps we'd find them in trousers, and asking us for Nestlé's milk.' I had travelled hopefully and I had not arrived. The Barama Caribs would remain always for me the Noble Savages to whom I could attribute all my romantic and sentimental notions of primitive life. I can think of them singing as they tease the wild cotton for their hammocks, can imagine the stories of their heroes, told as they sit round the fire, can visualize their ritual dances in full feather at the new moon. For some years I had been reading everything I could find about the Carib race, and looked on the Barama tribe as the nexus of it all, the ultimate True Caribs; I sighed as a lover and obeyed as a son of reason. I decided then and there, on that smooth black rock, that one day I would atone for my failure by writing down all that I knew or would come to know of the history and customs of the Caribs. The reader will find the modest result in Appendix B.

CARIB STOOL

Return

ON our last morning by the Barama I awoke to sounds that were to prove a misleading augury for our march, a birdsong of a liquid sweetness no magic flute could have emulated, notes that formed music so controlled and logical that it seemed some creating mind had composed it; a theme would be stated, repeated and followed by variations in harmony, sometimes given with all the power the little instrument was capable of, sometimes almost quavering and distant, as if the bird were spent with the passion of his own music. I lay still and listening in my hammock, making no attempt to go to the bush where the bird sang, in case I should frighten him and lose his song. And then, at last, having greeted the morning he ceased his music. I never heard him again. Cyril told me that he was called the Music Bird, and was small and brown. When I made inquiries in Georgetown I found that he was known as the Musical Wren, the Necklaced Jungle Wren or the Quadrille Bird; his scientific name is *Leucolepis arada*. From the drawings of him which I saw his appearance is nothing, but the order of creation so often gives glorious voices to the small dun-coloured birds of the lower forest, while the brilliantly plumaged trogons and parrots make the canopy hideous with their shrieks.

Robert and two other Indians politely came to wish us goodbye, and then we struck off into the forest. Within ten minutes saturation rain had begun and didn't cease all day, except for one or two short intervals, until we reached Pedro's place. But one's body can adapt to circumstance, and feeling fit and energetic that day, I looked on the rain as no more than a natural discomfort. The next day's march would have seemed no different if I hadn't twisted my ankle in a root during the first hour; it was not a bad twist but I had to place my foot in a special position as I walked, which used up energy and caused a rubbing which was a blister in no time. The rain had become, to my weakening senses, more intense than I had imagined possible, and my heavy breathing seemed about to draw water rather than air into my lungs. I fell far back behind the Marques and took the slightest incline like some old gentleman puffing up St James's. I told Cyril to unpack the sugar but there was no effect even after I'd eaten handfuls of it. When we had ten miles to go before reaching the manganese camp I felt the blister burst. By now my walk and actions were automatic, my mind had made a half-retreat; I walked over tree-trunk bridges without thinking of the drop below, and miraculously the hours and the miles went by, with the rain still unceasing and I beyond computing how far away the camp lay. And then, looking through the rain along the now widened trail, I saw a pale glint where sunlight had penetrated the clouds for a moment and struck the aluminium roofs of the camp. I could have shouted for joy; we had walked less than twenty miles that day, but it had seemed like two hundred.

Coffy and Smith greeted me from the mess as I hobbled miserably across the short grass, and Coffy called to his boy to put kettles on for a bath. Bathed, my blister seen to, in dry clothes and drinking Johnny Walker, I was a new man.

'You've come back just at the right moment,' Coffy said. 'We've got a rendezvous with the Grumman the day after tomorrow at midday, at Mount Everard. It's bringing in supplies and our tent-boat leaves to meet it tomorrow morning. Do you want to take it?'

I was glad to; I had not been looking forward to the long retracing of my steps. I went to bed early and we made an early start for Arakaka, where the tent-boat was waiting. The rains had raised the level of the river by nearly fifteen feet and the stratification of the rocks which had been revealed on my way up was now once more covered up. Tacoubas were less of an impediment, and the Indian wood-cutters had taken advantage of the rise to float their rafts down-river towards Mount Everard. The river was active once again.

I spent the night in a hut in an Indian village. Next morning we reached Mount Everard with an hour to spare and I sat reading in the sun. Shortly after midday we heard the distant hum of an aeroplane engine and a few minutes later the Grumman began to circle for the landing. She came down like a graceful bird until her floats skimmed the pool-smooth water. A small boat went out to receive the stores, and when the unloading was done it took Mr Khan, the proprietor of the sawmill, and myself out to the Grumman. A few minutes later I was looking down on the river as it wound off westwards; I could see the hazed and distant mountains of its watershed, the source, too, of the alluvial gold; and then the Barama and the white-flecked waters above the falls of Towakaima. The immensity of the forest, stretching as far as the eye could see and for hundreds of miles beyond, overwhelmed my imagination. I had walked through one minute particle of that immensity and come to know something of its life; was that particle a true symbol of the whole, or was the forest as infinite in its variety as it appeared to be in space?

In less than two hours we were above the copper-sulphate swamps that lay behind the cultivated coastland, and then the grid-iron streets of Georgetown, white in the sun, tilted as we banked downwards to the Demerara. We taxied across to the ramp, and after I had seen to the landing of my luggage I was given a lift to my hotel. Old ladies, widows of plantation managers, were playing bridge on the veranda-lounge. A store owner was having a siesta with his feet up on the projecting arms of a Berbice chair. The Indian waiters were quietly chatting in their usual row by the reception desk. Outside, the kiskadees were singing: *qu'est-ce-que dit? qu'est-ce-que dit?* How different their pert cry was from the ethereal music of the Necklaced Jungle Wren.

Interlude in Georgetown (1)

LIKE many of my generation who were at school during the 'thirties I felt the backwash of the political concern of the intellectuals of the period; I was an agent for the pamphlets of the Union of Democratic Control; I shouted myself hoarse in Hyde Park, one Sunday of the summer holidays, with cries of 'Arms for Spain', and on the same occasion found myself carrying one pole of a banner which read 'Square Deal for the Unemployed'; I kept Mass Observation informed on the political tenor of my school, and in my essays I never lost an opportunity to show how utterly I despised the pious piracy of the British Empire; our far-flung pro-consuls, all carriers of our burden in the imperial territories, were figures of fun representing an evil tyranny. How ridiculously little all we arrogant liberals of the time knew of the complexities of the Empire we were so anxious to dissolve. Without pausing to make the necessary historical comparisons we presumed that paternalism was a machiavellian method of maintaining the inferiority of subject peoples; Britain was indeed *il gran simulatore e dissimulatore*, her Empire a system for organized looting, capitalism without control. The truth is that all imperial career is governed by two vital forces, gain and idealism, and the greatest imperial powers are those in which the forces are balanced; Rome, with her sense of classical proportion, found the balance with ease; Spain, herself touched by the fanaticism of oriental domination, left her Black Legend in the New World because such men as Bartolomé de las Casas and Fray Motolinía had so little effect in comparison with the *conquistadores*, and the long line of rapacious colonizers that followed them. Even so the Spanish Empire in the New World lasted for three hundred years and created a new civilization by mixing the blood and culture of Europe with the bloods and cultures of Middle and South America.

I believe that when the historians of the future come to assess Britain as an imperial power they will see that a genuine balance was achieved; the crimes and misfortunes of the closing years of the Empire will be the proof of the social and educational advances made in an amazingly short time. Less than a hundred years ago Africa was as unknown as at any time since Aristotle sent his expedition to discover the source of the Nile. With almost too great a haste we have created intellectual élites throughout British Africa; in a few decades we have, with honest idealism, tried to make up for our economic plunder by transplanting modern European civilization to our dependent territories.[1] To future ages our mistake may be that we forced the pace of the new growth, made it an artificial insemination rather than, as with the Spaniards, a natural process arising from the mixture of bloods. But whatever we may be blamed for, it can never be said that the existing forces of imperial exploitation won the day; those forces, vested in the West Indian sugar plantocracy and the Calcutta merchants, would have preserved the Slave Trade, preserved slavery itself, have forbidden the education of colonial peoples; and maintained the Empire, perhaps, for another century.

It is a mere two hundred years since Britain, preparing to dominate Europe with her industrial revolution, began her imperial expansion. It would not be hard to find, in those two centuries, examples of barbarity, injustice and exploitation, but the miracle is that in spite of them the dependent peoples have moved from slavery through paternalism to a state of intellectual independence which will inevitably end in freedom from British control. Critics of British imperialism insist that Britain was forced into all these advances. But by whom? Such control from the democracies of the territories concerned is a modern phenomenon, and no government is wise which accepts democratic control unhesitatingly. In the past the force to improvement came, not from the still illiterate peoples under Britain's protection, but from an extreme moral consciousness on Britain's part. The proof that this consciousness was no mere meaningless dissimulation lies in the fact that we have accomplished our imperial task in a shorter time than any other imperial power in history, leaving us to hope that when our last legions move out of the last colonial territory a new Dark Age will not have begun.

---

[1] *'Nous voulons être des Congolais civilisés, non des Européens à peau noire'*, said an African manifesto published in 1956.

These jingoistic sentiments, of which I am a little astonished to find myself the author, were only indirectly inspired by what I saw of the coastal colony of British Guiana. From every aspect it is too special a case to allow generalizations, and the 146 years of British rule have not been years of wonderful advancement. When all products other than sugar had proved to be economic hazards the colony was cursed with a mono-culture; when sugar did well the colony was reasonably happy, but during the long years of the sugar slump, which was only ended by the First World War, life was bad. The move to find gold in the Interior was almost certainly a means to relieve the economic pressures of the Coast. For the past fifteen years sugar has been flourishing as it never flourished before. If it could be said that the considerable and certain profits of the sugar interests went merely to swell the incomes of British investors, one could feel nothing but shame for such exploitation. The truth is that for the first time the sugar interests have been able to make the improvements in the plantations and factories which will ensure some kind of economic stability and efficiency in the future; in fifteen years they and the Government have immensely alleviated the living conditions of the plantation workers, though they know that it is by a flourishing economy that the real alleviation must eventually come.

Yet British Guiana is an unhappy place, its people discontented with a standard of living which they know to be so much behind that of the advanced nations of the world. Its educated men return from foreign study and travel with a natural urge to raise their country to a European level. They reject the British argument that the present constitution of the colony's economy will not permit a higher form of existence, that this will come only by the slow and arduous efforts of the Guianese themselves. The pure intellectuals tend to retire from the frustrations of politics to tend some tiny garden of national culture, highly educated men who fear the results of uncontrolled nationalism. The nationalist leaders are men for whom education was a means towards power, who believe that the economic shape of the colony will only change for the better when British domination has been brought to an end. They have an obsessional hatred for British rule; ignoring the quiet advantages which membership of the Commonwealth must bring to so small a colony, they wish to sever the umbilical cord and run the country as they wish. Looking back after three years one can see that Britain did a remarkable thing when, in 1953, she gave British Guiana a new constitution and, for the first time, universal suffrage. The Intelligence Services must have known that the left-wing extremist nationalists would be elected to power, and that such men would not continue to accept the constitutional brakes which had been designed to keep ultimate power in British hands. With the elation produced by newly gained power the leaders of the People's Progressive Party felt that they were within sight of the complete liberation of their country. From the first they made it clear that they were going to make the new constitution unworkable, that they required nothing less than a constitution giving them complete liberty of action; the Governor was to be deprived of his powers of veto and the members of the Government nominated by the British were to be reduced almost to complete impotence. Meanwhile, the P.P.P., under Dr Cheddi Jagan, the Prime Minister, began a series of actions designed to disrupt the hated sugar interests — Jagan was brought up on a sugar plantation and his hatred has psychological roots. During the few months of P.P.P. government a comparative cosmos was turned into chaos. British officials, who had seen the new constitution as a magnificent opportunity for colonial territories to prove their political maturity, began to despair; the stupidity and intransigence of leaders who seemed incapable of a sense of responsibility towards the interests of their own people would inevitably end in general tears, and the whole political advancement of the colonies would be set back; diehards would say 'I told you so', socialists would say it was a case of vested British interests being endangered by a people stirred at last to political action in their own interests.

I think it is at this point, in studying the recent history of British Guiana, that anyone with genuinely liberal leanings must reach a crux. Has Britain allowed the Aristotelian balance to disintegrate? Had she, as well as the P.P.P leaders, no intention of allowing the new and liberal constitution to be a success? Were her revocation of the constitution and dispersal of a legally elected government acts dictated by the interests of 'colonialism', or were they sincerely made in the interests of the Guianese? My own belief is that what happened was inevitable, that by a hair's breadth the balance between

gain and idealism was maintained.   I say this largely because it is
impossible to spend as long as I did in British Guiana without
realizing that, almost to a man, the educated Englishmen in respons-
ible positions, whether as members of the Oversea Civil Service or
in sugar, are passionately concerned that the colony should advance
politically, socially and culturally.   They are surrounded by frustrations of every kind, they frequently curse the colony and everything
in it, but each man shows, in the various recurring obsessions of his
conversation, that he is in his way dedicated.   The sugar men give no
indication of schizophrenic anxiety produced by a division of their
loyalty between sugar and the Guianese.   They are absolutely convinced, without sophistry, that under the unique economic conditions
of the colony, the interests of sugar and the interests of the Guianese
themselves are identical.   This, I know, must sound like piously
fraudulent thought, an example of the hypocrisy on which the
Empire was built.   It produces an image of sugar magnates exerting
their pressures on the Colonial Office with tales of the misery which
will befall the unfortunate Guianese if sugar is not protected from all
possible assault.

British capital, on a vast scale, is invested in the sugar industry of
British Guiana; irrigation and drainage systems of a kind required
in no other place in the world, factories, distilleries, houses, land,
machinery, transport and stores.   We should be fools indeed if we
had no thought for these investments; but the anti-imperialist
argument does not blame Britain for looking after these interests; it
blames the capitalist-imperialist system for making such concern
inevitable, at the expense of the true interests of the people of the
colony.   For myself I can see no other system whatsoever that could
have made possible the existence of a colony in the first place.   In
God's eyes all colonization which takes advantage of the labour of
so-called inferior people is immoral; acts of ruthlessness must
follow the original sin.   To force the Negroes of the Virgin Islands
to work, the Danes cut down their soursop trees, and today in
British Guiana sugar must use a hundred subtle methods to maintain
a sufficient labour force — tropical people prefer a subsistence and
little work to hard work and a higher standard of living.   Most of
the evils in the sugar industry can be traced back to the fears of
labour shortage.   But the wonder is not that sugar has sinned so

much; it is that, given the system, it has honestly tried to avoid the gravest sins and has realized, particularly during the last fifteen years, that the general happiness of Guiana is the vital concern of sugar — and that the general happiness of sugar is the vital concern of the Guianese. This reciprocation was almost destroyed by the P.P.P. in its months of power. With the revocation of the constitution and a return to complete British domination, sugar might well have rested, returned to its old benevolent despotism. In fact it has not; sugar and government have agreed to join forces with the aim of creating a state in which sugar and self-determination can exist in harmony. 'Morality is the effective harmony of the whole', said Plato, and this is the ideal. But I think I detect a flaw in the ideal in British Guiana's case. True democracy must imply the possibility of choice from a number of possible ways of living. If there is only a limited number of such choices which can exist in harmony with sugar, and if the other choices will disrupt the sugar economy, where then has the ideal gone? The truth is, perhaps, that British Guiana is so strange, so unique a place that such conceptions as democracy, self-determination, self-government — even liberty itself — cannot be used in its context without modification. Because of the fundamental immorality of colonization British Guiana is politically immature. It was inevitable that chaos should come when Britain suddenly dressed the colony in clothes from the wardrobe of Western political thought. It was as if a welfare state had been proclaimed overnight in Plantagenet England.

When I arrived back in Georgetown from the North-West the threatened split in the P.P.P. had become a fact. Jagan, the leader of the party and one representative of the East Indians of the sugar estates, had been ousted from power by Mr L. F. S. Burnham, the Negro representative of the Africans, who are mainly centred in Georgetown. The P.P.P. had accused the British of a policy of divide and rule, an attempt to arouse mutual suspicion between East Indians and Negroes. Here, it seemed, a touch of racialism was entering quite naturally into the structure of the party. It was said that from the first only the tact and cleverness of Mrs Jagan, a Marxist from Chicago, had prevented a rift between Burnham and her husband. But she had been spending the last few months in gaol for holding illegal political meetings, and the split had come into the open. Some Englishmen, suspicious of the depths of subtlety in an oriental Marxist mind, still attributed the split to machiavellian tactics; Burnham, who had never admitted to being a communist, was pretending to deviate from the known extremists in the hope that the British would negotiate with him and back him as their man. I thought I might have a glimpse of the truth if I saw Jagan, and I telephoned him for an appointment. He asked me round to his surgery when his work for the day was over.

Jagan is the best dentist in British Guiana; many people wish that political differences did not make them uneasy about becoming his patient. His father was a sugar estate foreman who managed to make enough money to give his sons a good education. It was during his dental studies in Chicago that Jagan met his future wife, and learnt from her the principles of Marxism, and how they might be applied to his own country. She has inspired his whole political career.

Dr Jagan (the Dr is a courtesy title given to all dentists and veterinary surgeons in the colony) received me in the little office adjoining his modest surgery, dominated by a large coloured photograph of Stalin. The celebrated smile flashed on his handsome face, revealing teeth that were indeed a credit to his profession. In spite of his smile he did not immediately bathe me in the charm which has seduced so many. For him I was no doubt the hired accomplice of despots, and his attitude was suspicious and slightly truculent. I did my best to show him that my mind was open, that I wished simply to hear something of his case against the British. After a few carefully placed questions his words began to flow, and even in this confined space I sensed the persuasive orator, the demagogue made effective by the absolute sincerity of his beliefs. To enforce his attack on sugar's inhumanity, he described to me how he had seen his own mother, pregnant, working up to her middle in the flooded cane-fields. He talked of the 'sugar-coated government' which allows the exploitation of British Guiana to continue, claimed that the British had deliberately restricted educational opportunities so that the best jobs in the colony could be kept for expatriates, and that the present policy of 'Guianization' was yet another hypocrisy of the so-called new colonialism. His aim was the complete destruction of the domination of sugar; he would replace it by a diverse agricultural economy. When I asked him what the precise nature of this economy would be his thoughts groped for a moment and he shot out a random list of products, including coffee, cotton, rice, citrus fruits and bananas. I mentioned the difficulty of Panama Disease in banana cultivation in the colony, and the various failures of coffee growing I had seen in the North-West. He waved my objections aside; for him all was possible if one had the will. He seemed unaware of the long attempts made by government agro-scientists to produce a banana plant that could withstand Panama Disease on the coastlands, or of the years of patient research made by the sugar chemists to increase the sucrose yield of the poor quality Guianese cane. Every Guianese is brought up with British assur-ances ringing in his ears that without exception everything in his country is a special, difficult and often insoluble problem. No wonder that his answer, as in Dr Jagan's case, is a cynical disbelief and the certainty that, if only Government wished it, all and every-thing could be done. Jagan's wild schemes and manic certainty of their potential success are a frightening thing, for they are rooted in despair.

When I left the surgery I arranged to call on Dr Jagan and his wife one evening at his private house, where he would invite a few members of his party for me to talk with. It was a small white wooden house on stilts, in the colony fashion, simply but comfort-ably furnished. Mrs Jagan opened the door, a small bespectacled woman in her late thirties, a little sallow and thin after her confine-ment in the New Amsterdam gaol. Jagan had his six-year-old son on his knee, telling him a bed-time story and answering the intel-ligent questions arising from it which the little boy asked. It was clear that he was being very carefully trained from childhood to become a future leader of independent Guiana; it will be interesting to follow his career. He was put to bed, the other guests arrived and iced beer was produced. The first guest was a full-blooded Negro of about fifty, a gentle slow-spoken jeweller; next came a tall young Negro journalist with graceful manners and a sad voice; the last to arrive was a 'coloured' man with perhaps more European blood than African, small and knotty, a transport organizer and trade union official. Neither he nor the other two guests showed any truculence during the whole long evening of talk, their animosity to British rule was always expressed with courtesy; they were perplexed that things could not be better than they were, almost apologetic that they should have to place the responsibility on the British. Only once did one of them raise his voice. They had been saying that sugar capitalists were living in England, in a luxury made possible only by the exploitation of Guianese labour. I was able to quote in reply the $2\frac{1}{2}$ per cent dividend given by the sugar concern which dominated the colony, and to say that the dividend was so small not because profits were down but because greatly increased profits had been ploughed back into the industry, from which the colony in general must benefit. The knotty man did not reply, but with some emotion said that he remembered seeing during the war a film called 'Mistress Miniver' ('Mrs' is always 'Mistress' in the colony) in which Mistress Miniver had asked for a pound of sugar and had been charged $2\frac{1}{2}$d. for it—only a halfpenny more than they themselves had paid for colony white at the time, a halfpenny to cover transport, refining and packaging. 'You had your sugar cheap at our expense', he said, and my only answer was that today the Commonwealth Sugar Agreement has taken into account the special difficulties of sugar production in British Guiana and, accordingly, more is paid for it. But I knew that my answer had strained to the utmost my meagre understanding of economics.

During the whole evening Mrs Jagan lay in a hammock and contributed hardly a word to the discussion. Occasionally, when her husband's eloquence was in spate, as in his remarks on the rise in the power of the East Indians, she would make a quick potent remark which stopped him short on the brink of indiscretion. Then she would lie back in her hammock, *sphinge* but always ready for the pounce. She has the reputation of being the organizer of the party, the theoretician who keeps well in the background, but to whom everything is referred. She supplies the ideas which keep her loquacious husband primed. Dr Jagan did most of the talking during the evening, repeating most of the ideas which he had offered me at our first meeting. On one topic he was extremely interesting — the question of land reclamation on the coast and the riverain lands. He has seen that the enormously increasing population of the colony makes land shortage the first political question of the day. When he talked about this and the problems of land in general one could see that they were subjects he had studied closely and reasonably; some of his solutions had the wild impracticability of his general schemes for the betterment of the colony, but in general — as I found from my subsequent reading on the subject — he talked excellent sense.

This most interesting and revealing evening ended in the small hours of the morning. Although I had deliberately taken up an extreme attitude to encourage reaction I think we all felt amicably towards each other. For my part I had learnt a lot.

PART TWO

The Country of El Dorado

Aurum irrepertum et sic melius situm.
The gold unfound and thus the better placed.
Odes. HORACE III, iii, 49

Savannah

THE first time I climbed the stairs leading to the office of Mr James Bamford, Commissioner for the Interior of British Guiana, I had a clear image of the man I was to meet; he would be tall and in his fifties, greying at the temples, without an extra ounce of fat on him, his face the colour of a tobacco leaf in the first stage of curing; a fly whisk would be at hand, his manner would be polite, but a little severe to a somewhat tiresome amateur who wished to visit the Interior. The expected, however, rarely occurs in British Guiana, and as I entered the office, a smallish, plumpish, pinkish and baldish man rose from his desk and blinked at me humorously through his spectacles before offering me a cigarette in a highish voice full of the round vowels of Yorkshire. He had the north countryman's immediate friendliness, and within five minutes we were talking as if we had known each other for years. Maps were out, documents were summoned and the pile of papers in the in-tray was forgotten. We were planning the itinerary of a journey he had invited me to make with him to the Rupununi savannahs. Our planning was constantly interrupted by his story-telling; he had, as I soon realized, a quite insatiable appetite for anecdote. He told his stories with great incidental humour, in the true tradition of the Yorkshire comedian, and he reminded me, both in his manner and appearance, of that excellent comedian, the late Robb Wilton, whose stories, I remember, always began, 'The day war broke out . . . Jimmy's introductory line was usually, 'When I was on the Boundary Commission . . .' When I heard those words I would sit back and listen enchanted to some revelation of the wild life. He never talked local politics; I think they bored him.

In spite of his accent Jimmy was Guianese born and bred, and he counted his few periods of leave in England among the most miserable and lonely he had ever spent. His father came out to the colony as a young man and settled there. Jimmy had trained as a surveyor, and surveyed several sections of the colony before being appointed to the Boundary Commission in 1930. Until then, and in spite of the various disagreements with Brazil and Venezuela, the precise frontiers of the colony were unmarked and unsurveyed. The Boundary Commission was composed of Brazilians, Venezuelans and British, and its survey began at Mount Roraima, where the frontiers of the three territories converged. The Latin American Commission was an army unit under army officers, and they had expected the British to be a corps from the Royal Engineers, officered by men as dashing as themselves. They were rather disappointed to rendezvous with a handful of Georgetown surveyors and their Indian and Creole retinue. There were frequent disagreements over procedure and demarcation. One of Jimmy's funniest, and perhaps more imaginative, stories was of how the Brazilian leader had challenged the gentle, charming Mr Lord, leader of the British, to a duel. They were then on British territory and Mr Lord, playing for time and retaining a *bella figura*, said that duelling was forbidden on British soil, but that if they walked the few miles to Brazilian territory he would accept the challenge. No, said the Brazilian, duelling was also forbidden in Brazil, but it was permitted in Venezuela; they would walk the ten miles through the bush to Venezuela and fight there. But tempers had cooled by morning.

I think it was perhaps the final failure of the Boundary Commission that made Jimmy emphasize its hardships in his stories. Although an elaborate system of supply had been planned, the Commission found itself for a long period with very little food; beri-beri broke out and death would have followed in many cases if Mr Lord had not decided that the Commission must return to Georgetown with all speed, leaving the work unfinished. It was an ignominious end; the Royal Engineers completed the survey and received the commendations, while the original party was offered no recognition for its magnificent work. Jimmy became a District Officer, and was then made the District Commissioner of the Essequibo-Mazaruni District. He married a Portuguese girl, a sister of the man who dominated the diamond trade of the Mazaruni, created a little farm near Bartica, which he calls Bamford's Point, and finally was offered the highest post available to him, Commissioner for the Interior. This job is almost entirely concerned with administrating Indian areas, through District Commissioners and officers, and his duties would be more accurately described if he were called Commissioner for Indian Affairs. This concern for the Indians, who had been neglected for so long, is recent. The report of the Royal Commission on the West Indies of 1938-39 said, in reference to British Guiana, that 'special measures should be taken to protect the Amerindian peoples of the remote hinterland'. Two years later the Government of British Guiana applied for 'Colonial Development and Welfare' funds to appoint an officer to investigate Indian affairs. Part of the letter of application is worth quoting at length:

> The Amerindians of the interior of this colony have been at a disadvantage in facing economic and other developments through lack of a definite constructive policy with regard to education and social economic development. Mission schools have given a degree of literacy to some but there appear to be no cases of aborigines rising to fill any position of standing in the administrative or economic life of the country. It is proposed to appoint an officer to make investigations and recommendations as to the means that could best be adopted to attain their greater economic and cultural advancement. Eventually this officer would administer any schemes that were put into operation.

Three years later the grant was made, and from 1943 to 1947 Mr P. Storer Peberdy made his various tours of investigation. His report recommended the creation of three vast Indian Reservations in which cattle raising, timber cutting and other appropriate industries should be organized, from whose profits an Amerindian Trust Fund should be set up. The main outline of Mr Peberdy's excellent and detailed recommendations has been carried out during the past few years. In spite of the coastal difficulties the Colonial Office has faced its moral responsibility for the aboriginals of the Colony.

As part of his preparation for the Commissionership Jimmy Bamford made a tour of the Indian Reservations in Canada. It is said that during the tour the administrators of the reservations learnt a great deal about the reservations of British Guiana. Jimmy told me that what most impressed him about the Canadian reservations was the apparent lack of Indians. Generations of miscegenation had turned them into a race hardly distinguishable from the ordinary Canadian. They remained in the reservation because there were so many advantages in doing so. In one school Jimmy looked along the rows of Caucasoid faces and at last came upon one unmistakably mongoloid face. He turned to the teacher and, referring to the boy, said that he was the first real Indian he had seen in the schools. Alarmed, the teacher asked him not to mention this again; the boy had no right to be in the school, or in the reservation at all; he was Chinese.

The results of the new Indian policy in British Guiana have been rapid and dramatic. Malaria has been stamped out, and the tours of Dr Cenydd Jones, o.b.e., have so reduced the infant mortality rate that a once dwindling race is now increasing every year. This increase is at its greatest amongst the Makushi and Wapishana Indians of the Rupununi savannahs. The journey which Jimmy Bamford had invited me to make with him had a serious purpose — to discover what problems had arisen amongst the tribes as a result of the increase in population, to decide what plans should be made for the education and future employment of the children, and, more immediately important than all, to find some alternative employment for those Indians who had for so long lived by bleeding balata in the forests of the Kanuku mountains that divide the northern and southern savannahs.

Just before I left his office Jimmy looked at me, and a smile played on his mouth. 'By the way,' he said 'about twenty years ago that chap Evelyn Waugh went up to the Rupununi with a District Commissioner, old Haynes. He changed the H to B, called him Baynes, and put him in his book. Old Haynes swore like blue murder when he read it and said if he ever came face to face with Waugh he'd throw him to the ground and draw a knife across his throat. Now I hope I won't have to do the same to you.'

'Perhaps I'll change the B to H!' I said, 'but I promise I'll be kind.' 'Hamford!' he exclaimed, laughing. 'Now, I don't quite like that, and as for kindness — by God, Waugh was kind to Haynes! He got him to a T, but he could have gone much further.'

The matter settled rather inconclusively, we made arrangements for our rendezvous to meet the D.C.3 that was to fly us to the savannahs. The evening before our departure there was a telephone call for me at my hotel; it was Mr Bamford's secretary — Mr Bamford thought he'd better warn me that nights could be quite chilly in the Rupununi and he strongly advised me to include a couple of bottles of rum in my stores — he could recommend Booker's White Hart and Houston's Blue Label.

The inside of the D.C.3 was piled with an assortment of cargo for its whole length — spare parts for jeeps, tyres, crates of beer, cartons of tinned goods, an ancient wireless that had been sent down to Georgetown for repair, and a child's cot. The seats were small and made of metal, ranged along both sides of the hull of the aeroplane. Visibility was better than usual and I peered through the small window at the unfailingly fascinating terrain of forest, river and hill. To our right I could just see the grid-iron streets of Bartica at the confluence of the Essequibo and the Mazaruni; then the land began to rise and before us were the dim forest-covered outlines of the Pakaraima Mountains. The pilot did not make any more height, and gradually as the land rose I could see the contours of the hills in greater detail. At one point Jimmy suddenly put his hand to his ear and looked at me with an expression of extreme concern. 'Is there something wrong with the port engine?' he said. My heart fluttering, I said I couldn't hear any difference, and then he smiled, saying: 'No, it's all right, neither can I. Now, I remember once I was taking a visiting politician from England up to the Rupununi for one of those official one-night stands that don't do any good to a soul. I didn't take at all to this chap and I didn't think he was much of a man. So I did that one to him twenty minutes after take-off and he spent the rest of the flight getting paler and paler and looking at that port engine every minute to see if it had stopped.' I laughed, but wondered if I were going to be the victim of a series of such little jokes. Jimmy took up the rusty shotgun he had brought with him and began to clean its breech. No one bothers to keep his gun in good condition in the colony. The humidity makes rust-prevention impossible, and in place of pride in the spotless condition of one's gun there is pride in the greatest degree of dilapidation combined with accuracy of performance.

We were beyond the pinnacles of the mountains, and ahead, still too hazy to make out its nature, lay flat land, the Rupununi savannahs. Already, below us, bush on the hills had given way to desert-brown fissured earth with outcroppings of stone and no apparent sign of vegetation. A few minutes later Jimmy told me that we had reached the savannah proper. I looked down; the colour of the earth had not changed, not a touch of green relieved the desert. If this were cattle country how did the cattle exist? The truth is that they barely do. They wander freely over the vast open ranges of the ranches, the last open ranges in the world, in search of their meagre fodder, pathetically spending the baking hours of midday beneath the inadequate foliage of the sandpaper trees that dot the plains. The colour of these plains is as much an illusion from the ground as it is from the air; isolated tufts of feeble grass, lacking in many chemicals essential to animal life, cover the ground, always surrounded by a patch of unproductive soil, which is all that is seen from above. From ground level perspective draws the grasses together to form a green and apparently luxuriant plain. At one point, as I looked down I was surprised to see a series of white conical shapes, giving the appearance of a well-pitched encampment; they were, said Jimmy, ant-hills the size of Army bell-tents.

Jimmy knew the savannahs well; he had been roasted for days in the intense sun of the dry season as he traversed the plains on horseback, hoping that every evening would bring him to some isolated ranch house, or slinging his hammock in the full tropical forest that skirts the innumerable tributary creeks of the Ireng, the Takatu and the Rio Branco in Brazil, or the Rupununi,[1] whose waters flow into the Essequibo. In those days the country had been even more cut off from the Coast than it is today. No D.C.3s flew up to collect carcasses of meat — in fact no aeroplanes flew up at all, and the few settlers would make two journeys a year to Georgetown via the Rupununi river and the Essequibo to stock up with all they needed. There were others who never made the journey, were prepared to end their days doing odd jobs on a ranch where no questions would be asked them; roughneck Brazilians who had made even the traditional criminal air of the Amazonas district too hot to be borne; Central Europeans with graceful manners and fluency in several languages who said nothing of their past; honest adventurers who

[1] I was told on good authority that the name is derived from a small purple berry, the rapunun, found only in this district.

came for a while; lovers of the wilds who were content with a government lease of a few hundred acres of bad land so long as the fishing and the hunting were good; Negroes from the coast who would dominate an Indian village and live in idleness until the District Commissioner heard of them and sent them back to diamond prospecting in the forest; crackpots and men mad with religion. The most celebrated of these last had been a coloured man named Christie, of whom stories were legion. He lived permanently in a world of religious vision. A missionary had once called on him and offered him a medal bearing the head of Christ, which he had haughtily rejected, saying, 'Why should I want the image of the Lord when I speak to Him every night?' Then, looking more closely at the head, he added, 'Besides, that is a poor, poor likeness indeed.'

Evelyn Waugh, who passed a fantastic night with Christie, has recorded other remarks which are too good not to repeat here. When he arrived at the ranch Christie told him that he had known of his coming. 'I always know the character of any visitors by the visions I have of them. Sometimes I see a pig or a jackal, often a ravaging tiger.' 'How did you see me?' Waugh asked. 'As a sweetly toned harmonium,' was the reply. When his Indian mistress died he had heard, he said, a voice from Heaven saying 'The old horse is dead.' 'It did not mean that she was like a horse,' Christie explained. 'In some ways she was very pretty. It meant no more riding for me.' He had dedicated his life to spreading the gospel to the Indians, and each Sunday he would preach to them for four or five hours. Waugh asked him if he had been successful in his mission. 'No,' he replied, 'not successful, you could not call it successful. I have been here for thirty years and so far have made no converts at all. Even my own family have the devil in them.'

The aeroplane circled the landing strip, named Good Hope after the ranch house that stood some quarter of a mile away. A few jeeps and a handful of people stood beside the strip. As we landed we were asked to step in a tray of chemicals; foot and mouth disease had broken out in Brazil and all precautions were being taken to prevent the disease spreading across the border. The District Commissioner, Mr Cossou, came to greet us, a pale-skinned coloured man in his late thirties, keen-faced and very friendly in his manner. A tall distinguished man in a gaberdine suit, wearing a solar topee, was introduced to me as Mr Caesar Gorinsky. I took him for a successful American executive, but in fact he was the owner of Good Hope. He had come to the Rupununi twenty years ago and married Nelly Melville, the half Indian, half Scottish daughter of the first British settler in the country. With the marriage had come the ranch, but Mr Gorinsky was, I gathered, now less interested in cattle raising than in the possibilities of tobacco growing, and much of his time was spent in Georgetown, making his arrangements for the marketing of tobacco.

After the soft cloudy light of the coast the savannah light was intense, the glare striking up painfully from the cracked earth. The air, like the earth, was parched, and already I longed for draughts of cold water. We waved as the aeroplane took off on its way to the government station of Lethem and, with Mrs Gorinsky, drove over to the ranch house. It was a well-built house with a thatched roof, in a compound dominated by an avocado pear tree whose fruit hung large and pendulous but, alas, unripe. Revolver belts hung from a row of hooks in the entry, with *repoussée* designs on holsters from which elegant butts protruded. A slim handsome young man, Mrs Gorinsky's nephew, smilingly invited me to hang up my arms; here, as in Brazil, it was an insult not to surrender all weapons on entering a man's house.

The room where we sat drinking iced beer was simply furnished with homemade wooden furniture, and I noticed that no woodwork was painted. Paint is heavy and its air transport at six and a half cents a pound would have been expensive. Mrs Gorinsky's nephew's name was Harte, and I told him that I was looking forward to meeting his father, Ben Harte, about whom I had been told so much in Georgetown. 'He's married to my sister,' explained Mrs Gorinsky.

I had already realized that the whole Rupununi is dominated by an oligarchy which had its source, a mere two generations ago, in the fertile person of H. P. C. Melville. I had heard enough of this remarkable man for him to fascinate me; wherever I went I asked about him, and by careful repetition of the same questions to different people I gradually pieced together something of the story of his career.

He was born in Jamaica, the son of a Scottish parson. As a youngish man he was caught in the gold fever that broke out in British Guiana, but typically did not go to the known shouts, preferring to prospect unknown territory, such as the Upper Essequibo. He was not only unsuccessful; he contracted a fever and was found almost dead on a sandbank by some Wapishana Indians on their way to the southern savannahs. He asked them to take him with them, and on the journey the infusions of bark which they gave him cured the fever, and in the healthy air of the Rupununi his recovery was complete. The people of the southern savannahs were then in an entirely primitive state, untouched by the effects of the Anglican Mission at Pirara, in the northern savannahs, which had made converts among the Makushis until closed down by the territorial claims of Brazil. Melville loved the savannahs and the Indians, and was admired by them for his size and strength; he was certain that with their collaboration he could turn this vast territory into something more profitable than gold. He went barefoot with the Indians, took a fine Wapishana girl for his accepted wife, and encouraged the Indians in their hammock-making and crafts. Every few months he would pile a boat with these products, and sell them in Georgetown at a good profit. His return load would be guns, shot, powder, axe-heads, cutlasses, beads, fish-hooks and materials for the Indians.

Melville was not the first European to have settled on the savannahs; a man of Dutch extraction named De Rooy settled there in 1860, and bought a bull and a cow from one of the two ranches on the Brazilian side of the Takatu. He later left his herd of two hundred head to his heirs and went to live in Georgetown. In 1892 Melville bought the herd which he gradually increased in size, though he had no means of marketing the meat economically. Meanwhile he was rapidly becoming the Chief of the Wapishanas; his wife had borne him fine children. He treated her with a certain indifference, I gathered, and their relationship had little in it of Captain Smith's idyll with the Princess Pocahontas. He taught the Indians many things that were of use to them, and they, besides giving him their allegiance, sharpened arrow points so finely by drawing them through pirai teeth that he was able to use them as gramophone needles. He found them a meek, utterly passive people who accepted whatever fate brought them. As an old man he loved to tell how an

Indian had approached another, lying in his hammock, and said, 'I have come to kill you.' 'Very well,' said the other, wrapping himself more closely in the hammock that was to be his burial shroud.

Melville would probably not have stayed so long in the Rupununi if the Government had not recognized his work, offered him very large land concessions, and made him the local magistrate. It was fortunate for him that he stayed on, for the meat shortages brought about by the 1914 War forced the Government to recommence work on a cattle trail which had been abandoned in 1904. The trail was cut from Annai, to the north of the northern savannahs, through a hundred and eighty miles of bush to Takama, on the Berbice. From here the cattle were shipped to the Coast and fattened up after the losses of their trek. The going was hard and Melville didn't finish the cutting of the trail until after the War was over. The first herd made its way to the Coast in 1920. The losses were great; jaguars in large numbers were soon attracted to the area of the trail and made frequent attacks on the drove; stampedes brought further losses, and stragglers would stray off into the bush where they were killed by jaguars, or, in the case of cattle lost in the secondary growth resulting from forest fires, revert to the wild state. Yet some money could still be made and Georgetown interests saw a future in the Rupununi. They formed the Rupununi Development Company and bought out Melville's interests in the huge area of land surrounding the fine house he had built for himself at Dadanawa, the Hill of the Spirit of the Macaw.

At Dadanawa he had raised his family of ten sons and daughters, five of them by his Wapishana wife, Mamai Mary, the rest a younger generation born of a Patamona wife whom he had taken when parturition with Mamai Mary ceased. When the new wife had been brought to Dadanawa Mamai Mary had shown no resentment. 'Ah,' she murmured in Wapishana, the only tongue she knew, 'she can have him. I've had the best of him.' Melville had spent his long hours of leisure in omnivorous reading, and those who visited him were always impressed by his general knowledge. In 1924 he organized the aboriginal section of the British Guiana Pavilion at the Wembley Exhibition, and those who, on the opening day, saw the big distinguished man in the morning coat and silk hat did not suspect that he was an Indian chief with two squaws.

When he sold out to the Rupununi Development Company he moved a day's ride to Wichabai and built himself another fine airy house. His first family was now growing up and marrying — a daughter to Ben Harte, an American who had come up over the Brazilian frontier from Manaos, Nelly to Gorinsky; his eldest son John, made in his own image, had married a Brazilian girl, Teddy another Brazilian, another daughter a Brazilian named Orella. All the sons and daughters of the first family were given large ranchlands outside the Company's area, and set up with house and home. The younger family did not do so well. Lally is the best hunter in this part of the savannahs, seeming to have little else to occupy his time or thoughts. The youngest son is a government ranger, patrolling the northern savannahs by horse in long, lonely treks.

Old Melville did not die on the savannahs; in fact the end of his story is a little disappointing, an unromantic acceptance of the values of civilization. No wonder there is a slight mystery about it. What I am able to say here could perhaps be modified by those who know all. His sons and daughters were settled, his wives were old like himself; he felt that he had given the Rupununi all that was required of him. He put his two wives to live with their children and sailed away to the Scotland his father had left so many years before. Here he married at the kirk, and here, in or about the year 1930, he died.

It was easy to tell from her swift witty conversation that the blood of her remarkable father was dominant in Mrs Gorinsky. Her fine face had Indian characteristics; but her manner, as she directed conversation from the head of the great table, had none of the passivity of the Indian. It was interesting, as I travelled all over the savannahs and met the Melville children and many of the hundred or so grandchildren of the old man, to see the Mendelian sports that the mixed bloods had played. And I felt at the end that those powerful Scottish genes would be active till the end of time.

The various Melville ranches were by no means profitable, and the growing families, though self-supporting in many things, relied more on the balata trade than on the sale of cattle. Balata at one time ensured a reasonable income. Then came the War of 1939 and, like its predecessor, it brought the second great advancement in the Rupununi's history. Meat was needed urgently; the cattle trail had scarcely proved economic; Sir Gordon Lethem, one of the most farseeing Governors the colony has had, saw the emergency as the awaited chance to develop the savannahs. Cattle should be slaughtered in abattoirs at various points on the Rupununi and the carcasses flown down to the Coast in British Guiana Airways' new Dakotas. Abattoirs were built at the side of airstrips and four hundred miles of jeep trails were laid down, with bridges crossing the creeks, connecting ranch with ranch and abattoir. The scheme again took time to mature and the War was over by the time the first carcasses were flown to Georgetown. Today an aeroplane flies each day to one or other of the abattoirs, and the ranchers are making good money from their herds; their concern is now to improve and increase their stock, find some means of fertilizing the un-nutritious grasslands, to fence the ranges and to breed with scientific selection. I say 'their concern is', but perhaps I should have written in the conditional tense. The Melville Indian blood has made them prefer to let matters take their course. They now have money for the first time, they have jeeps, good clothes, and can fly to Georgetown when they wish. But the changes in their world have produced psychological problems for them. They have been brought up in a world where cattle live untended in a state of nature, wandering across the savannahs until the round-up. The idea of covering the stark, unhumanized plains with a series of little wire boxes clearly appals them. Whenever I spoke to a Melville on the subject he would agree that only by fencing and breeding could the stock be improved, and then he would add, by way of excuse for doing nothing about it, that they couldn't invest in the wire and the freight costs because the Government would only allow them to have the land on lease — a valid point — or that the Indians would look on the wire as a heaven-sent and unlimited source of excellent arrow-heads. I sensed that behind their conservatism lay a cause that they themselves had not rationalized. Civilization has brought them to a pleasant point of prosperity; they do not wish the savannahs to be settled by outsiders — perhaps the Negro from the Coast; they do not want progress and development — perhaps a township where the Indians will learn all that is worst in modern civilization. Already they refer to the cluster of houses and an hotel which form the government station as the City, and tend to hiss out

the word. Yet the oligarchy has acted typically in seeing to it that
Melville's second son, Teddy, is the proprietor of the hotel and the
manager of the airstrip which runs beside it. It might have been a
subtle psychological stroke if the Government had called its station
Melville instead of Lethem.

Our jeep left the parched flat lands surrounding Good Hope,
with the almost circular horizon of mid-ocean, on whose southern
quarter rose the blue-hazed Kanukus, where clouds seemed caught
by the shirt-tails on summit points, straining to be off into the
turquoise sky above the savannahs. Piled high, cumulus rolled at
intervals across the blue, but when it passed across the sun's face
the intense glare did not decrease, nor did the clarity of the light
that brought ant-hill and sandpaper tree so close. For an hour these
and an occasional creek were the only relief from the monotony of
the landscape, a monotony saved for me by the sad sense of remote-
ness which it gave, by its complete ignorance of humanity. In this
section of the country I saw no other tree than the sandpaper (*Cur-
atella americana*) which stood in dismal isolation, small with gnarled
grey trunk and branches of a kind of wood that has reached the
nadir of uselessness in its kingdom — it will not even burn. The
dry rough underside of its leaves is likely to give anyone sensitive
to the surfaces of things a strange tactile displeasure.

The trail at one point followed the fine blue waters of the Ireng
for a mile or two; Brazil lay beyond. In the normal way the whole
extent of the Brazilian frontier is unpatrolled by either the British
or Brazilians, whose police no doubt have more than enough to
keep them occupied in the unruly Territorio Federal de Rio Branco.
Because of the foot and mouth emergency, rangers were letting it be
known that the trafficking between the countries must cease till the
danger was past. Fences had been built along most of the border,
five miles inland, to lessen the possibilities of contagion. The
precious cattle of the Rupununi had indeed become a concern for
the Guianese Government.

In the late afternoon light a wind-pump appeared on the skyline,
turning in the slight breeze and glinting in the sun; then came a
group of buildings — we had reached Pirara, the ranch of Ben Harte
and his wife. Pirara is the only ranch in the Rupununi which may

facing, above: AKAWAIO WOMAN EXPRESSING POISONOUS ACID FROM CASSAVA
WITH A MATAPI
below: AKAWAIO GIRL MAKING A BEAD APRON

I

be said to have a history. In the 1830s Missionary Youd built his mission house here, and it was probably his presence which made the Brazilian Government, who rightly said that the savannahs belonged geographically to Brazil, send a detachment of troops to occupy Pirara as an earnest of their claim to the rest of the territory. The Governor of British Guiana sent twenty-nine coloured troops of the First West Indian Regiment under two lieutenants to dislodge the Brazilians. The British encamped some miles from Pirara and sent word that they expected the Brazilians to remove themselves to the other side of the Ireng. The Brazilians decided they were stronger and refused to budge. Poor Lieutenant Bingham was without orders for such an emergency and he dispatched a messenger back to the Coast to ask whether he should attack or not. Time went by and the British stores were exhausted; Lieutenant Bingham was reduced to the humiliation of asking his potential enemies for food, which was refused. The second detachment of soldiers arrived to find their compatriots half starved. The Brazilians, sizing up the new situation, departed for their homeland, allowing their half-breed troops the pleasure of a small night foray. An outpost of Empire had been successfully held.

The Schomburgk brothers were exploring the Rupununi at the time, and were witnesses of the triumph. Richard Schomburgk's account is worth quotation:

Shortly before supper Lieutenant Bingham had his black army drawn up and gave them an inspiriting harangue. He made known to them the condition of affairs but at the same time also warned them not to imagine that all danger was past, because it was easily possible for the Brazilians to come back now in doubly increased numbers, to try and drive them out of Pirara. At supper also many a sarcastic remark to be sure was let fall and many a satirical toast proposed; for without being a military genius, the impracticability of this monstrously costly and, if matters really came to a crisis, unsuccessful expedition was patent to everybody. Had the Brazilians wanted to remain owners of Pirara they could have easily crushed the small force to death before relief could even have been thought of. The presence at the mouth of the Amazon of a single frigate, of which many were lying at Barbados, would have produced the same effect at barely a sixth of the cost.

All ended happily, however. A Captain Leal arrived to negotiate, and that evening a gay and strangely attractive dinner party took place — British, Brazilian and Prussian vying with each other to contribute the most delicious dishes and wines. Missionary Youd sat amicably at table with his Brazilian rival for Indian souls, Friar José dos Santos Innocentes:

As the Commandant and the Friar were our guests during their stay [writes Schomburgk], the officers, like ourselves, supplied the table with all the delicacies in their possession, so as to make the first meal as sumptuous as possible, which we absolutely succeeded in doing. The Friar became especially lively after the emptying of only a few bottles of champagne which, as he asserted, he had not tasted for thirty years. Any stranger who might have noticed us would have had difficulty in imagining two hostile parties at this free and easy dinner party. At dessert Captain Leal drank to the health of the Queen of England, Lieutenant Bingham to that of the Emperor of Brazil, and I to the King of Prussia; during the toasting guns were fired, rockets were lighted, and God Save the Queen and Rule Britannia were struck up on the bugles.

Had I read this passage when we approached the wattle and daub buildings of the present Pirara I think I should have thought strongly of those black troops, uniforms in tatters from their long march through the forests, unloading from their corials on the Ireng innumerable crates marked Heidsieck or Mumm Extra Dry.

I had expected the arrival of our jeep to produce apparent life at Pirara, but no one appeared from the big house as we parked in the baked earth compound. An ancient Indian woman with long grey hair, dressed in a neat floral dress, was sitting in a wooden chair in front of the house, at work on what appeared to be an embroidery frame. She had looked at us, as we arrived, without curiosity, and now her eyes were concerned with her work alone. 'That', Jimmy said to me, 'is Mamai Mary. She doesn't know how old she is herself, but even if old Melville took her as a young girl she must be well towards her nineties.' I looked at her again with even greater interest, threading — as I discovered later — the minute beads into a *kewe-yo*, or little bead apron, the only form of dress which Indian women allow themselves in the natural state, and which they always wear under the garments which civilization has taught them to think proper.

There was an annexe to the ranch house, clearly recently built; it was open on all sides except for a wooden wall, some three feet high which surrounded it. As we approached we could see that figures lay asleep in hammocks, and dozing in a Berbice chair was a man whom I presumed to be Ben Harte himself. 'Hey there, Senator,' called Jimmy, and slowly the eyes opened, the head turned towards us, and the face lightened. He rose from his chair, and I understood why Jimmy had called him senator. He was a tall, heavily built man of about seventy, with white hair, white suit and the general appearance of the more distinguished type of American senator. 'Well I'll be bound,' he said in a gentle voice, coming forward to greet us.

Soon we were sitting talking, iced rum and lime juice at our elbows. 'What do you think of this, Jimmy?' Ben said, indicating the annexe with its well-laid floor of cedar planks. 'I'd been meaning to have an airy place like this built for approaching thirty years, and it's good to have it at last.'

'What made you get down to it, Ben?' said Jimmy.

'Why, the wedding, of course. You've heard about the wedding? My last boy got married two weeks ago to a damned fine Brazilian girl — time he settled down, too. You should have come then, it was a wedding — everyone agreed there hasn't been a wedding like it on the savannahs for years. Father Mather came over from St Ignatius to do the ceremony, and then we had tables all along that wall with turkey and hams and every damned thing you could think of, and drink all down that side and dancing here all day and all night. And you had better have me up in the caboose — I let the Indians have rum, too. Everybody was there; Tiny came over looking fine with his new teeth and did the carving — and you know what Tiny's carving's like. Ah, a good wedding. Only one regret for me; those Georgetown doctors, curse 'em, say I'm to keep off rum. I don't, of course. You'll agree with me, Jimmy, what's a man without his few snaps of rum?'

For answer Jimmy drank the rest of his rum in one long draught.

Ben had lived in Indian country all his life; he was born on a ranch in South Dakota at a time when the Cherokee Indians were still living in wigwams, dressing in buckskin and feathers, and resenting the westward course of the American empire. He showed me photographs of a tribal jamboree on the South Dakota plains, with himself as a very young man, posing with the chiefs. His parents had roamed the great plains and he himself was not a man to settle. He went to Panama and worked on the construction of the canal, and later left for the Amazon to work on the ill-fated Manaos railway that was intended to open up the region of Amazonas. With the little money he made here he trekked up to the savannahs of the Rio Branco. By now he had a partner, a man called James, a cousin of Jesse James. That was in 1913. In Boa Vista they heard rumours of gold in the upper reaches of the Rupununi, so they mounted their savannah ponies, strapped battels and jigs on pack-ponies and were off across the Takatu. The shout proved genuine; they struck well, but the rift was not loaded with ore and was soon washed out, leaving both men with a small capital. James drifted to England, where he enlisted in the first months of the War. Ben put his money into trade goods. The Brazilians in the Rio Branco were starved of materials and clothes; he brought up a boatload of cloth and felt hats from Georgetown and traded them for cattle; he would get a good steer for two felt hats and a belt. The boatload brought him twelve hundred head of cattle. He took a land concession, built himself a ranch-house and called his property Good Luck. The luck was not continuous. On one occasion he lost a boat on a stretch of Essequibo rapids; its cargo had been worth £600.

Melville recognized Harte as a good, kind and honest man, a man to be welcomed to the savannahs. He rewarded him with one of his daughters and later Pirara, the best of his ranches after Dadanawa and Wichabai. Ben has been faithful to this confidence; he is loved and respected all over the savannahs by whites, Indians and Creoles.

When I told him I was a writer he said: 'There was a writer came up here some twenty-five years ago and wrote a book. His name was Waugh, I think — Evelyn Waugh. He stayed with us here. I've often wondered what became of him. He was a fine fellow — a damned fine fellow.'

During the evening I encouraged him to reminisce about the old wild days, when law was administered by the individual, and a man had to use his guns and fists. At one point he leant over, showed me a scar on his knuckles and said, 'That's what I got from knocking out a black fellow called Ocean Shark.' I asked him to tell me the story, and in the dwindling light I listened for nearly half an hour as his gentle unemotional voice told me of his fight with Ocean Shark.

'This all happened my first year in the savannahs, nineteen-thirteen,' he began. 'In those days there was this fellow they all called Ocean Shark, the finest looking black man I ever set eyes on, well over six feet and muscles like an ox. The trouble was he was a bastard; he'd been a pork-knocker once, but the game was too rough for him, so he'd wait until another pork-knocker had got a good claim and then he'd come along and threaten to beat him up if he didn't clear out. Shark didn't give a damn for anybody. Old Walter Roth met him with a gun in his hand on the savannahs and asked to see his licence. "I ain't got no licence," said Shark, "but here is ma gun, you just come and git it." Roth hadn't even got a pistol so he had to move on. Well, I didn't like Shark or his methods, and I guess I was always doing things that got him hopping mad. Old Melville came to me one day and told me and my partner James that Shark was out to get us one day. "If he gives me half a chance I'll get him," I said, and Melville looked me up and down, because I was pretty slim in those days. Well, the chance came. Shark was a louse. There was a rancher a few days' ride from here called Macdonald; he'd taken a Makushi wife and he'd got a small herd and a few fields. He died and left it all to the Makushi. This was just the thing for Shark. He marched in one day on the Macdonald ranch along with a black fellow named Cecil who he always called his secretary. Now Makushis take anything that comes, and Shark was so big and strong he had every Indian in the place doing just what he wanted. He slept with the widow, had a fatted calf killed every few days and spent all day lying in a hammock under a tree. I got to hear of it. It was enough, I was going to do that devil Shark if it was the last thing I did. James was away so I saddled my horse and went off alone. I camped the night a mile from the Macdonald place.

'I rode over next morning. About a hundred yards from the house I came across some Indians and a black lad. I asked him who he was and he said, "Me is Mr Thomas's secretary." "And who in the name of hell is Mr Thomas?" I said. "They call Mr Thomas the Ocean Shark," said Cecil. Well, I walked over and found Shark lying asleep in a hammock outside the hut — without a weapon in sight. I'd got the upper hand. Even so my voice was trembling a little when I said, "Shark, wake up, Shark!" He looked up. "Don't move, Shark," I said, "or I'll fill you full of lead, you bastard. Now listen. I'm going to keep you covered, and you're going to collect your gear and you and your secretary are going to start walking north and over the Pakaraimas, and if I ever hear you're in the savannahs again by God I'll come and do you for good and all. Now, get out and stay out." I still today don't know how he did what he did do. No white man could have done it. That whole huge body seemed to just leap into the air from that lying position and he was at me. If I'd wanted to play really clean I guess I'd have switched my Webley to my left hand and punched him with my fist, but I didn't specially want to play clean. I brought that revolver butt down on the side of Shark's head with every bit of force I'd got. It would have finished anybody else. It split his ear wide open, but he didn't go down. I'd dazed him a bit — it just gave me time to smash my fist into his face. That, thank God, did bring him down, but not out. But he was in a bad way. "Right, Shark," I said, "I've been wanting to do that for a long long time." I told an Indian to get his things, but not his gun. Cecil was trembling away by now. "Shark," I said, "now you can get moving, both of you, you goddamned son of a bitch." I watched them both move off over the horizon. I knew they wouldn't come back to the Macdonald ranch. Shark knew the Makushis well enough. They'd seen him worsened, they wouldn't do a thing for him again.'

Ben's eyes were glistening as his mind went back to this day of his ancient triumph.

'And what happened to Ocean Shark in the end?' I asked. 'He

came back,' said Ben. 'Down south in Wapishana country. Up to his old tricks. He had another whole village waiting on him. But I didn't have to go down and finish him. Wapishanas are different from Makushis. They're more particular about not having black blood. Shark raped half a dozen of the girls, and one night the brothers of the girls all came into his hut, armed with bows and arrows. They filled him with six arrows where he lay in his hammock, and that was the end of Shark. Mind you, he wasn't all a bad fellow. When he'd got money he was generous to those who hadn't. There must have been some good in him somewhere.'[1]

And with those Christian words Ben finished his rum and gave the long sigh which old men give when they have summoned the vivid details of events that happened long ago. Time must have a different connotation on the savannahs, time must almost be away. We were all silent; we were at last conscious of the frog chorus from the pond; a horse neighed in the corral, a nightbird made unmusical sounds at intervals. It was time for us to go to our hammocks.

Next morning we set out across the savannahs once more in cool air; the landscape had slightly changed. The crippled curatellas were more frequent, the fronds of Ité palms formed their haloes on every horizon, and long wide bands of dense forest wound off along the hidden watercourses. But in the main it was the same scene of oceanlike grass, though the gentle rise and fall of its contours allowed the eye to search for form and shape.

At one point we drove for some minutes along what seemed to be a built up causeway with a flat expanse of grassland on either side. With splendid lack of dramatic emphasis Cossou said to me, 'You may be interested to know we're now driving across the Lake of El Dorado. Lake Parima they sometimes call it — we call it Lake Amuku. It's dry now, but in a month or two when the rains come it's quite a good-sized lake. You're seeing the savannahs at

[1] I am grateful to Mr Vincent Roth for the story about Ocean Shark and a telegram which he sent from Bartica to a Georgetown brothel proprietress. He had arrived with a good haul from the gold-fields and, going to the post office, said, 'Hey, Postmaster! knock the bakra wire for me. Say "'Ocean Shark' to 'Angel Baby': Expect me dogmatically tomorrow steamer. Order carriage, footman and lap-dog. If not got money, borrow. Gold in abundance."'

their best now; in the rainy season it's swamps, swamps everywhere, and all the cattle have to find out the little islands of higher land. It's the same all over. It's hell for us trying to travel about.'

I was not giving his last remarks the attention they deserved; so this — this was Lake Parima, the Mar del Dorado, the Mar de Aguas Blancas, on whose shores the mythical golden city of Manoa had been placed. I had seen early seventeenth-century maps of Guiana marked with a huge lake called Parima, the source of a score of great rivers and the size of the entire Rupununi. Hondius's map of 1599 makes the lake the size of the Caspian Sea, and his followers adapted his fantasy as they saw fit.[1] It is significant that it was not until after Raleigh's voyage of 1595 that the inland sea became fixed, by cartographers, in Guiana. Until then explorers and geographers had placed the lake in regions much farther westward.

Laurence Keymis, who shared the expenses of Raleigh's second voyage of 1596, learnt the position of the lake, which was fixed in both his and Raleigh's imaginations as the Mar del Dorado. 'The Indians', says Keymis, 'go up the Dessekebe [Essequibo] in twenty days, towards the south. To mark the greatness of the river, they call it "the brother of the Orinoco". After twenty days' navigating they convey their canoes by a porterage of one day from the river Dessekebe to a lake, which the Jaos call *Roponowini*, and the Caribees *Parime*. This lake is as large as a sea; it is covered with an infinite number of canoes; and I suppose that this lake is no other than that which contains the town of Manoa.'

In 1740 a German surgeon, Nicholas Hortsmann, was sent by Laurens Storm van's Gravesande, Governor of Dutch Guiana,[2] to explore the Upper Essequibo and the Rupununi, in search of precious metals and El Dorado. He found Lake Amuku in flood, and the Indians sent him in search of the mountain of Ucucuamo, the 'mountain of gold', and the river Mahu, where he would find silver, diamonds and emeralds. He found nothing but rock crystals, and his account of his long travels has a certain jaundiced air.

---

[1] Even after Humboldt's explorations and researches had proved the non-existence of the inland sea a map of America was published in Vienna, in 1818, '*dressée sur les observations de M. de Humboldt*', with Lake Parima dominating Guiana.

[2] This then comprised most of what is now the coastal section of British Guiana.

But the whole question of Lake Parima, El Dorado, Manoa, and the sagas and discoveries resulting from the quest for them, is too magnificent a subject to be treated in a few fugitive paragraphs. It demands an ample treatment.[1]

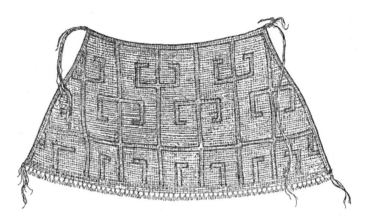

A BEAD APRON, OR QUEYU

[1] To avoid a long break in this narrative an account of the 'Search for El Dorado' appears as Appendix A of this book.

The Country of the Makushis

THE miserable lake of El Dorado was far behind us and we could now make out the forest-covered clefts of the Kanukus, rising sharply from the plain, mountains on whose fertile lower slopes the Indians have their garden places. We passed through an area well covered with palm, and then on the horizon I saw a Union Jack fluttering from a mast; a scattering of white houses rose over the hill-line and corrugated aluminium roofing glinted in the sun. We had come to the city — Lethem, successor to Bon Success, the post which had itself succeeded the Brazilian Bom Successo. The hotel lay, with the abattoir, a few hundred yards from the government buildings, beside the airstrip. It was well built with brick and stucco, set in a garden compound. A cloud of flies greeted us as we entered and made our way along a dark, dank corridor to the bar — a bare cement-floored room with a counter running along the far end. We quenched our thirsts with a few beers and talked on through the rest of the afternoon till it was dark.

Imagine the dimly lit room; the unexpressive faces of Makushi Indians looking hour-long through the windows, knowing that with the Commissioner here they can buy no rum. Others with their women stand at the open doors content with the entertainment of watching the white men talk, laugh and drink, their beautiful dark eyes caught in the light, their burnished copper faces shining. Standing at the bar are Bamford, Cossou and myself; sitting are Lally Melville and the vet, Smith, who has recently come over from Jamaica. Lally is talking about an alligator that wounded him in the calf a few days before, and orders another snap of rum. 'I forbid it,' cries Jimmy. 'Amerindians can't have liquor!' But Barrie, the tough little Mancunian behind the bar pours out a stiff tot, while another Mancunian, Lewis, tall and thin, also behind the bar, waits for an opportunity to ask Jimmy whether his claim for land in the Kanukus has gone through yet. Sitting on a chair away from the bar is a sturdy young Brazilian, with a spotless nylon shirt and beautifully tailored trousers. His name is Senhor Brazil. He lights a Chesterfield with a gold cigarette lighter, puts it to burn away in an ashtray, and begins to sing gently to his guitar. He sings Brazilian songs. He is waiting for a truck to come over to take him to his home in Boa Vista. He finishes his song and I ask him if he will sing 'O Cangaceiro' ('The Bandit'). 'No!' he snaps with undisguised anger, and I do not then realize that his father is Adolf Brazil, once the most powerful bandit of the Rio Branco territory, and now the owner of vast ranches and a small plateau mountain composed, it seems, largely of diamonds.

The vet tells us the story of a Chinese called Wun Fung who did him out of two thousand dollars in Singapore five years before. 'That reminds me of the time,' says Jimmy at the end, 'when, after I was on the Boundary Commission, I was holding court at Bartica. There was a black up before me. The blighter had got hold of an Indian girl and kidded her that if she went at full moon to a certain tree and buried her jewellery under it she'd find it had doubled by next full moon. She did it and he went off with the lot. "Sah," he says to me in the dock, "me ain't no liard fellow, me don't play no bold game, 'tall 'tall. When me is discoursin' wid dat Amerindian girl me had no thought of storyin' she. Me tells yo', sah, since me is young young me is psychic, sah, psychic. Some terrible t'ing he happen dat dat unfortunate young lady should no' retrieve her jewellery. Becausin me *is* psychic." "So you are psychic are you," I said to him. "That's a strange coincidence because I am psychic myself. In fact I'm so psychic that I know exactly what you're going to be doing for the next six months." '

Lewis chooses this moment to ask about his land claim, and is given a non-committal reply; Jimmy and Cossou have some business to arrange and go back to the District Commissioner's house. I remain, talking with Lewis, Barrie, Lally and his younger brother, a ranger.

Lewis and Barrie were fond of talking, and before long I knew their history. They had first met in the army and had been through the Burma campaign together. Though Barrie's straightforward plainspoken temperament was quite opposite to Lewis's more contemplative, more contorted nature they had decided to share each other's fortunes. Lewis married after the war, but the partnership did not break up. Life in Manchester had little to offer these two young men who had tasted adventure and wanted more. They were interviewed for jobs as overseers on the sugar plantations of British Guiana and dreamt of quick advancement and various pleasures of colonial life. The reality was less pleasant; the life was hard and isolated, they learnt that the East Indian labourers looked upon the overseers as their natural enemy. When Lewis talked of the East Indians his eyes blazed, and he paled. They did not stay long on the plantations — the adventure to be found in the Interior was too strong an enticement, and they went off to the North-West to help survey the manganese concession, and to do a little prospecting of their own. Then came a diamond shout in the upper Mazaruni and Lewis went to make his claims. His diggings were good and he told me that they had brought him sufficient money to keep him going for a few years. Meanwhile Barrie had left to try his luck in the Rupununi. His openness and obvious decency had brought him one of the rewards of the Rupununi; he married Teddy Melville's daughter Anita, and was given the job of running the bar. Lewis, who had no love for the Coast, accepted the invitation to be assistant barman, and there he had been for some months waiting for his land concession to be granted.

His knowledge of the flora and the fauna of the forest and savannah was remarkable; he had trained himself rigorously for the wild life, and now he had centred all his wishes on those few fertile acres. With his own hands he would hack down the trees and up-root them, clear the vegetation and plough the earth. He would build a simple hut and watch his crops grow — tomatoes, vegetables, fruit trees. He would fly his produce down to the Coast and with his profits he would subdue more land. Then he would take an Indian girl for his wife and beget the children who would inherit his holding. As he talked his eyes would stray away in the direction of the invisible Kanukus, his El Dorado.

It was unfortunate that his fine pioneering spirit had the corollary of such hatred for the Coast and all that went with it. Both he and Barrie feared that the new prosperity of the savannahs would bring coastal Creoles to the Rupununi. They hated Africans almost as much as East Indians. With an extraordinary naivety of mind, with which I could not argue, they seriously told me that all the Negroes in the colony should be sent back to Africa, and the East Indians to India. They had come, they said, to British Guiana because it was a British colony, and the purpose of a British colony was to give opportunities for Britons to make good. Instead they were treated as if they were outsiders, as if the place belonged to the bloody niggers and wogs. 'My answer,' said Lewis, 'is to send the blighters back to Africa or drown the lot.' 'Why', put in Barrie, 'should my old man back home have to pay taxes so that they can have an extra bit of irrigated coastland?' They were convinced, they said, that if the bloody Labour Party were elected in Britain they would hand the colony over to Cheddi Jagan. They had made their arrangements; they knew somebody in Manaos — they would slip over the border into Brazil and start a new life in Manaos.

At first I tried to give a little reality to their views of the situation on the Coast, and to suggest that the purpose of colonies was no longer what they supposed it to be, but neither seemed to have a glimmering of what I meant. I became plainer; Lewis's face glowered and his facial muscles twitched, Barrie became pleasantly dogmatic. I had drunk too much to realize that our conversation could lead nowhere profitable. I raised my voice and returned their dogmatic statements with angry statements just as dogmatic. The evening did not end pleasantly. I don't suppose Lewis to this day has forgiven me for some of the things I told him. Next morning I learnt that our conversation had been reported in detail at the District Commissioner's office. I was never quite sure whether my attitude was officially approved of or not.

Lewis and Barrie were extreme cases in their resentment of Britain's growing concern for the advancement of colonial peoples. They spoke from ignorance and from contempt borne of a new-found sense of superiority. Their attitude is by no means typical of the white British attitude as a whole, but in its extreme form it is typical of undercurrents of thought which are strangled by many, sublimated by others, and given considered expression by very few. Lewis and Barrie wished for an actual stake in the land and they had so far been frustrated. They resented Britain's unconcern in their careers. It is a pity, perhaps, that the colonies can no longer canalize the great qualities of such men.

That night, from my bedroom window, I saw the sky lit by fires scattered all over the savannahs. Every night we spent in Indian country was illuminated in the same way. It is a tradition from which Indians cannot be broken, even though the grass experts say it harms the productivity of the soil. The Indians, who certainly get pleasure from the flames, say that their cattle like the sweet green shoots that spring up from the ash-covered soil. A man I met once travelled with old Melville across the savannahs, who told him of the impossibility of breaking the Indians of this bad habit. That evening he looked back from his saddle to see Melville himself busily striking matches and throwing them on to the grass.

An hour or so after breakfast the next morning I walked across soft sand down to a creek that flows into the Takatu. Two grey and twisted tree-trunks formed the only bridge and I made my way carefully across, for the river was high. Then up the rise and on across the flat dull sandy country with hardly a tree in sight. I passed some adobe huts, outside which sat Makushi women with children at their breasts, staring at me as I approached them to ask the way to the St Ignatius Mission. Eventually three buildings came in sight, simple enough but unmistakably the mission. They were made of adobe and of Indian workmanship, but a European mind had conceived the open loggia on the second floor of the nearest building, which seemed to have been inspired by the wool-drying loggias at the top of Florentine palaces. I stood in the silence of the compound and called out. A moment later the tall figure of an Englishman appeared at a doorway, dressed in grey flannel trousers and a white shirt; he was in his seventies, his face and body extremely thin, his skin yellow and sunken from the one-time ravages of malaria. We walked towards each other with hands outstretched. 'Swan,' I said, and he replied 'Mather.'

He was Father Mather, the Jesuit priest in charge of the mission. He took me into his house; the first room we entered was his workshop. Benches were covered with the insides of clocks and watches, complicated pieces of jeep machinery, a rancher's Leica which had fallen into the river, now stripped down for cleaning. I later gathered that machinery of this kind was a mere part of Father Mather's interest in handicraft; he was a carpenter, a cabinet maker, a worker in leather, and a clever converter of motor car inner tubes into other useful things. He had not used his gifts to make his mission house more comfortable, for every room I saw was furnished with an absolute minimum of comfortless furniture — although, with typical hospitality, he opened out a home-made deck chair for me in the loggia. Here we sat all the morning talking, and looking at the blue Kanukus as the strong wind whistled through the open spaces.

Father Mather was an enchanting talker, liberal in his attitudes and willing to give freely from the stored results of his intense curiosity. He had come to the mission in 1923, and had never returned to England since. He had spent those years at St Ignatius, except for a short term in Georgetown, which he had looked upon as an interruption of his ethnological, zoological, botanical and ornithological studies. He believes that he has succeeded in finding the means by which the old social forms of the Indians may survive the teaching of Christianity and the destruction of their more harmful aspects. He showed no animosity towards other sects who are evangelizing the Interior, but he was genuinely alarmed that certain odd American sects were forbidding the drinking of cassiri and paiwari. 'Their bodies *need* it,' he said. 'It's good for them. I've tried to make the Government realize that their whole metabolisms will be affected if they don't drink it.' His great fear was that the variety of Christian teaching would produce as many forms of belief as ever before, that a new tribalism could be based on Catholicism, Seventh Day Adventism, Methodism and the rest.

I asked him about the problem of the coastal Negroes who were coming up to the Rupununi, and he admitted that this worried him. There was, he said, a quiet, progressive Negro colony of settlers at Annai and he admired them. But the men who had come up to work at the abattoirs did not behave well. They tended to terrorize the Indians, teach them bad habits and rape their women. Governor Lethem, he said, had intended the Rupununi to continue to be a different world from the Coast, an Amerindian not an African world. He had found an administrator with exactly the vision for the task but he was killed during the War, and without him the development of the Rupununi had proceeded without a great deal of inspiration.

We lunched in the mess adjoining the mission house, and to celebrate my visit Father Mather unlocked a cupboard and produced a

facing, above: THE HEADMAN OF A SAVANNAH VILLAGE DEMONSTRATING THE BLOWPIPE
below: SCENE IN AN INDIAN HUT

dust-covered bottle of Scotch whisky. He told me about Wapishana
travelling hammocks that were a triumph of craftsmanship, the type
of wild cotton which they used, the special reeds from which they
made their baskets; he told me about the excited dances performed
on the flat surface of a rock by those brilliant yellow and orange
birds, the cock-of-the-rock (*Rupicola rupicola*); he told me which
part of the Kanukus I might go to if I wished to gather the leaves of
the *Erythroxylum coca*, whose active principle is an alkaloid cocaine.
The Indians use it as a tonic, he said, chewing the leaves with lime
and ashes. An infusion of this leaf is the famous secret constituent
of Coca-Cola — or was.

After lunch we returned to the windy loggia. The light had
changed on the Kanukus and their blue haze had lifted. Father
Mather pointed to the peak of the highest mountain and said, 'You
see that mountain, Mount Iramaikpang — it has a very special place
in Makushi history. An epiphytic liana grows on the top of it,
probably the finest species of its genus in the whole of the tropical
forests. Without it the Makushis would never have become famous
as the best makers of urari, and they could never have traded the
stuff right through the Amazonas.'

'Urari?' I said.

'Come with me,' said Father Mather, with the air of a man who
knows he has made his intended effect.

We went to a back room, and from a locked cupboard Father
Mather produced a dozen black gourds of various sizes, each with
two small holes on either side through which a piece of bush-string
had been looped. Each gourd was heavy with a dull black substance,
fissured like sunbaked bitumen.

'There's enough there to kill the whole Black Watch in Georgetown,' said Father Mather. 'And the entire P.P.P. too.'

'Urari?' I repeated, still a little mystified.

'You've probably heard of it under its detective story name —
curare. You remember the Sherlock Holmes tale? It's the original
South American poison, unknown to science and leaving no trace.
Except that it's been known to science for donkey's years — they
were using it for nervous diseases in Europe nearly a century ago.
One might say it fascinates scientists — it has all the romance they
could ask for. These gourds are left over from a consignment I sent

facing, above: WILLIAM AND CECILIA AT THE CAMP NEAR THE FOOT OF RORAIMA
ESCARPMENT
below: AT THE FOOT OF THE MURAL FACE *(see p. 245)*

K

last year to some laboratories in England where they've been making urari experiments.'

'It certainly fascinates me,' I said, holding a gourd a little gingerly and examining its contents.

'It's perfectly safe,' said Father Mather. 'You could eat the lot and it would have no effect, but if you'd got the slightest scratch on your finger and touched it I should have to perform the last rites over you in approximately seven minutes. This Makushi stuff is the quickest. Most of the other Indians have their own version of urari — "devil-doer" they sometimes call it — but it takes much longer. Later I'll show you a photograph of an old Indian who told me most of what I know about the stuff. As a boy he went up Mount Iramaik-pang with the Schomburgks and picked the right lianas for them.'

Later I looked up Richard Schomburgk's account of this expedition:

> When we had climbed about 600 feet [he wrote], my guide pointed out the first plant with the exclamation 'Urari-yeh! Urari-yeh!' With a certain amount of dread I regarded this mischief-making plant,[1] the rapidly-acting properties of which I had now so frequently seen, and still was so often to see again, and for which an antidote had so far not been discovered. Even its external conformation had something suspicious about it. The brown hairy young twigs and leaves, the rough dark-coloured bark of the older shoots, everything betrayed its awful properties. . . .

As far as I am able to discover, the first account of the effects of curare are given, with his usual accuracy in such matters, by Raleigh, who says that a man shot by a curare-tipped arrow 'abideth a most vglie and lamentable death'. He found that the Indians in general were ignorant of its composition: 'But euery one of these Indians know it not, no not one among thousands, but their soothsaiers and priests, who do conceale it, and onely teach it but from the father to the sonne.'

Waterton wrote the best-known account of the poison in his

---

[1] There seems to be an agreement among modern writers on the South American forests to preserve the idea that the active principle of curare is known only to Indian witch-doctors. In fact the actual poison was isolated a century ago.

Wanderings, cleverly making the quest for 'wourali' (as he called it) the theme of his book. He says that the juice of the vine is mixed with the fangs of the labarri and counacouchi snakes, with pepper and the pounded bodies of two species of ants. The mixture is boiled on a slow fire, the scum being removed with a leaf until the liquor has been reduced to a thick black syrup. The hut in which the poison is made is considered polluted after each brewing, and abandoned. The maker of the poison, aware of the evil nature of his art, appears to produce a psychosomatic illness when he has completed his task, retiring to his hammock for some days. Robert Schomburgk managed to make a poison strong enough to kill a fowl in twenty-five minutes simply by making a weak infusion of the vine bark. Neither Waterton nor Schomburgk mentions that the purpose of the other components is to make the thin poison viscous enough for it to stick to the points of arrows and blowpipe darts.

Although during my travels in the Interior, I passed through country where curare was in constant use and saw poison darts in action, I never came across a death from curare poisoning, though I saw bush-hogs which had been killed by curare-tipped arrows being brought in from the chase. Birds die in two or three minutes, bush-hogs in about ten minutes. The alkaloid, curarine, contained in the poison has a paralysing effect on the peripheral nerves; as the paralysis creeps, the muscles slowly cease to function and respiration becomes impossible; the animal finally dies of asphyxiation. Raleigh did not exaggerate when he talked of men dying 'starke mad' from the poison.[1] This terrible death, which I am glad not to have seen, leaves the flesh of the animal untainted.

A century ago curare was used in some experiments to trace which part of the human body was served by which nerve. The recent experiments for which Father Mather had made his collection will make some amends for the agony which curare has caused for so many centuries. Isolated curarine is being used to relax certain muscles before a surgical operation is made; it has also been used to break down tetanus rigor. The poison masters in the Makushi villages need no longer pay the penalty of psychosomatic illness after their visits to the summit of Mount Iramaikpang; they can be

[1] During the First World War, I have been told, an attempt was made to assassinate Lloyd George with curare.

happy that by the art handed down to them from their fathers they are contributing to the medical advancement of the world.

I looked up to the summit of the mountain and thought of those dark and hairy leaves, the winding woody tendrils perhaps asphyxiating the hospitable tree, the little scented white flowers that bloom so rarely.

Uncertainty is the greatest delight of travel; not to know where your bed will be, or whether there will be a bed at all, to be prepared to travel at an hour's notice in whichever point of the compass the greatest interest lies, to have made plans in the knowledge that they will be broken. That night, when I was scraping the last spoonful of blancmange from its thick pink carapace, three Indians came quietly into the room. I was dining with Macleod, the handsome young policeman from Rhodesia, who had returned that day from an inspection of the Ireng border. The spokesman of the Indians approached our table and said to Macleod, 'We find tiger, big big black tiger him kill pig and dog. We no gun big big for he. You come kill he for we.'

Macleod's face lit up. This black jaguar had been plaguing some Wapishana villages for weeks and he had told the villagers that when they had found its lair he would come over and help in the hunt. True to their word the Indians had walked the whole day to Lethem to bring him the news. I asked Macleod if I could join him on the hunt.

'We might have to keep on the run for the whole morning,' he said. 'These big cats can move.' I shrugged my shoulders as if such exertions were nothing to me, and it was agreed that I should come.

I sent word to Bamford and Cossou to pick me up at Charley Melville's ranch in two days and packed my luggage into Macleod's jeep. He brought nothing except his hammock and the beautiful sporting rifle with which he had hunted game on the plains of Rhodesia. We moved off across the savannahs in a darkness that now seemed hardly lessened by the burning patches of grass. Now and then, when the trail passed near a fire, Macleod would stop and take the three Indians to the flames and try to stamp them out. I would see the Indians' figures, silhouetted against the light, inefficiently performing an action which was entirely contrary to their principles of correct conduct. Looking even more miserable than usual they would climb back into the jeep and sit mumbling to each other. I have no doubt that if they had had matches they would have blazed a trail of fires in our wake.

When a small moon appeared I could make out the Kanukus always to our left, and from the stars I knew that we were slowly rounding them, moving into the southern savannahs. The trail now traversed long dense patches of bush and dried-up, rock-strewn watercourses. At last we turned off the trail, along a rutted path at the end of which stood a low unlighted building. It was Charley Melville's ranch. A door opened and Charley himself, bearing a lantern, came down to the compound wire and greeted us. He knew about the jaguar hunt and was expecting Macleod to spend a few hours of the night at his ranch. As for myself, he and his wife had been told that I should call on them sometime and they'd had a bed made up for me for weeks. Warning me that we should start off at three-forty-five next morning Macleod slung his hammock in the compound, and I went into the dark house, where Mrs Melville greeted me charmingly and took me by candlelight to the little room where the bed was ready for me.

I slept well, and a moment only seemed to have passed before I heard Macleod calling to me through the window that it was time to get up. The air was cold in the open jeep and my body froze beneath my bush shirt. Macleod sat at the wheel controlling his dreams of the black jaguar well enough to make his way across trackless country to the Indian village. After an hour of fast driving we reached the village. There had evidently been no sleep at all for the Indians that night; men, women and children sat and stood in the darkness, while the whippet dogs roamed round, impatient after sensing that a hunt was on. The tuchau, or elected headman of the village, showed us a poor cur that had been mauled by the jaguar and from the clawmarks one could tell that this was not the usual small cat of the savannah, but an animal of circumstance. 'It should have a fine coat,' Macleod said.

The tuchau told us that the villagers had lost many pigs and chickens, and they were frightened that the jaguar might attack their children. If he had, the jaguar would have had a wide choice of victims; children toddled everywhere — not a woman was without a suckling child. The tuchau pointed down towards a river and said that the jaguar's lair was on a bush-covered island in the river. The riverbed was dry except for pools along its course, so that the jaguar could make a quick retreat from it if necessary. The plan was to place a party on either side of the river before dawn to receive the jaguar when he came back to his lair after the night's hunting. The sky was just beginning to lighten when we set off for the river. The dogs and some Indians kept to the left bank, while Macleod, the rest of the men and I made our way across the rocks of the river-bed, and walked quietly along the right bank. We stopped at a patch of Ité palms, and waited, my ears feeling as erect as a bird-dog's. Sweet dawn birds trilled and made their dovelike calls, and for the first time that morning I became conscious, in the expectant silence, of a murmurous brek-ek-ek-ex. A whippet dog over the river barked faintly. The sky lightened, and to the east above the Kanukus the sky became a pale rose. I could see to the west, where the land rolled for some miles, a range of isolated hills beyond which lay the territory of the Rio Branco. Twenty minutes went by and it was full dawn. Suddenly the dogs began a furious barking and the sound seemed to be approaching us as if they were in full chase. We rushed down towards the river from the Ité palms and broke through the bush that fringed the bank. A pool lay in our way and we splashed through it to make the centre of the river. The dogs had now reached us and passed us in a flash, while the running Indians pointed down-stream. The jaguar had been seen. We ran with them up the bank, through the bush once more and then veering left again across rising country whose horizon was close, but divided from us by two long slopes.

At last we made that horizon and looked down towards a river course bounded on either side by heavy bush. We were in time, by less than a minute, to see half a mile away the black jaguar leaping across the grass, knowing that he had outpaced the pack and that in the bush he would be master. Macleod, knowing that he was simply making a votive-offering of gunpowder to Diana, raised his rifle and fired one round. But the great black jaguar was gone.

If we had had plenty of beaters it might just have been possible to pursue him with success, but as we walked on towards the bush we knew that from now on the chase would be merely good exercise. The dogs came out of the bush as we approached it, having lost the scent, and as there was no trail through the bush at this point we skirted it. A spur of hill swept down towards the river, and after some minutes an Indian village appeared on its silhouette — three adobe huts.

'Makushis,' said one of the Wapishanas.

In this border country between the Makushi and the Wapishana territory one finds a few isolated Makushi villages or nomadic encampments. The two tribes may have shared the land for centuries but they have ignored each other's existence. The Makushis belong to the Carib stock, the Wapishanas to some stock which perhaps has its source deep in the Amazonian forest. There is no similarity at all between the Makushi Carib dialect and Wapishana speech. There has been little or no intermarriage and the two tribes have maintained their differences of character. The Makushi is solemn, introverted, completely fatalistic and easily confused into decadence by the influence of civilization; the Wapishanas, though I found them often solemn enough, are gay among themselves and laughter-loving. They have adapted themselves better to what civilization they have seen and make good *vaqueiros*, or cowboys, on the ranches. Less than ten years ago, before the new development of the Rupununi, the Makushis were an unhappy, dying people. They would say themselves that they were doomed, that their children all died of malaria, that there was no point in planting, it was better to lie in one's hammock and prepare for death. They starved; game and fish were scarce, and what there was they preferred to leave, stealing a cow now and then when they felt the need to gorge themselves with meat. They allowed their fine hunting dogs to degenerate into curs that lived on their own and human excrement.

Unlike some Indian tribes, where the women have a degree of power, Makushi women are the willing slaves of their menfolk. The men of the forest Carib tribes are tireless carriers, but Makushi men will carry nothing on their shoulders. I have seen them walking across the savannahs with nothing in their hands except a bow or a shotgun, while their women walk behind bent over with a laden warishi. Even the smallest sons treat their mothers with a kind of contempt. In the village we came to that morning a woman sat grinding cassava, with great flat breasts hanging from her as she worked. A boy of four came up to her and, with an action that strangely expressed his indifference to her, took one of her breasts in his hands and raised it to his mouth as if it were no more than some flaccid vessel for quenching his thirst. He took his fill and picked up the miniature bow which had been given him as soon as he could walk.

The Makushis are a little happier today, now that their health is better and they are benefiting from the new money economy of the Rupununi. A man poured a drink called shabbi into a calabash and handed it to us. It was a refreshing, non-alcoholic drink made from water, salt and cassava flour, or farine. Farine is one of the two staple foods of the savannahs, tasteless but nutritious. The other staple is tasso — hard, dried, jerked beef, which I had seen hanging, black with smoke, in every ranch I had visited. When the *vaqueiros* go out on the range — perhaps for a few weeks — they live entirely on tasso and farine. They take with them a long woollen receptacle, like a long stocking, which has a hole in its middle. One side of the stocking is stuffed with farine and the other with tasso. When you meet a *vaqueiro* on the savannahs you see this food bag hanging on either side of his saddle. He carries no other rations.

We drank the shabbi and were on our way. At the river crossing we found a party of small Makushi boys standing beside one of the pools formed by the retreating waters of the river. They would study the surface of the water, see a fish, make allowances for the refraction of light and shoot an arrow. Never once did the arrow not shake furiously in the water as the fish struggled for life. The boys were more active than their fathers, who usually do not bother to use bow and arrow when the fish are trapped in pools, but squeeze a few drops of hiari root into the water, which brings the narcotized fish to the surface of the pool.

Some way beyond the creek we came to the fences separating the Indian reserve from the land of the Rupununi Development Company, whose vast lands, stretching across the southern savannahs, support no more head of cattle than a large Devonshire dairy farm. Ten minutes later we reached one of the Company's outstations—an adobe hut for the headman of the station, stables for horses and a long hut for the *vaqueiros*. It was Sunday and no one was out on the range; the *vaqueiros* lay in their hammocks singing Brazilian songs to a guitar, their straw hats on pegs above them. A lean, leather-skinned old man came out of the hut and spoke to us in rapid Portuguese. One of our Indians, who had been a *vaqueiro* and spoke a little Portuguese, told him that Macleod was the police chief, and he smiled and shook our hands warmly, inviting us to sit in the airy anteroom to his hut. Raking up the remnants of my Spanish I tried to make conversation with the old man, Vasco, and we found that we could make some kind of contact, enough for me to tell that he was an odd character, with a past I longed to know. In the darkness of the inner room I could see two girls preparing the coffee which Vasco had ordered, and quite half an hour later these two pretty daughters of the house brought out the small delicate cups and the pot of coffee. It was coffee in Brazilian style, and as in all countries where the drink is really understood it was hot as hell, sweet as an angel and black as night. Even if it were not a delight to taste good coffee again after the wretched *liberica* of the colony, I think I would call this the finest cup of coffee I have ever drunk. We showed our appreciation to the two shy girls, and I said I should like to photograph them. Vasco said that he had a third daughter who was paralysed in both her legs, and he would like to have her photographed too. The girls went off to prepare themselves and I continued to make what I could of Vasco's flow of talk.

A quarter of an hour later the three girls appeared, in bright pretty dresses, their hair beribboned, powder on their cheeks and lipstick on their lips. They were three very pretty girls, and it was sad to see the prettiest of them all sitting helplessly in a wheel-chair; she had been struck by paralysis some years before. When we had taken our photographs and listened to the girls' songs we took our leave. Although I knew that Macleod would disapprove I asked Vasco if I might borrow a horse to get back to the Wapishana village. Macleod planned to retrace his steps, but I much preferred to return by a different, longer route, and to know what it was like to ride one of the fiery little savannah ponies.

Vasco saddled me a pony and gave me one of his Wapishana *vaqueiros* as a guide. I mounted the horse, and Vasco explained how to use the reins of heavy plaited leather that fitted, bitless, into the horse's mouth. Then we started, and a roar of laughter greeted my obvious discomfiture at the unexpected movements of the horse. It had been trained, like all horses of the region, for the 'savannah trot', which produced a motion unlike that of any horse with European manners. Whatever I did, the saddle seemed determined to come up and strike me sharply on the behind as I was going down towards it. My whole body was soon making large vibrations, and when we were far enough from the outstation for my bad horsemanship not to be seen I whipped the horse into a canter, a motion which at least was more familiar to me. But for someone like me who is only just able to ride, the canter was too tiring, so I forced the horse into a walk which, I learnt later, is far more tiring to a savannah horse than the trot. It was an unwise step, and I should have realized that my entirely inefficient handling of the horse was irritating him. Andrew, the *vaqueiro*, was far ahead, and we were moving across a large area of grassland with one solitary sandpaper tree two hundred yards to my left. I started another canter to overtake Andrew, but a few seconds later I realized that the horse was not responding to my pressures on the reins; he was making a full canter for the tree, and had every intention of giving me the big brush-off. I panicked slightly, my camera became a nuisance and my feet lost the stirrups, but as we reached the tree I was able to put my arms around the horse's neck and lean far enough over to one side for the branches not to touch me. He went twice round the tree with me in this undignified position, and then began an amiable trot in the direction he knew I had wished to go. Rearranging myself I looked ahead to see Andrew, fifty yards away, rocking up and down in his saddle in uncontrollable laughter, which had not abated when I reached him.

The horse was evidently more impressed than Andrew by my ability to remain seated, for he now seemed to make some effort to move at a comfortable walking pace. Andrew walked beside and we made a little conversation as we went. He had learnt some English in the mission school at Sand Creek, and in ways which I was unable to fathom had gathered various strange notions of civilization. He was sophisticated and knew it, expressing it in a certain cheekiness of manner. He was seventeen years old, he told me, and at seventeen a man should be earning more than $20 (£4 3s. 4d.) a month — why, he had clothes and brilliantine to buy; at this point he raised his Brazilian hat to reveal hair gleaming with evil-scented pomade. It was strange to hear an Indian talking like some aggrieved British workman, and I had a vision of a *vaqueiro* strike on the grounds that wages had not kept pace with the rising cost of brilliantine. It is the Government's policy to see that the Indians are paid with money rather than with kind, part of the Indians' preparation to undertake one day full responsibility in a money economy. At the moment, however, dollar bills mean only the ability to make luxury purchases at the stores. At one ranch I was to find signs of a greater sophistication than brilliantine; the magic of peroxide had been discovered and everywhere bottle-blond Wapishanas strutted, feeling that they had at last gained one of the admired attributes of the white man.

'Is England a place?' Andrew suddenly asked me. 'Yes,' I replied, 'it is a large place, and the Queen owns all the Rupununi.' As I spoke I felt strangely outdated, as if the Queen were still Victoria and Britain an imperial power.

'The Queen?' said Andrew, 'me no hear of Queen.' I did my best to explain who she was, but his only reply was, 'Me want go to America.'

He had no conception of America either, but had gathered, probably from some overheard conversation, that America was an excellent place to live in.

'If you go to America,' I said dampeningly, 'you'll need fifty horseloads of farine and tasso, and it'll take you a year to ride there.'

'Plenty plenty long way,' he said and laughed.

When conversation flagged I asked him to sing some of his people's songs, encouraging him by singing 'Three Blind Mice' myself. Eventually he sang sad little songs, clearly Brazilian in origin but with a touch of Indian modulation to them.

In this way we arrived, in the full heat of the sun, back at the Wapishana village where we had begun the hunt. Ten minutes later Macleod arrived and we set off in the jeep for another outstation, a quarter of an hour away, where Macleod wanted to see a horse that had been poisoned by drinking from a pool polluted by hiari. He knew, incidentally, that the two Brazilian *vaqueiros* who lived there would give us a decent lunch.

The outstation was a simple building, in the Indian benab style, without walls, and on arriving we both dropped with relief into large colourful Brazilian hammocks. Lunch came; buttered eggs, followed by farine and hot tasso, which, though one had to Fletcherize it before swallowing, proved to be less horrible than it looked. The pudding was a heaped plate of quariad, the savannah curds and whey, sprinkled with brown sugar. Quariad is made every day on the ranches and outstations in a bucket which is never washed because washing would destroy the precious culture which transforms the milk into the delicious curd. Like *vignerons* on vineyards or genealogists on great family descendancies, the ranchers discuss the cultures at the various ranches, usually deciding that the Dadanawa culture reigns supreme. All the Melville men have eaten a plate of quariad at every meal for as long as they can remember, and it is suggested that there is a relationship between quariad and the high fertility rate of the Melville clan.

After some coffee I fell back once more into the hammock and slept soundly for two hours.

It was late afternoon when I arrived back at Charley Melville's, and the family was waiting for the sun to set behind the hills before going down to the creek for their bath; when the sun was up, kaboura flies, minute pests that move in swarms, made it impossible to go to the creek. I now saw my hosts by daylight for the first time; Charley was a handsome, heavily built man in his middle forties, with the slightly strained expression of an intellectual who has understood the misery of the world; his wife Edwina was a slight girl in her twenties, delicately pretty with the palest of skins. She was, she told me later in the evening, an octoroon, born and brought up in Georgetown.

While they bathed I waited for them in the large room of the ranch house, rather bare of comfort, with walls of darkened undressed timber. The family came back, and while Edwina put her two small children to bed Charley and I drank lime juice and talked. He gave me a list of Wapishana words and smiled when I asked him for some Indian stories, saying that most Wapishana and Makushi stories were too pornographic to bear translation. However, he would tell me the legend of Murapa-yeng, the Bat-mountain in the Pakaraimas.

'The Makushis say,' he began, 'that long ago a huge bat lived on the top of Murapa-yeng and all the Indians on the northern savannahs were frightened of him. At sunset the bat would come down and circle above a village to see if anybody had stayed out of his hut, and if anyone had he'd sweep down, pick him up in his claws and take him off to the top of the mountain, where he'd eat him. Every night he'd get one or two people, and all the Makushis thought that as time went by the bat would get them all and there'd be no Makushi tribe left. The piaiman tried to exorcize the spirit of the bat, but it was no good; an expedition went to the top of Murapa-yeng to kill the bat, but that was no good either. Then an old woman said that to prevent the destruction of the tribe she would offer her life as a sacrifice. Night came and she stood in the middle of the village with nothing in her hand but a covered firestick. Then they heard the heavy beat of the bat's wings and they knew that the old woman was being carried away. They came out into the open and saw a moving ball of fire in the sky with a trail of small pieces of fire behind. The old woman had uncovered her firestick so that they would see whereabouts on the mountain the bat came to rest; then they could set out to kill him. Next morning they could see the burning nest of the bat, and they went with bows and spears and killed him. The Makushis will tell you that if you go to this spot you'll still find a great heap of bleached bones.'

We talked of more mundane things. Charley agreed that air freight was bringing some prosperity to the Rupununi; but as his cattle stock was low and he did little slaughtering it had not brought him much personal prosperity. What he wanted was a cattle *road* to Georgetown, a road which would take large trucks. He had fertile land in the Kanukus, where he could grow almost anything, including coffee. But there was no use making the long journey two or three times a week to see to his crops when there was no outlet for them, air freight being too expensive. So he had left his land to return to nature. His ranch land, he added, was very poor and needed two years without cattle grazing in order to recover itself. He finished off his picture by telling me that his stock needed improvement, but he didn't have the money to buy a good bull.

Edwina came and sat with us, fresh after her bathe. She had married Charley two or three years before, but still had not let the romantic spell of her new life wear off. I had read some articles she had written for Coast papers on life in the Rupununi, and some charming poems in the intellectuals' magazine, *Kyk-over-al*, so that I knew her attitude. She was strongly against the civilizing of the Indians, feeling that their happiness lay in the preservation of their tribal ways and traditions. She distrusted the influence of Christianity, and she told me how one day she had gone to the door to find Father McKenna, the Jesuit missionary. He had read one of her articles that morning and had ridden over all day from Sand Creek to warn her, in strong terms, not to write such things — that they were harming the advancement of the Indians.

We talked for some time on this point. From my small experience of primitive society I had found it impossible to generalize about the beauty of the gentle savage's life. In Mexico I had seen, at one point, an idyllic primitive society that had managed to preserve itself entire, within a few miles of an oil town; but the villagers had been descendants of a tribe which had once been strong and, according to its lights, civilized. I had seen evidence of the beastliness of some tribal societies when completely untouched by civilization, and seen both degeneration and advancement as the influences of civilization. But from what I had seen I realized the sentimentalism of Rousseau's approach. I was interested in savage society not because I wished to return to it in any way, but because I wished to see the life from which the civilization I loved had sprung.

Although I could not wholly agree with Edwina's stand against secular and spiritual civilizing, I was to see enough in the Rupununi to understand the dangers of the break-up of ancient traditions. Living in such places one's views must be extreme to be heard at all and Edwina's brave fight, though irritating to authority, was necessary.

We dined off labba that night, and before he carved the roasted rodent Charley made the ritual comparison. 'You'll find it rather like chicken,' he said. I found it, indeed, better than chicken, a flaky pink-white flesh that melted in the mouth and left behind a lingering subtle taste. There is a saying that you will return to the colony if you eat labba and drink creek water. I had now done both, and I sincerely hope I shall one day return to British Guiana — so long as I'm assured I will not be received on the quayside by a black and white mob crying 'A la lanterne!' and 'Give he a good cut-arse.'

During dinner we talked about El Dorado and gold. There was

gold, Charley said, in the Morudi mountains lying to the south of the savannahs. A Canadian company had taken a large concession some years before, but had retired after extraction costs had proved too great. They had kept their concession and employed a watchman to patrol the land and keep poachers out. Charley had met a pork-knocker who had managed to make only one trip into the claim, who said, 'Baas, me tell yo', dat patrolman him never sleep, him never never sleep.' From the one bag of soil he had been able to take away he had washed out thirty dollars' worth of gold dust.

We went early to bed, in the custom of the country, and were up to enjoy the cool early morning. I walked with Edwina and her little girl across some fields to gather firewood and to visit a wild cashew tree whose fruit was ripe. It was a low, well branched and leafed tree, heavy with the drooping dark green fruit, at the end of which was attached the kidney-shaped pericarp containing the oily delicious nut. I ate the fruit, a sharp refreshing flesh, with a pleasantly turpentiney flavour not unlike the July mango. I was about to skin the pericarp to eat the nut when Edwina called out to me to stop. Between the folds of the skin a caustic oil forms, which burns the tongue and lips and turns them black. Unless the skin is removed carefully the acid coats the kernel itself. She took out the nut for me — it had a pleasantly sweet taste, but rather different from the roasted cashews I was used to. Edwina told me that this caustic oil can be used to preserve wood against worms and decay. I later suggested to Jimmy Bamford that a little cashew oil industry might prove a blessing to his procreating Wapishanas, but I don't think the idea was thought economically realistic. Cashew wine is a common drink in the savannahs, and has an unusual quality, according to the story; if you drink enough of it you can become drunk again next morning simply by drinking a pint or two of water. I did not put the matter to the test.

Wapishanas

BAMFORD and Cossou arrived for me later in the morning, and after Edwina had made various propositions about Indian welfare we drove across the savannahs to a large Makushi village which had been warned of our arrival. The men were dressed in their best trousers and shirts, the women sitting in the shadows with their children and babies. All watched us in dogged silence as we climbed out of the jeep, and perhaps as a sign of reverence to authority not even the tuchau came forward to make the act of shaking hands which is usually the Indian prelude to all conversation.

Extreme seriousness came over Jimmy's face for the first time since I had known him, and he stood in front of the men, with Cossou a little behind him. Jimmy turned to his interpreter, a not very bright-looking Indian boy, and said, 'Tell them that much must have happened since I last came to their village two years ago, and I wish I could come to them more, but I have to see many many Indians. But now I want them to tell me all they think is not good. I shan't come for a long time again, and now is the time to let me know everything.'

The Makushi language must be very compressed in its meaning, for the interpreter turned to the tuchau and released a short staccato sentence. The tuchau was not so concise; he rambled on for what seemed minutes, and the interpreter, turning to Jimmy, said, 'Him say Makushi hear land to be taken from they.'

'No, no,' said Jimmy, 'tell them the Company's land is going to be fenced and we may do a little fencing on Indian land, but they lose no land at all. Tell them that they must promise not to use the fence-wire for arrowheads. Make a big point of that.'

'Tell them,' Jimmy said later, 'that I want to know if they are pleased with the way their children are growing up and have they got any ideas what to do with them when they leave the mission school.'

The tuchau's reply to this was longer than his first reply, and I

160

could see that its meaning, let alone its implications, was proving too much for the wretched interpreter, who at the end turned to Jimmy and said, 'Him say yes.'

Jimmy raised his hands in despair. He shook the tuchau's hand, climbed back into the jeep and ran his handkerchief over his face. The palaver was over. 'I couldn't tell them what we're planning to do for the village', he told me as we drove away. 'They take everything for promises, and then if we can't in the end do the things, they get annoyed with us.'

Our next halt was at Mountain Foot, an emergency abattoir which had been built at the foot of the Kanukus. Cossou pressed on the accelerator as we rushed along the airstrip towards the aluminium huts. Carcasses hung in line in the open-sided abattoir, and Creoles, standing in alleys of running blood, were dressing the last animal before the arrival of the Dakota. Ten minutes after our arrival the Dakota appeared over the mountains, circled once and touched down. The carcasses were loaded in another ten minutes, and as we were leaving the airstrip the Dakota roared above us and was away to Georgetown.

Towards lunchtime a wind vane and a fine high-stilted house appeared on the skyline. From the distance the house had the solid proportions of a small Queen Anne country house, with large sash windows divided into panes. It was the most impressive building I had yet seen on the savannahs; it was Wichabai, built by Melville after he had sold Dadanawa to the Rupununi Development Company. A jeep stood outside, and a big bespectacled man rose from the examination of its engine; he was John Melville, the eldest son of the family. He came forward, and after greetings said, 'The pump's gone again. I'll have to send down to Georgetown for a new one.'

'Machines!' exclaimed Jimmy. 'Now hosses don't have pumps, you don't have to send down to Georgetown for spare parts for hosses.'

He had hit John on one of the sensitive spots of all the ranchers. When I had come to Rupununi I had expected to hear talk of the fecundity of stallions, the beauty of a bay mare, talk of bridles, martingales, stirrup leathers and gallings; instead it was talk of the superiority of Land Rovers over jeeps, miles to gallon, big ends,

facing, above: THE BENAB NEAR THE TOWAKAIMA FALLS: *centre,* THE ELDER
MARQUES; *right,* ROBERT
below: INDIAN BOYS AT BLOWPIPE CONTEST

gearboxes and four-wheel drives. Yet the ranchers drove their new mounts as if they were fine horses, galloping them across the plains, exulting in the new speed brought to them by the engine.

The big airy living- and dining-room at Wichabai was filled with Berbice chairs, and we relaxed in them drinking rum and ginger, while Jimmy and John Melville talked over the gossip of the savannahs. John spoke with earnest authority and sense of responsibility; one could sense in his kind manner something of the Scottish clergyman who had been his grandfather. Lunch was served by a pretty girl with an olive complexion, his daughter by his first, Brazilian, wife. A year or two before John had married his third wife, a Wapishana, and their second child had been born recently. Lunch was an excellent kidney soup, steaks, fried potatoes and a dish of quariad.

There was little time for siesta that afternoon. We had to make a detour to visit the Sand Creek Mission, and we hoped to get to Dadanawa by sunset. The drive to Sand Creek was through the most beautiful country we had seen so far, the land rising eastwards into the great plains of the Kanukus, and patterned with trees and ribbons of bush, rising and falling so that the eye was never bored. We crossed the dry bed of the Rupununi twice, easing the jeep gently over the boulders. Sand Creek came into sight, and we saw scores of children hurrying to form themselves in position beneath a flagpole from which fluttered the Union Jack. We drove into the compound before the mission school; as we climbed out Father McKenna cut the air with his hand and the assembled children broke into a somewhat Schönbergian version of 'God Save the Queen'. In fluent and expressive Wapishana, Father McKenna spoke to the children and then said to Jimmy, 'I have been telling them who you are, that you have been made their white father by the Great White Queen. Will you say something to them? It doesn't matter that they won't understand it, just let them hear your voice and I'll tell them the gist of it.'

Jimmy's loquacity failed him when he thought that he would not be understood, and in a rather flat small voice gave them a few words of greeting. Father McKenna interpreted into Wapishana and we went into the bare living-room of the mission house for tea and Madeira cake. After tea the men of the village, led by their tuchau, came for the palaver. With Father McKenna as interpreter, I now expected to hear the problems of the village and the question of rising population thrashed out in detail, but the tuchau seemed to have nothing to say, and Jimmy contented himself by saying that the Indians need not fear that any of their lands were to be taken from them, and that they must promise not to use the Company's new fences for arrowheads.

The palaver was over; I think it might have been more productive if Father McKenna had done more than interpret. I learnt from him, as he took me round the village, that he had little faith in the Government's Indian policy, and had for a long time looked on the Indians of the southern savannahs as the private concern of the Jesuit mission. It is an attitude which runs through the history of Jesuit missions and, in the eighteenth century, led to the creation of powerful Jesuit-led Indian communist states in Paraguay and Lower California — states which were crushed when Rome saw in them the possible abuse of power. Father McKenna had no such grandiose schemes, but he was determined to bring the Wapishana Indians to a reasonable state of religion, civilization and education.

He was a thin man with a long grey beard and steel-rimmed spectacles; I would have supposed him to be in his fifties, but learnt to my surprise that he was thirty-five. He had been a padre during the War and his experiences on the battlefield had made it impossible for him to live amid the noise of a town. He had chosen the Rupununi for his mission because of its isolation. When he had arrived at Sand Creek just after the War there had been forty children of school age; now, with the health improvements, there were a hundred and forty-nine. 'Twenty-five years ago,' he said, 'these people were all wearing laps and bead aprons. Now, if they've got some money, they'll go into Lethem and buy a pair of spectacles because they think it's a sign of white superiority. The older people don't know how to take civilization, so we concentrate on the young ones, train them. We teach them English and arithmetic. When the Rupununi is developed they must know how to live in a money economy and respect money.[1] We must have an organized labour force ready for when the place is developed.'

---

[1] Boswell has an instructive story about an Indian, who, when told of the advantages of money, said, 'But will it buy occupation?'

'But,' I said, slightly confused, 'you speak as if the whole of the savannahs was going to be industrialized, as if you had to get the Indians ready for it quickly. From what I'd gathered there are only vague plans for developing the place, and the biggest headache the Government has is to know what on earth to do with the increased population.'

'Yes,' said Father McKenna, reflectively, as if knowing his earlier words had been some form of support for ideas that were not as simple as they seemed. 'That is a headache. Eventually there won't be enough subsistence crops for the population, and everyone is getting too used to buying dress material — the handicrafts are dying out, I can't even get the old women to make hammocks.'

We went into the school. At one end an East Indian teacher was giving an English lesson to some sixty children of ages between five and seven. At the other end was a class of five children of eight to twelve. The teacher asked me if I would like to hear the infants sing, and they broke into a strange rendering of 'The Ash Grove'. 'Could I hear some of their own songs?' I asked. 'That's what really interests me.' I regretted my words immediately, for I realized that they implied a criticism of his teaching. 'They haven't any,' he said, and I left it at that. In the higher class I picked out an intelligent little boy and asked him what he wanted to do when he grew up. He eventually understood my question and haltingly said that he wanted to go to live in Georgetown.

The main concern of the Jesuits is to teach the Indians Christian dogma and morality, and to make both penetrate deep into the Indian nature. Civilizing is necessary for this — tribal construction must be broken, sexual and courtship customs must be changed. Father Mather had believed that the tribal forms could be maintained side by side with Christianity, but I do not think Father McKenna would have agreed with this. The Government's policy of assimilating the Indians into the community apparently fits into the Jesuit civilizing schemes on the Rupununi; but the apt question is, what are the Wapishanas to be assimilated into? They live in isolation, their economic situation is not developed; their children are being prepared for a kind of life that may never come. They will be all dressed up with nowhere to go. The little boy told me he wanted to go to Georgetown. He was typical of many boys

whom I talked to in other villages. Will they grow up into youths
and men dissatisfied with the life the savannahs can offer them, and
drift down to swell the population of Georgetown, taking the lowest
menial jobs that are reserved for the 'buck'?

The Jesuits are singleminded; the spiritual end of their work
justifies the means, and what they are doing is irreproachable by their
own tenets. But I felt strongly, by the end of my tour, that they are
detribalizing the Indians, teaching them to despise their own culture,
even their own language, and in the process teaching them to lose
the habit of work, creating a bewildered people who even in their
superficial adherence to Christianity are self-interested. They go to
church for fear of the missionaries' 'big fire' if they don't. Christianity's promises appeal to them, but their own nature is opposed
to the morality of Christianity. No action in a harsh society such
as theirs is made with thought of kindness or charity. You take a
traveller in and give him food because when you yourself are travelling you want to be taken in and given food. Nothing is done
without thought of return. The missionaries were nonplussed to
find the Indians demanding trade goods for services to the church.
The Indian conception of sin is wholly unlike the Christian conception. You lie because to do so may prevent pain to yourself and
others; it is not important that you should not lie. A girl's chastity
does not decide her marriage ability; amiability and domestic
qualities come first. No man marries a girl before he has made her
pregnant, thus making sure of her fertility. Homicide and infanticide
are permissible on occasions, and a man who has killed another is
not necessarily disapproved of. The one unforgivable sin is to
take food secretly from the family's store. To substitute a Christian
morality for this is difficult; concepts that do not exist in the Indian
language or minds must be conveyed, and the result must be con-
fusing. I was told that sins which the Wapishanas had never even
conceived had been introduced into their country by the Ten
Commandments. Father McKenna told me that Wapishana contains
only verbs and adjectives and no abstract words at all. Part of the
Lord's Prayer has to be translated as 'Do not get annoyed with us
just as we will not get annoyed with those who offend us' — '*Mana
pu Fourana waunauat pakawan aununi wa touran kidmudwaitiknau-
namat.*' Christianity has brought new desires, new concepts; it

may eventually succeed in its civilizing task, or it may wantonly destroy that state of innocence of which Socrates thought when he said, 'Those who want least approach nearest to the Gods, who want nothing.'

In the beautiful late afternoon light we made the return journey to Wichabai, arranged for John Melville to act as interpreter for the rest of the tour, and roared off across the savannahs to Dadanawa. As we approached the Company's land I could see that the grass was noticeably greener and thicker, and the large paddocks round the ranch, where horses and dairy cattle grazed, had an unnatural lushness produced by fertilizers. Unfortunately fertilizers can only be used on a small scale in the Rupununi — in most areas the rains would wash them into the creeks before they had done their work.

The ranch house at Dadanawa was, like Wichabai, well built and large, though without its classic proportions. A big fair-haired man in flannel trousers and a spotless white shirt came down the steps, clapped Jimmy on the back and asked him what lies he'd been telling the Indians. He was Mr Turner, the manager of the Company, and when I was introduced to him as a writer, his hands went to imaginary holsters and he said, 'Where's my gun.' Standing shyly behind him was his assistant manager, a tall thin bespectacled man in his late thirties, dressed in khaki. We washed in the guest house and then went across for rum and lime in the ranch house, sitting back in Berbice chairs covered with the various jaguar skins which Mr Turner had shot during his thirty or more years in the Rupununi. The isolation of his life had not affected his enormous zest and good spirits; it seemed strange to me that this most sociable of men should tell me that the only place in the whole world where he could live and be happy was the savannahs — he only wished his wife and daughter thought the same, and would come back soon from England. Brown, the assistant manager, was as fervent in his love of the country. He had come out to the ranch as a boy, and after many years of service the Company had persuaded him to spend a long leave in his native England. He had managed to endure nearly half his leave, and then the call had been too great. One day Mr Turner had seen his figure riding across the grassland towards the ranch; he had made the long overland journey up the cattle trail.

'Well, Jimmy,' said Mr Turner, 'what government nonsense have you brought with you this time? Why don't you fellows leave us alone to get on with our own business? God, we came up here for freedom and now we're being told what to do by a crowd of bureaucrats sitting on their arses in Georgetown. Now let me tell you what to do. Stop crippling us with taxation, stop ruining the Indians, and ban the infernal combustion engine from the savannahs for good and all. All these newfangled ideas are ruining the place.' He turned his humorous blue eyes on me and said, 'So you're a writer, eh? Why do you fellows come up here in the dry season? You go back and say how beautiful it all is, and you haven't seen it just one enormous marsh when the rains come, with the cattle splashing about trying to get at some shoots of grass. Now Evelyn Waugh, he should have come up here then. He wrote a damn' good book about it all the same, the only honest thing that's ever been written about the Rupununi. I met him in Georgetown before he started out. They told me he was a Mayfair novelist, and I thought he was a dude, so I tore a few strips off him when we met. But by God he went through it up the cattle trail and over to Bo' Vist'. A good fellow. He lost his way coming to Dadanawa and if he hadn't been picked up by the Wapishanas that might have been the last of him. The hills are very misleading, you can't tell where you are.'

After dinner we drank whisky and smoked Havana cigars late into the night.

South of Dadanawa the savannahs reach the height of their stark beauty; they are no longer plains, but rolling downland rimmed with hills, scattered with dark granitic rocks worn to strange shapes by rain and wind — shapes that might have been carved by some primitive hand. At one point, a huge smoothed slope of granite rose for a thousand feet or more above the horizon, its quartz-veins sparkling in the sunlight, set off by the darkness of the rock itself. Was it report of these hills that made Raleigh write: 'Every mountain, every stone . . . shines like the precious metals; if it be not gold, it is *madre del oro*.'

Our first destination was the village of Shea, whose name, meaning 'swelling', derives from a near-by granite hill. The villagers had been given notice of our arrival but there was no crowd to meet us, only a few women who told John Melville that as the village had nothing to ask the Commissioner, the men had gone to work in their fields. Mr Melville, who is looked upon as the Big Chief by all the savannah Indians, gave the women an angry reprimand for this lack of interest and told them to go and find the men.

The men arrived; they, like the women, had noticeably negroid features, a legacy from two Negro runaway slaves, named Boney and Fredericks, who came to the village over a century ago and took Indian wives. Richard Schomburgk has a description of one of their 'capoucre' daughters, and is full of admiration for what he calls her musculature. Then, as now, the Indians in general did not admire the Negro or wish to share his blood. Indians from other villages would not intermarry with capoucres from Shea, and the village began to interbreed, with the result that all now have Negro blood. In the southern savannahs Shea is looked on as a pariah village and, to judge from the behaviour of the men when they assembled for the inconclusive palaver, its level of intelligence is below that of the other villages. Cossou told me that he looks on it as the most difficult and unco-operative village in his district.

John Melville's jeep moved off across the hills towards Arwarnaunau, the Windcreek Hill, and we followed him, doing a gainly canter to his wild gallop. Arwarnaunau was a large village, bursting with healthy small boys and girls playing boisterously together, whilst almost every woman sat suckling a child. As we came into the village we saw the end of a queue of children, each being served with a mug of milk by the East Indian schoolmaster. I remarked on this to Cossou and he said that free milk was served to the children in all the villages every day. 'Free?' I queried. 'But isn't it their own milk from their own cows?' 'No,' he replied, 'they don't keep dairy herds. It's all powdered milk sent up from the Coast, a gift from UNICEF. It's ironical, I know, that they should have to drink dried milk in cattle country.'

The people of the village were without doubt livelier and more independent in their spirit than any of the other villagers we had seen. I don't know whether or not this is because they lie outside the range of civilizing contacts; I can only record that they and the other Indians of the extreme south seemed to be of a race apart from the bewildered and listless people farther north. The tuchau told us with dignity that the village water was so bad that they were ashamed to offer it to strangers who came to the village. Two years before the Government had promised to dig them a new well where the water was sweet, but no one had come. Jimmy renewed the promise, and explained to them the purpose of the fences that were going to be erected on their land. He made them promise that they would not use the barbed wire for arrowheads.

We lunched here and then moved on, through the dark overcast afternoon towards the village of Maruanawa, the Hill of the Armadillo, and then to Ishalton, the Island of Ishal — a bush-rope used as a fish poison, which contains a property once used in the manufacture of Flit. Ishalton was a large village spread out on a large open space of slightly sloping land. The sun had returned and busy figures cast long shadows as the men sat fashioning arrows, bows, making baskets with black geometrical designs, or the women found the eyes of minute beads and set them in the beautiful patterns of their aprons. Other women were patting cassava paste into circular cakes two feet in diameter. After they had cooked them on the griddle they threw them to form white, Breughelesque patterns on the roofs of their huts. For the first time, in the Rupununi, I had the sense of an active natural Indian life, though the next morning was to prove that all was not as well as it seemed.

John Melville's daughter Olga was the school teacher of Ishalton, and she had prepared a hut for our party. We washed, slung our hammocks, and the servant whom Jimmy had brought with him from Georgetown began to unpack an enormous wooden trunk. Jimmy had told me that his days of roughing it in the Interior were over, and I realized what he meant when decorated china plates, cups and saucers, a canteen of silver and a safari Thermos full of ice were produced. My own contribution was an inflatable nylon bucket and a packet of Norwegian flat bread, which Jimmy took and asked if one had to blow that up too. We ate an excellent four-course dinner, and then over coffee and rum in the dim lantern light I managed to get John Melville to talk about the Indians. He told me he had read books in which the Indians were attacked for believing only in evil spirits, for having no good spirits. 'It's true,' he said, 'but nobody seems to see why. The Indians think that the natural state is when things are good, and there's no need to have spirits at all when things are good. Evil spirits come along and make things bad, and you've got to trick them somehow to get things back to normal. That's the job of the piaiman,[1] the medicine-man, and they're always sly old frauds who trick anybody. There are three in Ishalton at the moment and they're great rivals. If there's sickness in a house one of them's called in and he burns garlic leaves and then blows. If you want to get rid of an evil spirit you have to blow him away. You can also blow on people to bring them good luck. When I was here a few weeks ago I found one of the piaimen with an old rear light from a bicycle that he'd picked up somewhere, and he was holding it over a man's chest and saying that he could see through it into the man's heart. Then he turned to me and started moaning "Tiger spirit is coming, tiger spirit is coming". Maybe that's Jimmy. But these piaimen have to go through a lot to get the village's confidence. They have to prove themselves with long fasts and go wandering alone for weeks in the forest without even a bow. When they're doing an important job like chasing away the really evil spirit, kenaima, they work themselves into a trance with tobacco juice mixed with water and they wail and move about frantically, and in the end they usually have convulsions on the ground when they're supposed to be battling with kenaima. They have their sessions in their hut at night in the dark, and they're wonderful ventriloquists. They can fill a hut with strange noises that they say are the spirits. They're terrible frauds.'

Almost the whole village gathered for the palaver next morning, and an intelligent man had been elected to put Ishalton's various troubles before authority, speaking in English. He was a born advocate, subtly conveying in his pidgin English that here was a village whose people wished to improve themselves and should be helped to do so by the Government. He said that Ishalton was far from the Company's land and didn't benefit from the money that

[1] Generally used, anglicized form of *peartʒan, piaiyen* or *piaichan.*

the Company had brought to the district. Its water was bad, and
no one had enough to eat (John Melville later said this was an
exaggeration), that they wanted to produce something which they
could sell and with the money make their village a finer place to live
in. Could they not grow tobacco and sell it to the white people?
Jimmy told them that a tobacco expert would be coming to see
them very soon to teach them how to grow good tobacco. The
young man went on to say that some men from the village had
found gold in the Marudi mountains but they didn't know whether
they were allowed to take it. Cossou explained to them that if
they showed him where their finds were and they were not on land
belonging to the white men he would give them paper which would
mean that no one else could dig for gold where they had found it. It
was a successful palaver; one felt that although these people had
learnt a measure of discontent, it was a discontent that might prove
fruitful. They had the wish to work; there was no sign of an attitude
of crushed resignation.

I will not describe the remaining three days of our tour, since
each day followed a similar pattern, and the landscape, in spite of
its incidental variations, did not change. We would see Indian
families travelling on the backs of great white oxen, on their way
to a hunting ground, a stretch of good fishing, or a garden place.
We saw, above all, signs of a larger and healthy younger generation
— children who in ten or twelve years would decide the fate of
Indian life in the savannahs. I sympathized with Jimmy Bamford.
The object of his tour had been to lay plans for the beneficial
occupation of this generation; but, as he discussed with John
Melville the possibilities of brazil nuts, cashew nuts, tonka beans
for scent manufacture, tobacco growing or cotton cultivation, I
could see that he wished deer still roamed in herds across the
savannahs, to be pursued by feathered men in laps who did not make
awkward requests for new water-holes. But the old happy hunting
grounds were no more. The Indian had offered his independence
to the state. One could only hope that wild Nature's vigour was
still active at the root.

The
Little World of Tiny McTurk

K ARANAMBO RANCH lies some miles north of the Kanukus, on an acre or two of grassland skirting a tributary of the Rupununi. It is a unique site for a ranch in the Rupununi since it is surrounded by the forest that runs for a mile on either side of the watercourse. The near-by savannah is unseen and you must walk a mile for a sight of the Kanukus. Here I felt I was back in the world of the tropical forest, though the presence of an ancient motor car standing under a fine grapefruit tree in the compound suggested easier communication than the forest allows. The ranch house itself looked more like some Indian ceremonial building than the home of an Irishman and his English wife. Its high gabled front formed a wooden isosceles triangle and the sloping roofs were made of fine kokerite palm thatching. One side and the back of the house had wooden, windowed walls, but the part where the day's life was passed was a large loggia depending from the front gable, roofed with corrugated iron and supported by a series of rough posts. In this loggia coloured Brazilian hammocks hung from the posts, there was a large English oak dining table with fruit boxes beneath it, a shelf of Indian basketwork and headdresses made from the feathers of the cock-of-the-rock; there was a large case of battered books, a shelf of fish-hooks of all sizes, and a fish harpoon that looked more suitable for game-fish hunting in the north Caribbean; a blowpipe stood next to a nine-foot bow; in one corner were the score of heavy accumulators that provided the house with electric light, in another a tame, long-beaked yellow and black bird studied a parakeet from a pile of magazines.

This was the world of Mr and Mrs McTurk. They greeted me on my unexpected arrival with the unquestioning friendliness and hospitality of the Rupununi. They had no idea who I was or why

I should be there until, over glasses of iced grapefruit juice, I told them something about myself. In spite of his name, Tiny McTurk was a lean man of average height. He was in his late fifties, with humorous blue eyes, a four-day stubble, wearing a pair of hard-worn khaki trousers caked with mud. His wife in blue overall jeans was small and delicate-looking, her hair drawn back in a way that emphasized the sensitivity of her face. Tiny's flow of talk was exactly as I had expected it to be; all over the savannahs I had heard people speak of Tiny McTurk, and their talk had formed an image in my mind of a man unique even in this unique world of the Rupununi. For once my image was borne out by reality.

Tiny was born in British Guiana; his father, Michael McTurk, had run away to sea from Liverpool, and found in British Guiana the freedom and excitement he was looking for. He made the usual bushman's progress from government surveyor to magistrate to Commissioner for the Essequibo, ending with a C.M.G. and a comfortable house on a hill near Bartica which he named Kalacoon, the Arawak word for Turkey which had been his nickname at school. Here he fished and hunted, studied the things of nature and the customs of the Indians, wrote tales in Negro dialect, and brought up his children to a strict but kindly discipline. He only made one journey to England, for a conference of colonial officials, and found himself staying at the Savoy. The first morning after his arrival the chambermaid found him sleeping in a hammock; he no longer found it possible to sleep in a bed.

From earliest childhood Tiny had learnt to hunt with gun, bow or blowpipe, to prefer fishing with bow and arrow in the Indian style to fishing with rod and line; he had learnt the calls of birds and the mating sounds of animals, had grown up to speak the Indian languages as if they were his own. He had interrupted his life in the bush to become a pilot in the 1914 War and had spent some time in hospital after daredevil exploits in his fighter aeroplane. I think he remembered those days with a passion almost equalling his love of fishing and hunting. After the War he had wandered the colony by river and by foot, for the joy of seeing the far corners of the hills and forests; a certain puritanism in his character made him quite uninterested in prospecting for gold or diamonds. Then, thirty years ago, he had taken a lease of the land round Karanambo, and built the ranch house that now stands there. Although he had to make a living by some means Tiny had chosen this unlikely spot for one reason only; the giant arapaima fish, which could only be found in the creeks, the kirahaghs, of this section of the Rupununi.[1] He would keep a few cattle, and he might trade with the Makushis for balata, but the pursuit of this largest freshwater fish in the world was to become the main occupation of his life. For thirty years he has hunted it and brought in monsters weighing five hundred pounds; he has perfected methods of hunting and landing it which are described with awe in the classical literature of big-game fishing where they appear under the title of 'McTurk's Method'. Occasionally a party of rich American sportsmen who have caught his arapaima fever arrive at Karanambo, and he gives them the pleasure of speeding in a corial along the kirahaghs with an arapaima on the traces.

The balata trading brought him good money and he added to this by supplying zoos and aquariums with animals, snakes, birds and fishes. Then he went down to Georgetown to find himself a wife who could bear to share this life with him. He found a colony-born English girl who has proved the perfect wife. Mrs McTurk described her honeymoon to me. It took the form of a long boat journey to her future home, which she had never seen. Indians and Creoles had paddled the boat and portaged it over the rapids. Two had died from malaria on the way, and at last they had reached the Karanambo landing late one night. They entered the house, and as Tiny lit the lantern she had screamed; in the middle of the floor lay a coiled eighteen-foot anaconda. With delight Tiny had popped it in a sack, exclaiming that it was just what the Berlin Tiergarten wanted. Then he went into an inner room, returning to warn her not to enter it. 'There's a very dangerous bushmaster in there', he said. 'He might take a bit of getting.'

Unknowingly, I had similar experiences at Karanambo. During the night I spent there I heard continuous movements in the loft beneath the thatching, which I took to be those merely of rats and mice. I learned later that Tiny has the habit of throwing into the loft the small snakes which are brought him by the Indians. He

.[1] The only other rivers in the world where arapaimas are found are the Rio Branco, the Rio Negro and the Amazon.

says they are warm and cosy there, have all the food they need in the form of rats and mice, and never come down into the parts where people live. I am glad he didn't give me these assurances until the end of my visit.

Mr and Mrs McTurk had three children; one daughter is married to a plantation official on the Coast; another works in London; and a young son is at a public school in England.

Although I had not been expected to lunch that day, Mrs McTurk produced a meal I shall never forget. The fruit boxes were withdrawn from under the table and Tiny said: 'Sorry these boxes are a bit rickety. They've got to last. They stand just the right height. Last year the fruit company changed the size of its boxes and the new ones are no good at all for dining chairs.' A marvellous minestrone was served, followed by brown melting steaks of lukanani fish, cooked in butter; then a superb duckling with orange sauce, buttered young carrots and peas, potatoes roasted in butter; exhausted, I did my best with a plate of fruit salad of exotic fruits, dressed with quariad.

After allowing me twenty minutes in a hammock Tiny suggested we should go down to the kirahagh to shoot lukanani. He handed me a bow and arrow, and within a few minutes we came to the sluggish waters of the creek where markings on a sand bank on the opposite shore showed how low the river was. We stood on a sheer cliff of black granite rocks that rose some twenty feet above the river, and at a point where the rocks curved I could see their weird conformation; they were like a series of huge shiny black torsos, and when I exclaimed at the sight Tiny said, 'Yes, they're supposed to be the bodies of a crowd of Karanam Indians who wanted to come to a paiwari feast this side of the river, and came even though the piaiman told them not to. He let them get as far as this bank and when they got out of their woodskins he froze them on the spot — and a very nice lookout position they make for seeing lukanani. The Makushis won't come on them — they still get a bit scared when they pass them on the water. Only a few years ago they covered their eyes as they went past, and if by any chance they'd seen the rocks they'd wet a paddle, hold it above their faces, and as the drops of water fell into their eyes they'd squeeze pepper-juice into it. Must have been quite some pain. The idea was that the pain would chase out the bad spirits that had got in from their seeing the rocks.'

He was not concentrating on his last words; his practised eyes were searching the waters for the subtle signs of lukanani, and suddenly having made the split-second judgment of the refraction of light on the water, he had drawn the bow and released an arrow; the arrow threshed on the surface of the creek, and agile as an animal Tiny had bounded down the rocks and was splashing through the shallows up to his middle; he drew the fighting fish out of the water, some ten pounds in weight, came back to the rocks and with a blow of the flat of his cutlass had stilled the struggles. When he rejoined me he described how the female lukanani carries its eggs in its mouth, and how, when the time comes for it to feed, it hands over its burden to the keeping of the male for a short time.

We continued our walk and then returned to the landings. Tiny suggested that we should go out in a corial in order to give me a chance to use my bow and arrow. As we paddled into deep waters Tiny passed his hand vaguely towards the farther shore and said in his inimitable, slightly hushed voice, 'I was over there in the savannahs a month or two back when a couple of Makushis came up to me and told me they've found diamonds on my land there. Well, I'm not interested in diamonds, but I can tell diamonds from crystal in the rough and I said to them "Let me see the diamonds". I looked at them and by God! they'd got a couple of carat stones. Now, I thought quick. If they had a diamond shout up here I'd have a crowd of pork-knockers raping the girls before you could say knife. The sort of amenities of the place would go down. So I said to the Makushis, "No, these aren't diamonds, these are crystals," and to show them I wasn't humbugging them I threw them away as far as I could.' He slapped his cutlass at the memory of his cleverness.

Now followed two remarkable acts on my part which delighted Tiny as much as they mystified us both. He threw a piece of wood some ten yards ahead of us and invited me to shoot it with an arrow. I stood up, drew my bow and the arrow flew with ridiculous precision straight into the wood. Amazed, I pulled the bow again; this time the arrow entered the water about five yards from the wood, but instead of lying flat on the water it began to move like

the arrow which had pierced the lukanani. 'By God,' said Tiny, 'you've got something!' It proved not to be a lukanani, but a deeper-bodied fish some two feet long, which Tiny held out to me, pointing to the rows of small, beautiful saw-edged teeth which were revealed as the fish struggled with its respiration. Tiny took a piece of cord, and as the mouth opened, lower jaw out-thrust, he put the cord in; the teeth closed on it, and with horrible eyes staring the creature hacked at the cord with a frantic ferocity, driving its teeth through the fibres with a power that suggested an amazing muscular activity of the jaws. It was an ugly sight, as if I were watching an action of unmotivated evil and destruction.[1]

'Damn it!' said Tiny. 'Do you know you've just shot the wickedest fish in the world. That's a pirai.'

I knew about pirai, or piranha, the cannibal fish that has frozen the blood of many readers of Amazonian travel; the fish that is reputed to be able to reduce a cow to a skeleton in five minutes, and a man in three. The actual performance of the pirai may have been exaggerated, but it is impossible to exaggerate its vicious potentialities. It is to be found in all the rivers of British Guiana which link with the Amazonian system, and hardly an Indian who lives on these rivers has not had a toe bitten off by a pirai or a piece of his heel torn away. Tiny, to demonstrate the particular fortitude and resignation of the Makushis, described to me how a party of Indians had walked barefoot through the shallows to get into his corial. They had made no sign that anything unusual had happened, but he suddenly noticed that all were bleeding from foot wounds. Each had been attacked by pirai, but had not thought it worth while to warn the next man.

Pirai are found in piratical shoals in slow-moving currents far from the white water of the rapids. They move near the surface of the water, pursuing the smaller fish that are their usual food. Blood is their great delight, a drug that makes them mad with carnivorous fury. I once saw a piece of bloody iguana meat thrown to a shoal, and it had disintegrated in a moment in the fury of their attack. Pirai will on occasions attack a swimming man, even if he has no open wound, but if he has the smallest wound they are certain to attack, and if given time and opportunity would strip

---

[1] Tiny assures me that the teeth can bite through a heavy fish-hook in one stroke.

facing, above: THE SOUTHERN SAVANNAHS OF THE RUPUNUNI
     below: TINY McTURK IN THE LIVING-ROOM OF HIS RANCH-HOUSE

his body to the bone. Negroes are likely to fare best with pirai since black skin does not attract them even when it is bloody — but the Negro has his Achilles heel in the shape of the white soles of his feet. Wounded animals are frequently attacked, and Colonel Roosevelt tells how he saw an alligator half devoured by the fish. The feet of ducks in pirai waters are an attraction, and it is rare to see a duck with whole webs to his feet. Kingfishers diving for fish may find themselves caught in the vicelike mouth of pirai. It has well earned its other name of cannibal fish. Even the blood of its own species produces a fury of craving, and a wounded pirai will defend itself from the teeth of other pirai until, weakened, it allows itself to be devoured.

The flesh is soft and bony, but the Indians eat it. Knowing that fish-hooks are useless they have other ways of landing it. The bloody entrails of some animal are fixed to a stick and allowed to trail in the water from a woodksin. When the pirai come to eat the entrails they are shot with an arrow. The jaw and teeth of the fish form one of the most useful instruments the Indian has — it was on this machine that old Melville would have his gramophone needles sharpened. The Indian sharpens his poison darts on pirai teeth, and with it he partially severs the poison tip from the shaft of the dart, so that if the dart breaks from the victim the point will remain in the flesh and the curare can perform its task. I never heard of one authenticated case of a large animal being reduced to a skeleton in a few minutes, or even an hour, but this story turns up so constantly in travel books that there is perhaps some basis for it.

On the way back to the ranch Tiny pointed to a pile of bricks lying on the grass. 'Those,' he said with a laugh, 'have been there for twenty years. I brought them up to build a new house. But every time I think I'll start building I look at the old house and think — well, maybe it is a bit broken down, but I really wouldn't be happy with it looking any other way.' For Tiny the sin against the Holy Ghost was any waste of the precious hours of daylight, and as soon as tea was over he said, 'Well, if I'm going to take you after arapaima tomorrow we've got to get the bait — an aruana. There's a pond in the bush where we ought to get one this time of day. They're big fellows, you have to shoot them with a gun.' He handed me a gun and some cartridges. Then he went to a round red toffee tin, from which I was expecting him to produce some other article for the hunt. In fact it was full of Sharp's Kreemy Toffees, and after thrusting a handful into his pocket he bade me do the same. He neither smoked nor drank alcohol, but his tooth was sweet and he indulged it. He picked up his cutlass, a much larger weapon than the one he had brought to the creek. Quietly, but perfectly aware of the effect of his words, he said, 'This is what I call my alligator pacifier.'

We entered the cool, dark forest, following the merest trail which had been trodden by Tiny during his years of visiting the pond. It was not high forest, and the ground vegetation was heavier than I had seen before. There were long patches of sword grass — appropriately called *Scleria flagellum* — to be walked through, and my legs and arms became patterned with thin lines of beading blood. At one point we came across a mound of fresh excrement, and Tiny said a tapir was probably in the vicinity. 'He made a meal over there,' he added, pointing to a tree where the bark had been eaten off in patches. I hoped we would get a sight of this strange animal that forms a zoological link between the pig and the elephant, and seems indeed to be some lonely survivor from the Jurassic age. At another point Tiny stopped, sniffed, and pointing to a tree crown said: 'There's a howler monkey in that tree.' To my insensitive nostrils the air had not changed at all.

At last we came to the shores of the pond, Tiny's Walden. I had been thinking of Thoreau as Tiny talked to me about the animals and the plants — of that time when Thoreau, in Walden Woods, had said to his companion, 'You sometimes find Indian axe-heads in the woods', and, looking down into the grass, had picked one up. Tiny had those same qualities of intuition, of an almost mystical oneness with the scene he had chosen. But he had no Concord to walk into when he felt like it, or kind Emersons to dine with three times a week.

The pond was half a mile long, a sluggish ellipse, its dark surface unlit by the sun that was now below the treeline. Trees on the bank bowed towards the water, and here and there fallen trunks emerged from its surface like animals far more weird than the tapir. I had seen, and was to see, no water in Guiana that suggested primaeval nature more; its silence did not seem to be broken by the few distant birds that sang; had a pterodactyl emerged from its depths I would hardly have been surprised. Quietly we walked out along a fallen trunk, and as we did so two four-foot alligators moved slowly towards the shallows of the mud bank. Tiny's hand did not even move towards his pacifier — he knew the quiet habits of these sated caymans. He studied the water for eddies caused by aruana surfacing for air, but there were none. We returned to the bank and he climbed a tree for a better view before moving on to the next tacouba. It was here, while Tiny was waiting for the eddies, that I heard crisp sounds of some largish animal moving through the bush in our direction. I waited quietly, knowing that to move or speak might scare it away. At last I could make out, dark against the surroundings, the ungainly form of a tapir, the size of a small donkey. Some suddenly released primitive instinct of the hunter made me raise my gun; fortunately the movement was seen, and the tapir leapt off through the bush, disappearing, until with a great splash he dived into the pond some hundred yards away, where he submerged, leaving a surface trail to mark his immensely swift passage. In a moment he was on the farther bank and was lost in the forest, leaving me ashamed that I had ever thought of shooting him.

Tiny returned to his study of the water, and a minute or two later he fired into it; he thought he had hit the aruana and plunged towards it to take the wounded fish in his hands. But the shot had missed. We began to make a slow progress round the pond, walking to the end of each tree-mole. While I was balanced precariously on one slender trunk a sound came that almost shook me into the water. It was as if some giant had brought a huge oar with all his force flat on to the surface of the water. The crack reverberated like sharp summer thunder. 'That,' said Tiny, looking across the pond, 'was arapaima, coming up for air. Look over there, he'll come up again.' A minute later the great fish, some eight feet long, leapt out of the water and cracked down on the surface once more. 'Quite a big one,' said Tiny. 'But we don't get that if we don't get aruana.'

Alas, we found no aruana that afternoon, and as there was no opportunity to find the bait before I had to leave Karanambo I had to be content with Tiny's descriptions of arapaima and its capture. Arapaima is not actually the largest freshwater fish in the world —

the extremely rare laulau and pacumo live in Amazonian waters —
but it is the largest fish that one is likely to see. In Brazil it is caught
regularly and, dried, makes an equivalent to the Portuguese *bacalhao*.
'Those Brazilians are fishing it too much,' said Tiny. 'There aren't
as many today in the Rupununi as there used to be because they
get taken in the Rio Branco or the Rio Negro.' He did not say it,
but I knew that if the day should ever come when the Rupununi
was without arapaima, half the reason for his life would be gone.
'Arapaima's a sporting fish,' he went on. 'He gives you the best
sport you'll ever find. I tell you, I've seen jaguar waiting till one
comes inshore and boxing it with his paws, and the arapaima puts up
a fight before he gocs into deeper water. Sometimes the jaguar
gets him, though. I fish him from a corial. First we sight him and
follow, and I shoot an arrow in his flank to mark him more easily.
Then we chase with all the power the outboard's got; the fellow can
move like blazes. When I get close enough I shoot a small harpoon
into him, attached to a long line — shoot it from a bow. Then the
fun begins. No outboard — the fellow gives us a long tow and I
have to play him carefully and exhaust him. Then we creep up
and I bash him dead with a club before boating him. I had one
fellow with the strength of twenty men. He tugged and pulled —
I tell you, he had two corials tipped over before we got him. That's
how I like 'em. Ah, arapaima! Give me arapaima before anything
in the world.'

It was dusk as we walked back to the ranch, talking and eating
toffees. The electric light was on in the house, and we lay in the
hammocks, drinking grapefruit juice while dinner was cooked. One
of Tiny's Indians, who had returned after some weeks gathering
brazil nuts, came up to greet him. They talked for a while in
Makushi and when he had gone Tiny smiled and said, 'Funny
language, Makushi. You can't say "How are you?" in it. It's got
to be something more definite. That Indian said to me just then,
"Is you wife dead yet?" And when I said no he knew that all was
all right. It's a really bad thing for a Makushi to lose his wife,
specially since the missionaries have been down on them having
more than one. There used to be a Jesuit at Sand Creek, a fine
chap, but one day he made a Makushi give up his second wife. The
Makushi didn't like it so he went into the bush and got a nice little

collection of poisons. Nothing deadly, you know — he didn't want to do any real harm. So he made them up into a nice little potion and popped them into this Jesuit's coffee. Ten minutes later the poor man's mouth and throat were burning away and water would do nothing. It drove him mad for two days. He went out into the savannah and rushed around like a madman for two whole days before it passed off. But the Jesuits won in the end. They only have one wife now. All the same, Christianity's paper thin up here — all the old ways are surviving, really. You wouldn't know, the Jesuits wouldn't know. You've got to be brought up with Indians to really know them. They won't tell you anything. They won't even tell you their Indian names. They say they haven't got Indian names. They won't sing you their songs or tell you their legends — pretty filthy most of them — they'll just say there aren't any. Funny people. I had a piaiman once come to work for me, and like all piaimen he was very fond of his hammock, wouldn't do a hand's turn unless I forced him. Well, we didn't see eye to eye over something and he came up and blew on me — that means sort of cursing you. "Right," I said, "you've blown on me in Makushi. I can blow on you in Akawaio' — they all know that Akawaio-blowing is the strongest of the lot. So I did, and I said that in two or three weeks his mouth was going to close up and he wouldn't speak and then he'd die. Well, three weeks later a crowd of Makushis came to kneel in front of me and said it had happened just as I said. I was the greatest piaiman they'd ever known.'

He paused and I said, earnestly, 'What do you think it was. Auto-suggestion?'

'No,' he answered, smiling, 'you don't live in the bush all your life without knowing tetanus symptoms when you see them. I knew that fellow would get lockjaw before the month was up. In those days, I'm afraid there was nothing we could do about it.'

We dined as well as we had lunched, and over coffee Tiny talked about the old days when all power in the Rupununi was in the hands of the ranchers, a time when Tiny himself had played his part in the maintenance of order; he remembered Ocean Shark and had had a similar experience in running a Brazilian named Pedro Rodriguez off the savannahs. His father had brought him up to have no fear in the defence of order against the bad men, even if the defence was not entirely within the law. Michael McTurk had once burnt down the house of an undesirable Italian who had taken no notice of his warning to go — with the result that the Government was successfully sued for £700 for the worthless contents of the house. Tiny's action against Rodriguez, and his leadership of a small band which had chased some Brazilians off British territory, had earned Tiny a reputation in the Rio Branco area. He had been shot at twice when he paid a visit to Boa Vista. In those days, and up until the mid-1930s, Boa Vista was a bad town, dominated by bandits and hostile to strangers on principle. At the time of Tiny's visit the bandit leaders were contending for the domination — Adolf Brazil, the father of the guitarist I had insulted in the hotel at Lethem, and Alonso Cruz. Eventually Brazil had won, after a gunfight in the main street of the town. Brazil had seen Cruz in the distance, drawn his automatic and fired; Cruz had replied with his revolver. After two shots Brazil's automatic jammed and Cruz fired two shots into his stomach, the last shots in his chamber. But Brazil managed to get up, staggered towards Cruz and knocked him out with the butt of his automatic. He was never seen again.

The moon was up and the chorus of the tree-frogs loud. Occasionally we would hear the crack of a leaping arapaima, and each time we did so a light would come into Tiny's eyes. The black and yellow troupiole hopped on to my shoulder and pecked at my ear. Mrs McTurk, tired after her heavy day of cooking and housework, swung gently in a hammock. The sudden high trill of a tinamou would come from the bush and, unaccountably, not repeat its call; a woodhewer would raise its voice in a crescendo and then fall silent. Far away the no longer chilling roar of the red howler monkeys caught the currents of the wind. Night had fallen, and day for the McTurks was over until the first light of dawn brought them once more from their bed. Tiny, at last, was tired, and we went to our rooms. I felt I had spent the day with the happiest man I had ever known.

Interlude in Georgetown (2)

Bishop of Guiana's sermon. He says that the colony is on the edge of a volcano, but by this I don't think he means literally that there are signs of an uprising. His volcano has deeper implications. He feels evils are not so much political and economic as moral and social. Moral standards have gone down — sensibly he doesn't harp on sexual immorality, but concentrates on the corruption of local officials, nepotism, profiteering by local traders. Crimes of violence, and theft, have gone up. Talks of abuses of wealth and privilege among *local* people. 'The small man is always the loser, and with his sense of helpless frustration he has become embittered, revengeful and even desperate.' He says that small men are punished for crimes, bigger men evade punishment by influence. 'The trouble is that the whole country today lies prostrate in the merciless grip of that evil tyrant, whose name is FEAR.' An atmosphere of suspicion everywhere. 'You may call Georgetown the Garden City, but I can only think of it as the City of the Hungry Children ... Can you blame the small man if he follows some extremist politician who feeds him with wild promises of a new order of society?'

Negro Dialect. Negro is emotional in thought, has a common phrase 'me mind gi'e me ...' as in 'Me mind gi'e me dis land ent gwine gi'e no good returns'. The dialect 'talkie talkie' is dying slowly but still survives. The slaves were deliberately chosen from different African areas so that they couldn't get together to talk their own language — had to learn some kind of English. New slaves learnt it from the old ones. They knew the Bible well and their speech has been influenced by Biblical rhythms. Today I heard two small boys in Main Street discussing where they should go that Saturday afternoon. One said, 'Me think that very lonely and desolate place.' 'Kinna' is taboo food. Everybody has his own kinna that will give him a disease, and if a girl has a child she will make every effort to find out the father's kinna so that she'll know how to combine it with her own for the child's safety. Presumably kinnas are inheritable.

'Heavy' means 'important', 'sweet mouth' is 'flattery', 'strong eye' is to play a bold game, 'upstrated' is 'bumptious'; a common intensitive is to say 'bad too bad' or 'sweet too sweet'. Typical proverb: 'What in yo' belly yo' own, but not what in yo' jaw.' 'Presently' always used in Shakespearean sense. A taxi-driver said to me, 'Is it true, sah, that since the Duke of Windsor ran away with Mrs Simpson the younger generation in England have shown a noticeable increase of freeness in their behaviour?'

Talk with Bookers.[1] Bookers's policy is based primarily on the wish to induce sugar workers who feel rootless and not indigenous to take over serious responsibilities in sugar. Bookers find all the time that they are suspected and resented, in spite of the good they are doing. Yet when Guianese are asked outright what their criticisms are they hedge. They have come to rely on Bookers to do so much for them that they expect still more. Bookers specially resent accusation that they exploit the colony, point to the amount of money that has been ploughed back since the War.

Population. In 1952 population was 450,000; in 1955 45 per cent East Indian, 36 per cent African, 11 per cent mixed, 4 per cent Amerindian, rest Europeans and Chinese. East Indian population has had greatest rise. The 1927 Committee found each race had different interests, etc. All human problems spring from this root. European has disadvantages, being legatee of the old plantocracy. East Indians form a community within a community. Africans assimilate European life, get educational and public appointments. East Indians less assimilable to Western conceptions, no doubt because of their own culture. Their aloofness less than it used to be — they now want to play part in control of the colony.

---

[1] Bookers own seventy-five per cent of the sugar estates.

PART THREE

The Road to Roraima

Great things are done when men and mountains meet.

BLAKE

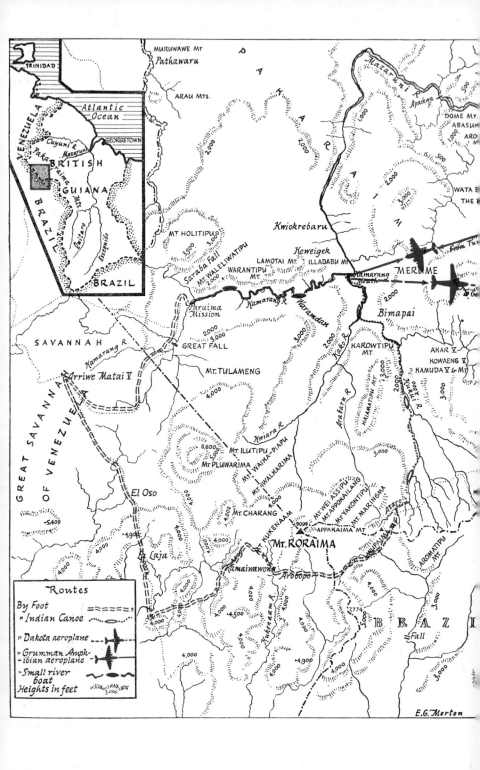

Up the Wide Mazaruni

I N the first section of this book I referred to Mount Roraima, the great mountain on whose plateau summit the boundaries of Venezuela, Brazil and British Guiana converge. In my ignorance I had never heard of the mountain until I began to make my preparations to travel in British Guiana; but as soon as I had read the first account of it deep memories began to stir in me. It was a summer Sunday afternoon, and I was ten or eleven: instead of taking the chance to pursue meadow browns and cabbage whites across the school fields, I read the adventures of Professor Challenger and his expedition that penetrated the Amazonian forest to find the Lost World — the table mountain with the precipitous mural cliffs on which, preserved from evolutionary change, lived monstrous prehistoric animals. There was no mistaking; Roraima was that lost world of Conan Doyle's imagination realized in fact, and from my vivid memories of the book it seemed to me that this was no mere coincidence, that Conan Doyle must have read accounts of this amazing mountain. My suspicion proved to be true. At the beginning of the century Roraima caught the interest of the scientific world. There had been a dispute for some years in the learned journals; supposing, thousands of years ago, the earth had thrown up by volcanic eruption a large area of earth, so that it was isolated from its surroundings by impassable precipices? What would happen to its flora and fauna? One school denied the possibility of suspended development, or an evolutionary development quite different from that of the rest of the world. The other believed that life in this static environment would be unique. A search was made for places with the required conditions, and expeditions set out for Roraima to study the ecology of its slopes and summit. Conan Doyle's novel was a dramatization of this pursuit of lost worlds.

From the moment I first read of Roraima I knew that I would

never allow myself to leave the colony without climbing it. Some great objective is essential to a journey. In the past these great objectives had been, for me, the isolated works of man, the ruins of Maya cities in the forests of southern Mexico, or the sacrificial temples of the Zapotecs on the mountain above Oaxaca. But Man had left no memorable sign of his passing in the marches of El Dorado, nothing except the primitive 'Timehri' scratches on rocks and the walls of caves. Nature only had left a great monument when, at some moment of cataclysmic change, great areas of red sandstone had been thrust fifteen hundred feet out of the forest and savannah, to form the series of plateau mountains which is dominated by Roraima. Wherever I went in the colony Roraima was never far from my thoughts; I would repeat its beautiful name to myself as if it were the name of some woman with whom I was in love.

When I returned to England I wrote to my friend, Mr Gerald Brenan, to tell him that I had climbed Roraima, sensing that in his wide knowledge of the physical world the mountain would have its place. I was delighted to find that his life had been haunted by thoughts of the mountain, and I quote from his letter to show the enduring influence which Roraima can have on a mind that has once fallen under her spell:

> I can't tell you how jealous I feel, when you tell me you have climbed Roraima. I fell in love with that mountain at my prep school, read everything I could on it, felt the world had nothing left to offer when I learned that someone had climbed it, was revived by seeing some photographs of it and very nearly called my daughter after it. And I have not been the only one. I am sure that the image of that curtain of rock rising out of the steaming rain forest has been the Laura or Dulcinea of thousands of lonely Scotchmen drinking themselves to death in the worst corners of the world. And now you have climbed it (Venezuelans don't count), and found black butterflies on top. . . .

At last, my work on the Coast as complete as such work could ever be, I was ready to make the long and difficult journey to

Roraima. Apart from taking the Grumman to Bartica, thus avoiding a dreary day on the estuary of the Essequibo, I would try to take no short cuts, would travel overland by whatever means I could find, and know the joy of slow travel through inhospitable terrain, the improvisation that such travel demands and the sense of physical contact with the country which even the intimate vistas of low level air travel can never give.

I spent hours in the Georgetown stores buying the necessary food and equipment, paring down to the various minimums. There would be four hundred miles or more in which all would have to be carried on the backs of droghers. Tinned steak had to be rejected for the more concentrated corned beef, and I had to decide on the relative importance of another tin of Dundee cake or two pounds more of beads, fish-hooks and trading salt. At last all my food was packed in its cartons; what I was not taking with me had been sent by air to Tumereng and Kamerang, caches placed at the farthest points of the airways system, but still three hundred miles from Mount Roraima. Eventually I ran the Venezuelan consul to earth and was given a visa, in case by some strange chance I should run into a police patrol as I crossed the almost uninhabited vastness of the Gran Sabaña.

Then, one Saturday morning, I packed my gear into the Grumman, and twenty minutes later saw below, lying in the great fork made by the convergence of the Essequibo and the Mazaruni, the grid-iron streets of Bartica, surrounded by low bush hills of citrus fruit trees, vegetable gardens, and here and there green cattle meadows cut from the bush. We touched down on the water and a small boat came out to meet us. The District Commissioner took me in his jeep to the hotel, and half an hour later I was making my first reconnaissance of the place.

There is a strange ghostliness about Bartica; its streets and house-plots form the skeleton of a proper town, but for every plot that boasts its tumbledown shack there are half a dozen that have not been built on. The great entrepôt city of the Interior, imagined during the hopeful years of the gold shouts, has been relegated to village status after its brief decades as a township. Only the brothels and the rum-shops with their swing doors remind one of its glory as a diggers' town, and as I walked along its phantom avenues I heard some gloriously drunken pork-knocker, down from the upper Mazaruni, singing a calypso in the 100 Carat Bar:

> Last year in Venezuela
> I gave the mechanic man his instructions . . .

Outside the Freitas Bakery was a roughly scrawled sign which read, 'Eat good bread and live longer'; outside the next-door shack, belonging to the carpenter-undertaker, was a complementary sign: 'Why live? — We bury you so cheap.' Girls in bright silk Saturday clothes, wearing the hats that are the indispensable sign of respectability among African women, walked in gaily talking groups, and old, grizzle-haired men with tales to tell of gold and diamonds sat on the house steps in the shadows. Grass verges ran beside the streets of the red earth which has given the village its Indian name. I walked over to the wooden church, where the wind blew cool from across the broads of the two rivers. Near the church was a simple monument to the memory of the Rev. Thomas Pierce who, in 1876, had been drowned with his family while going over the Mazaruni rapids. The words startled me for a moment, since I hoped to be riding the rapids myself within a few days.

There are more ancient ghosts in this Bartica triangle than the skeletal village itself. There is the ghost of the Dutch sugar plantation, Vryheid, which, in the seventeenth century, occupied the site of the village, and if you fly over the triangle you can make out the traces of plantations Duinenberg, Fortuin and Poelwyck; for it was there, beyond the coastal swamps and on land defensible against corsairs, that the first Dutch settlers cut down the forest trees and set up their primitive mills for crushing the cane. They built a fort on an island in the Mazaruni and called it Kijk-over-Al — See over all — but all was not seen, and in 1708 a French pirate took the settlements, refusing to leave until the settlers had bankrupted themselves to pay him off. And then the good red earth, abused, began to fail, and down the years the Dutch moved to the coastlands until finally the seat of government was transferred from the Two Rivers to the future Georgetown. The forest closed in on Duinenberg, Fortuin, Poelwyck and Vryheid, and at Bartica Point there was nothing but a scattering of Indian benabs. Then, under the British, the Church Missionary Society set up its station there in 1829, and called the village Bartica Grove. Within fifty years, as the objects of their salvation migrated inland, the missionaries pursued their prey on foot and by river, leaving Bartica to the Negroes and the descendants of Negroes and Indians. Then came the shouts, the hopes, the promotion to town status, followed once more by the gentle decline. Today Bartica grows the best fruit in the colony; I ate grapefruit from the tree so sweet that it needed no sugar, and its pineapples supported once more my theory that tinned pineapple preserves the true taste of the fruit, that the tart and stringy flesh which one eats in Europe bears no relation to this princess of fruits when eaten ripe from the tree.

I had been told by Vincent Roth, in Georgetown, that the most interesting men to be met in Bartica were the boat captains who had commanded the tent-boats plying up the Mazaruni and the Essequibo. They were a fine race of men, he said, usually of mixed Negro and Indian parentage, fearless and possessed by a dedicated love for the rivers. The old ones would be able to talk of the days before the outboard engine, when the journey against strong waters had been done 'raw-rank', by paddle. I had been studying the maps of the Bartica triangle. The Essequibo is navigable to large boats for some miles above Bartica; ocean steamers can go as far as Wineperu to pick up the great hewn greenheart trunks — the finest stands of this imperishable tree are found in the triangle. The Mazaruni has a different geography. The Cuyuni flows into the Mazaruni three miles above Bartica, and after this confluence the Mazaruni is blocked for a hundred and twenty miles with thousands of islands, rapids and waterfalls. In the old days a passage had to be found through this ceaselessly dangerous water if the still waters of the upper stretches were to be reached. It was here that the boat captains learnt their skill and their fearlessness, here that the Rev. Thomas Pierce and his family lost their lives, and here that no month went by without loss of life.[1] Finally, two decades ago, the Government decided that this death-trap must be bypassed. A corduroy road, surfaced with lateral logs, was cut through the triangle to Issano, a village above the islands. Today trucks go

---

[1] From Vincent Roth's journals I learn that in June and July of 1923 twelve lives were lost at Paiarimap alone, the most dangerous of the series of falls.

regularly from Bartica to Issano, where the traffic continues by boat on up the Mazaruni. The one hundred and twenty miles have returned to the dominance of Nature, never visited, but ripe in the memories of the captains.

That evening I entertained three of these boat captains to a bottle of rum in my hotel. There was Captain Pequeno, a fresh-faced, blond-moustached man of pure Portuguese stock, the only European to command a boat on the Mazaruni; he had made good money and now owned a stores in Bartica; Captain Holder, a powerful coloured man who had known a year or two of the raw-rank days and now managed the truck service between Bartica and Issano; and the more taciturn Captain Ned, who assisted him in the garage. Holder had the typical Guianese gift of dramatic, image-laden speech, though he did not speak with the grammatical licence of pure Creolese. He dominated the conversation — a little to the annoyance, I think, of Captain Pequeno, whose experience of the river was greater. Together they told me of the hazards of the lower river. 'Oh,' said Holder, 'we needed every hand we could find in the raw-rank days to fight against that white water, and usually we'd give free passage to pork-knockers — that's what we call prospectors — who'd be willing to break their backs with a paddle. There was never a lack — pork-knockers going back to the fields were men without a cent, often as not. But if they were lazy but provident they might keep back the passage money, and then they'd sit up atop the cargo and sing and lie in the cool day's sun. Chibats we'd call them, I never knew why, but chibats it always was. But even they would have to help in the potashes — potash is a word meaning portage and comes from it always being pronounced in the French fashion — for the French had this colony once, you know. It was always a fine struggle over the potashes and at each pull of the rope the bowman would shout "Mandey" and the men would make reply "Mandey" and pull. Mandey is a word signifying "Is the man there?" and it was in the manner of a warning. And then, often, the chibats would start up a song and give a rhythm to the raw-rank men and to save their lungs. Come, Captain Pequeno and Captain Ned, let us sing the old shanties together for Mr Swan.'

In strong voices, with the slow, insistent rhythms of the river they sang the songs:

Johnny Fernandes was a Portuguey man
A Portuguey man and a dandy young man
Whe-e-y-ho whe-e-y-ho.
It's a long time and a very long time of it,
It's a long time ago, you know.

or

M'lover's goin' to find me carat stone
M'lover's goin' to find me carat stone

or

God made d' white man in d' day
God made d' white man in d' day;
God made d' black man in d' night
And den God forgit to paint he white.

or

I put my hand on Lulu's breast,
Lulu faint away ...

or

Blow d'man down wid a bottle ob rum
Blow, blow, blow d'man down,
Blow d'man down or I'll cut his white arse,
Blow, blow, blow d'man down.

or

Oh Madeline, sweet, sweet Madeline,
Tell me where you get that belly from.

Each song was prefaced with the call 'Mandey?' from Captain Holder, and all replied 'Mandey' before the shanty was sung.

We were all merrily tight when something occurred to change the mood of the evening. Providence seemed determined that I should have my wish of passing through the hundred and twenty miles of dangerous water. Late that night the door of the hotel opened and a rugged-faced Englishman came in. Captain Pequeno hailed him as 'Reggie', and asked him what he was doing in Bartica. He was, he told me later, managing a small mining camp some miles below Issano. He told us that the child of one of his Indian workers had fallen on to a sharp pole in the river and wounded himself badly. It was no good taking him to Issano as there would be no truck to Bartica for three days. He knew that a doctor was needed urgently, and the quickest way to get the child to Bartica was down-river, taking advantage of the following current. His boat captain, an East Indian named Captain Sugrim, had navigated this section in the old days but had not been too willing to put his memory of its waters to the test. However, they had set out, and Sugrim's instinct and memories had brought them to Bartica in excellent time and without mishap. The Indian boy was in the hands of the doctor and the Grumman was calling next morning to fly him to Georgetown. The boat was returning to the camp in a couple of days.

I asked Reggie Hill if he could give me a passage in his boat, and after warning me of the possible dangers as a matter of duty he agreed to take me. He finished the bottle of plum-cured rum and while we waited for the fierce rainstorm to abate Captain Pequeno told us a pork-knocker story.

'You know,' he explained to me, 'these pork-knocker fellows are, and always have been, fellows to spend every spot of money they make in the fields in one go. Why, one even came into my shop once with a bag of gold and told me he wanted to buy Bartica. Well, this one I am telling you about came down from the fields one day and went straight to the post office. They always liked to send off plenty of telegrams to Georgetown and this one said to the telegraph clerk, "Young fella me wan' to send wire from B.G. to B.G." and the clerk thinking he meant British Guiana said the thing made no sense. "You an ignorant fellow," says the pork-knocker. "That means from Bartica Grove to Booker's Garage. An' me wan' d'wire him say, 'Have motor car waiting on stelling chauffeur well-adorned,' an' sign it d'Tsar of Russia, fo' dat is ma name." So the wire goes off and next day the Tsar turns up in the boat at the stelling in Georgetown and there is a motor car with a chauffeur. The Tsar gets in and says to the chauffeur, "Make he go fo'wards," and the car goes forwards. "Make he go backwards," and the car goes backwards. "Now," he says with a great laugh, "make he go *sideways.*" '

And with those words we heard no more than the heavy drip of
rain falling from the eaves on to the ground below. The squall was
over and the boat captains returned to their homes.

Before dawn, two mornings later, three Indians came to carry my
luggage and stores down to the tent-boat. Torrential rain came
from a cold grey sky and wind rushed across the Essequibo. I
needed the mug of hot sweet tea which Brown, the Negro bowman,
offered me as I stepped over the gunwale of the thirty-five-foot tent-
boat. Reggie was tinkering with the engine, Captain Sugrim eating
a solid breakfast of curried fish and rice. Two Negroes lay in a
half-sleep and the dozen or so squat Indians sat talking quietly
together. Dawn came, the rain ceased, and as the air began to warm
a little in the sun we chugged off across the choppy water, past
Bamford's Point, where cows grazed, past the stone quarry whose
stones so unaccountably never reach the burnt-earth roads of the
Coast. To the right a group of severe greystone Victorian buildings
appeared high on a green bluff above the river. It was the Penal
Settlement, whose beautiful and fruitful ground has been claimed
from the forest by convict labour. It is in a magnificent position
and it is no wonder that some Guianese criminals prefer to be
convicted for the more serious crimes, and thus receive a sentence
to this health resort.

Half an hour later, the mists at last quite risen and the sky clear,
Katabo Point came into view, where the Mazaruni narrowed and
the wide waters of the Cuyuni joined it from the right. Defiantly
a miniature island stood midstream in the Mazaruni opposite the
point, and on it were the romantic ruins of a stone and red-brick
arch, an arch from some Ossianic poem. It was the remains of Kijk-
over-Al, the star-shaped fort which the Dutch built in the seventeenth century, on the site of a Portuguese fort. I could not ask
Reggie to give me time to land and examine the ruins, and from
the boat I could barely make out the incised keystone to the arch,
which had once made a journey to England to prove the Dutch
origin of the fort to the arbitrators examining Venezuelan claims
to this region of British Guiana.

As soon as Kijk-over-Al was passed Brown stirred his great
muscular body from sleep and stood at the bows with his paddle,

searching the water for hidden rocks. The river banks still formed
a regular channel on either side; no islets were visible yet, but flecks
of white showed that the current was swift and breaking on rocks.
The engine strained a little and our speed lessened; but I did not
realize the strength of the water until two rafts of silverballi logs
rounded a point, moving at great speed with the current, alert
black bodies guiding them with paddles through hidden lanes
between the rocks. Some minutes later we saw another silverballi
raft, caught on a projecting rock in midstream, straining for freedom
to hurtle onward. It must have been manned by one or two men,
and I wondered if they had been able to make the shore in safety.
The peculiar horror of the lower Mazaruni was always that men
could drown in full view of other craft. There was no turning back
to aid anyone in distress; in fact to do so would have been a humane
action punishable by law. No one was allowed to turn back while
in the dangerous water. They had to wait till they reached calmer
water. This law has produced a saying among the rivermen
with connotations distant from its origin: 'Boat gone a-falls, 'e
can't turn back.'

Beyond the abandoned raft lay the first bush-covered island, and
now the Mazaruni divided into two channels. Captain Sugrim
studied the water and the tide marks on the river bank. It was his
first, and comparatively simple, decision of the journey. There is no
fixed route along the thousand lanes, or itabos, formed by the islets.
Each subtly varying river level may mean that it is wiser to take one
itabo rather than another. We rounded the island to the right and
regained the open water. It seemed that the mainland ran to either
side, but in fact from now on it was impossible to tell whether the
land we saw was river bank or island. We would burst from itabos
to beautiful broads and back into wide channels between islands.
Sometimes the itabos were so narrow that the tree-crowns from
one island would meet those of the next, to form a dark corridor
down which the water rushed with concentrated fury. The Indians
now came into their own, pulling the boat upstream by rope until
the engine could again combat the current in the lustrous black
water of the broads. If it were a good stretch with no white water
Brown would lay down his paddle and chew on hard pickled berries
like crab-apples, an offer of which I accepted and learnt the extent

of the Creoles' liking for things that are hot. Sometimes Brown would sing a quiet song, the song of the greenheart cutter talking to his boss:

> Timberman, me weary work,
> Oh-ho, see sun a-go,
> Timberman, me wan' go home,
> Timberman, me weary work
> Oh-ho, see punt a-come-o,
> Timberman, me wan' go home.

A rather louder song went,

> Oh, you blow, Potaro, blow,
> Oh, you blow, Potaro, blow,
> An' d'spade-man spade,
> An' d'hoe-man, hoe,
> An' d'pully, pully, pully,
> An' d'batel tell,
> An' d'manager shout, 'Potaro gold,
> Potaro coa'se, coa'se gold.'

Rain came at intervals all day, and there was no time without magnificent banks of cumulus drifting from the sea, eventually to be cut by the ridges of the Pakaraimas. The trees grew higher and finer the farther we went up the river, and it was the hope of still finer trees that relieved the monotony of the broads, a monotony that yet so hypnotized me that I was unable to sleep or read all day.

Before dusk we reached an old overgrown loggers' landing, encircled by the buttressed stumps of greenheart cut long ago. Soon the forest was ringing with the metallic sound of cutlasses hacking at the slim yari-yari trees, the trees that were once used for lances and pikes. With incredible speed, and delight in their skill, the Indians built a benab, roofed with a tarpaulin and secure enough to support a dozen men in their hammocks. Reggie and I lay luxuriously smoking in ours while his boy boiled us a billy-can of tea. Soup, corned beef, rice and carrots followed, with sweet grapefruit for dessert. Darkness came, and then the night chorus; we talked for a little through our mosquito nets and then fell into a deep sleep.

Next morning I was for the first time really grateful for my mosquito net. An Indian who had been sleeping close to me had a deep wound in his foot from which blood flowed freely until Reggie insisted on stanching it — the Indian showed no concern. 'Him sure has had a visit from Dr Blair,' said Brown — Dr Blair being a onetime surgeon in the colony with an old-fashioned belief in blood-letting. The Indian had been attacked by a vampire bat, the creature I had come to dread most in the forest, and which was specially prevalent in the Mazaruni-Cuyuni area. There are two kinds of vampire bat in British Guiana; the smaller, a little larger than the European bat, usually confines himself to birds and animals, though Waterton observed him eating berries and succulent plants. The larger, the one with a taste for human blood, has a wingspan of some two feet, and is equipped with teeth as sharp as chisels. He comes silently to the hammock and usually chooses the foot, particularly the big toe, for his operation, very gently scraping away at the skin until the blood oozes through a triangular-shaped hole, upon which he begins to suck — sometimes removing as much as ten ounces of blood in a night. The victim is not only unaware that he is being attacked but apparently is lulled into a deeper sleep by the gentle action. If your foot is in contact with the mosquito net the bat will chisel through the muslin and get down to work, and, not having Waterton's scientific curiosity, I always made sure that my feet were surrounded by air. Waterton slept night after night with his foot thrust out of his net in invitation to the bat, so that he might study its method of work. Although his Indians were attacked he was always left alone. A Scottish friend with whom he was travelling was sucked, and Waterton, with his usual odd humour, comforted him by telling him that in Europe he would have been charged a couple of guineas for such a good job of blood-letting. Reggie Hill had overcome his fears of the vampires, although he told me that he would never take risks because one could never tell whether a rabid bat might not appear. When rabid the bat flies round madly day and night sucking whatever it can find in its wild flight, leaving rabies in its trail. It even attacks other bats; finally after two days and nights of unceasing flight it dies of exhaustion.

Dawn on the river was a swirl of mist, which cleared in the sun long before we reached the great obstacle of the Mazaruni; the amazing confluence of unchartable water formed by the falls of Paiarimap, Kaburi, Kaburi-mamma, Wara-wara, Pabracash and Anizet. It is here that the Kaburi river flows into the Mazaruni, and where the Mazaruni itself drops eighty feet in a series of rapids; the river has widened with the force of the waters, making a great island-dotted bend where current beats against current, where black water is continually made white, and rocks abound. Captain Sugrim studied the water and decided that our best passage was through the Mutusi itabo. We strained with all the engine's strength across to this dark passage, bowered with meeting trees. An Indian jumped into the water with the bowline, or warp, in his hand and secured it to a tree; another followed him with the long sternline. Others then took their positions in the line, leaning against the current in the shallows and holding to trees for support. The method of easing the boat up the passage was to secure the bowline always to a tree, and to man-haul the boat by the sternline till the bowline was quite slack; then the bowline was taken up to the next tree while the boys played tug-of-war with the boat. It was during these moments when the bowline was being transferred that one felt most insecure; if the boys had let go of the rope we should have been flung uncontrollably backwards, and the current would have taken us where it wished. But all was well, and we reached the largest area of rapids where on all sides the waters rushed towards Pabracash, Paiarimap, Wara-wara and Anizet — falls which we could not see but whose distant sounds we could hear, and whose smokelike mists rose on all sides. The portage to the upper level of the Mazaruni was at Kaburi falls, which lay half a mile away across the water, a small tumbling mass of foam. It took us nearly an hour slowly and painfully to wend our passage through to the artificial landing at the foot of the main rapids, but at last the loop of the bowline was thrown round the iron post, and the boat secured to the landing which had been con-structed on an islet of rock dividing the rapids. It seemed strange to step out on to this secure island, and, by climbing to its highest level, to see the partly surrounding area of swirling torrent. Above, with that sinister innocence which the water of rivers assumes before it plunges over the falls, the Mazaruni lay with hardly a fleck of white on its black surface.

We now had to make the 'potash' up the Kaburi falls. Everything movable was taken from the boat and carried up the islet to the highest level. Then came the preparation for the portage of the boat up and over the falls themselves, and thus round the islet to the higher landing. During the tug through the Mutusi itabo I had seen the immense emotion expressed by the glistening bodies of the Indians and by Brown's straining muscles as he pulled the paddle against the bow; it is not until the body strains with all its strength to preserve itself against the antagonism of Nature that one realizes the extent to which it can express emotion. It had been too dark to photograph these extraordinary forms in the itabo, and I decided to go up the falls in the boat and photograph an action which promised to be far more severe than the passage of the itabo.

I sat on the roof while Brown was at the bow and Captain Sugrim attended to matters at the stern. An Indian knotted the bowline round his arm, and holding to the trees on the island climbed up the fall until the line was taut; then he secured it to the tree. The same process as in the Matusi followed—though now, of course, the strength and the incline of the water was greater. Everything was ready for the first haul, and Brown broke into the fury of excitement which did not abate for the whole half-hour of the portage. 'Mandey?' he shouted, and the reply came back. 'Right, boys!' he shouted. 'Haul on the warp, Haul—haul—haul . . . that's it—steady—ease the sternline . . . ease it . . . ease it . . . ease it . . . hold—now haul away, boys—haul, haul, haul, haul on the warp that's it she's coming boys she's coming she's coming—ha-a-a-u-l on the wa-a-r-p!' His own body pulled on the paddle and the great muscles bulged and glistened with sweat, and slowly the boat, its bows so much higher than its stern that I had difficulty in keeping balance as I photographed, moved up the falls. For sheer sound and excitement I have known nothing to approach it in my life. There was not a moment for the thought that if the Indians had missed their footing and lost their hold on the warp we should have been washed down over the falls of Paiarimap.

At last we reached the calm water and the boat rode gaily in its unaccustomed lightness, while the Indians loaded it once more. I had, or so I imagined, finished my film and went into the bush to change the cassette. I felt that I had taken a remarkable set of photographs. To my horror I discovered that in my haste to load the camera before the portage I had not fixed the film securely enough on to its receiving spool. The virgin film lay in its cassette. I had not taken one photograph.

The character of the Mazaruni changed above the falls; it became broad and majestic, with forest-covered hills visible on either hand, the trees taller and more luxuriant in their foliage. The islets still continued, but there seemed to be more order than in the chaos below. The exhilarating sense of danger was passed. In the late afternoon we approached the columbite camp,[1] huts strewn over a long wide clearing on the slope of a hill. It was a superb position, dominating a great bend of the river, and in the soft light of the cooling sun seemed almost paradisial.

Reggie's hut was on stilts, a pleasant combination of ancient and modern: the roof was aluminium, the walls and floor corrugated with the malleable bark of the slim ballamanni tree. There were two rooms, and a slip-room with a tin bath. I sat in one of the two deck chairs and Reggie poured some beer for us, ice cold from a kerosene refrigerator which stood oddly against the ballamanni walls. The Negro cook came up to ask if we would like to eat fish that night — an anaconda had that afternoon eaten the pullet he'd been fattening.

We ate well and settled in the deck chairs with more beer. I was looking forward to Reggie's talk; I knew now, from my experience of these remarkable Englishmen who live in wild places, that the talk would be good and uninhibited; Reggie was no exception. He had left England as a very young man to prospect in Canada, but after nine years the cold had proved too much for him and he had come to British Guiana to try his luck. He had prospected, surveyed, worked for wildcat gold companies, and now, at sixty-four, he was the camp manager of an American columbite company, working on a small scale with portable equipment for placer workings. It was a quiet, well-paid job and he was happy to have it after all his years on the river. He talked about the pork-knockers he had known and worked with, and I asked him what was his explanation of the word — most people have their own private etymology for it. Reggie's was the most convincing I had heard; he said that in the old days when the Government grubstaked the prospectors the

[1] Columbite is a valuable mineral used in the case-hardening of jet engines.

rations were rice and pork-tails, so that when a prospector went into the fields he would say that he was going to 'knock the pork', i.e. eat the pork. Reggie told me that when he was in charge of some pork-knockers in a gold area he noticed that all of them had very long nails, which at first he put down to misplaced Negro vanity. Later he learnt that the nails were kept long, and coated with wax, so that they could smuggle gold dust from the workings by this means.

During our conversation I told him about the wild man of the woods which the Negro at the manganese camp in the North-West had talked of, and his face set seriously. 'I don't take these things lightly,' he said. 'When you've lived in the bush as long as I have you don't. That must have been a kind of massakruman, although a real massakruman lives in the water and has a beard and tusks like a sea lion's. There are supposed to be a few of them in the Mazaruni by the penal settlement. That's why, whenever the convicts make a breakaway, they'll never swim for it — they always build a raft. I remember another story about a massakruman. Years ago there was a black fellow lived above Bartica at Barakara, on the Essequibo. One day he went down to a bathing place and found a massakruman sitting on the rocks combing his beard. He turned and ran for his life. Now a week later his little sister went down there to wash clothes, and didn't come back. They went down to look for her and found her drowned at the bottom of the pool. Now, the clothes she'd been washing were twelve feet up in a tree. *She* couldn't have put them there. Of course, I don't believe it really was the massakruman. . . .'

I did not look into his eyes, but if I had I think I would have seen some measure of belief that the little girl had been drowned by the wild man. Superstition must come easily to people who pass their lives in the forest. The moon came up, and Reggie changed the subject.

'Indians'll tell you', he began, 'never to cut trulli palm for a hut roof when there's a moon, and you might think that a silly story. But if you cut during the day or when there's moonlight the sap will be rising, and sap means worms, and worms'll stay after cutting, so that when you've built your hut it'll be full of insects come to get the worms.'

Before we went to sleep Reggie said to me, 'If we make a six o'clock start we can get you to Issano before midday. I've got to pick some stuff up there. You might have to wait a day or two for a boat up-river. If you do go and see the local baker he's a fine old pork-knocker — the Sultan of Turkey. He'll have some stories to tell you.'

The morning journey to Issano was dull; a mile or two before the village the islets finally ended, and at last we knew that the land on either side marked the course of the actual river whose breadth was roughly that of the Thames at London Bridge. Issano was a village of shacks on a bluff, orderless and streetless, living on the traffic of the river. Reggie and I ate our sandwiches on the terrace of the rest-house. Then I went over to see Captain More, who organized the river boats up to Tumereng, in the diamond fields. 'You're lucky,' he said, 'there's a silly-week boat goes up day after tomorrow.'

'Silly-week boat?' I asked.

He smiled and explained that the regular service was once a fortnight, but that an irregular boat always went up during the intervening period, and was called the silly-week boat.

I saw Reggie off in his boat and returned to the terrace to spend the afternoon reading Boswell's *Johnson*. When evening came I strolled up to the baker's shop and saw, sitting outside in a wicker chair, a fine old Creole who I thought must inevitably be the Sultan of Turkey. His big face beamed when I introduced myself and mentioned Reggie's name.

'A veritable pleasure to receive yo',' said the Sultan, 'an' a great great honour. Ah wiz jus' t'inking of takin' a snap o' somet'in an' now me hopes dat me can look fo'ward to company.'

He brought out another chair and a bottle of rum; he poured himself three fingers and knocked them back with more relish, I daresay, than he had ever knocked the pork-tails. We chatted for some time, and then, when I imagined him to be approaching his full spate of loquacity, I said, 'Could you tell me about the time you celebrated your own funeral?'

'Dog bust ma innards,' he cried, 'how come yo' know 'bout dat?'

'Mr Hill mentioned it.'

'Fo' true? A bigable man like he know d'story o' I an' d'Tsar of Russia? Dat is a heavy t'ing, a major t'ing. Sah, me will discourse dat story presently. Niggah forgit, dey say, bakra remember, but me remembers. It was a long time ago, yo' know, an' me an d'Tsar of Russia is partners up d'Mazaruni, but d'gold and d'dymonds them no good an' yo' has to have strong eye to perceive dey. So Tsar and me we goes to d'stores and we gets a grubstake fo' a trip aback, and d'storeman him good in giving we plenty rum. Now us look for gold and dymonds — me no hard fellow — but when us get back widout one damn t'ing d'storeman him seems t'ink us has jus' drunk d'rum and done no work, which is agin d'facts of d'case. Howsomever, when us goes on d'next trip, d'storeman him give we no rum 'tall 'tall. Now Tsar him spend all d'time aback givin' ruction 'gainst dis ridicerlous upstrated fellow an' him an' me works a means fo' procurin' both d'revenge an' plenty rum.

'Us gits back to d'waterside and Tsar comes to d'storeman an' he says, "Yo' has on yo' conscience d'death o' d'finest o' all d'pork-knockers on d'Mazaruni, d'great Sultan o' Turkey. In d'bush dat fellow gets d'fever an' as all knows rum is d'finest medicament fo' d'fever, and us has no rum, no nothin'. An' Sultan him die. We is now celebratin' d'fellow's wake in d'village an' if yo' wishes to have d'salvation of yo' conscience me suggests yo' comes and brings d'rum dat yo' should have provided in d'first case!" So long-faced over him comes, an' sees I lyin' in dat coffin as fine a dead as ever yo' did see, while d'fellows look in on me, crying out, "Sultan dead, him de-e-e-ad, d-e-e-e-a-d! O-oh, o-oh!" an' knockin' back dat rum. An' everybody gits tight, and every now an' agin, accordin' to d'plan, Tsar says, "Me goes see old Sultan, him poor ol' dead," and him slips I a snap o' rum in d'coffin. Well, me supposes dat him gets plenty plenty tight, becausin' him no' mo' comes wid rum though him and d'others has plenty. So me waits an' waits until me has waited nuff nuff. An' den me suddenly rises in ma shroud from d'coffin ejaculatin' a great howl as me does so dat even dose who knows dat me ain't a dead is substantially affected by d'proceedings an' dose dat t'ink me is a dead gives out d'biggest noise yo' ever heard, an' d'storeman him t'inks me is goin' to take he along to Hell wid I. But no, me calls out to dat Tsar of Russia, "Brudda Tsar, d'man me had preferenced most in dis colony, if me had d'knowledge me wud cuss yo' in arithmetic, geography an' Latin. Me is lyin' dere a fine 'live dead in dat coffin an' yo' forgits d'existence o' yo friend, me lyin' dere in dat t'ing an' yo' no bring I one snap o' rum. An' so me makes ruction wid yo', eh eh?" But by dis time d'store-man him has cleared off into d'bush an' we is left alone wid d'rum an', sah, we cleans up dose bottles o' rum and decides dat dis is d'finest wake d'both o' we has ever attended in he life.'

He broke into a glorious belly laugh, to which I added my own treble.

The next afternoon I hired a small boat to take me some five miles up-river to the landing of Hillfoot. Inland from Hillfoot was a large columbite mining camp where I planned to spend the night. It was a glorious, almost cloudless day as we chugged slowly up the Mazaruni, whose water, now like a sheet of rippled obsidian, dazzled the eyes. At Hillfoot the Creole guardian of the landing told me that unless I wanted to walk the ten miles into the camp I would have to send an Indian in with a message, and a truck would come down for me. William, the boat hand, agreed to go to the camp, and I slung my hammock on the veranda of the guardian's hut, where I lay for the next two and a half hours. During that time there was never a moment without the sweetest harmony of birdsong I have ever heard; I didn't know then that this area of the Mazaruni is distinguished from the rest of the colony by the magnifi-cence of its forest and the variety of its birds. What birds they were I do not know; perhaps it was some virtuoso colony, an ornitho-logical family Mozart, ceaselessly varying both tune and harmony, or it may have been birds of many species which, by inhabiting the same neck of the forest, have learnt to sing in counterpoint and to harmonize with each other. I can only say that this orchestral sound was of such sweetness that I felt that strange tearful pain which comes with too much beauty.

The concert was disturbed by the arrival of a heavy truck, lurch-ing down the last rutted slope. The road to the camp had been cut over a series of ravines and each steep fall seemed as perilous as a switchback, a ribbon of track edged by magnificent moras and purpleheart, vast in their girth and higher than any I had yet seen. Writhing lianas hung in festoons and epiphytes swagged from crown to crown. It was strange, after penetrating the forest, to burst suddenly into a square mile of open land which had been completely razed by bulldozers. Here stood the miners' shacks, the offices, the manager's bungalow and the great refining plant that had recently been put up at great cost. Later, when the manager took me over the plant, he sighed as he looked up at the silent machinery. The prospecting of the region, he told me, had been so haphazard that the plant had been erected before the true concentrations of the ore were known. Now it seemed as if the ore lay in isolated reefs at all points of the compass, and often many miles from the camp. His task was to find a means of bringing tons of ore through the forest to the plant. To build a truck road was an expensive business and not justified economically. He couldn't build a system of radial roads. He knew that the central plant was a white elephant. They should have had a portable plant to go to each working in turn. He pointed to a barrel containing a black gravel — the entire columbite production of the mine to date.

I spent the night at the camp and returned early next morning to Hillfoot. An hour later the silly-week boat rounded the point and came towards the landing. It was a battered-looking launch, some fifty feet in length and laden to the gunwales. In the stern sat pork-knockers with battels, jigs, pickaxes and spades; midships was piled high with cargo covered by a tarpaulin, on which sat half a dozen gaily dressed Negresses; in the small first-class section in the bows four policemen sat under cover, and I jumped in beside them, adding my baggage to the confusion of theirs. Then on we went. I asked the policemen where they were going, and with a sigh a sergeant replied, 'Tumereng'. They would be stationed at Tumereng for two years; no more the civilized life of Georgetown — they were going into exile to live on a little piece of river bank reclaimed from the forest. 'New skies the exile finds,' says Horace, 'but the same heart.' The hearts of those policemen that day, and the day that followed, were heavy with unconcealed misery. They hardly exchanged a word with each other, and after a few attempts at conversation I realized that their minds were too preoccupied for speech.

The day for me passed mainly in reading, for the serene sameness of the river soon became monotonous. Once I climbed through to sit on the cargo in the clouded sun, and my appearance caused a slight giggle among the women. One of the girls was a slim, very

facing, above left: A SEVEN-FOOT ARAPAIMA LANDED BY TINY MCTURK
right: THE PIRAI (OR PIRANHA) CANNIBAL FISH
below: TAKING A POWER-DRIVEN BOAT THROUGH WHITE WATER

pretty light-skinned girl of twenty or so, who sat apart from the others, and looked a little apprehensive, while the other full-black women talked and laughed among themselves. I did not realize at the time that these women were prostitutes; two of them had worked the fields for years and were returning from a junketing in Georgetown. Three others were younger and probably coming to the fields to make quick, good money from the generous pork-knockers. In Tumereng, I was told that the pretty young girl was in the fields as the reputed wife of a pork-knocker with a bad reputation. He was planning to be her 'bully', and make a fortune from pork-knockers who would be willing to lose the money for a whole packet of diamonds if they could have a *poule* as *luxe* as she.

Now and then the pork-knockers would throw up some remark to the women and then return to their incessant talk. There were two young men, evidently partners, who never ceased talking about the bonanza they would find and how they would go back to Georgetown with their pockets weighed down with dollar bills. Beside them sat a thin old man with a gentle face, a week's grizzled beard, a far away, infinitely sad look on his face, as if he were making yet one more journey to the fields and knew that he would die without ever knowing the joy of a bonanza. I was making some notes in my journal when the two young men raised their voices in argument; they began to abuse each other, for what cause I couldn't gather. One started a flow of invective which came with wonderful effortlessness, and as he spoke I wrote down what I could — he spoke too fast for me to keep up with each sentence. I print here what I recorded; the passages of Creolese elsewhere in this book are, of necessity, a little factitious, but this passage can be taken as *echt* Creolese. It seems to me to have the imagery and form of natural poetry, and its first phrase is like the opening of some early Elizabethan sonnet:

'When you me vex so grieviously me no care wit' yo' foolishness. You musta come from Mars, man, yo' so low in t'inking and fright me, funny man. Now realize, yo' vex stupidly. Me carry mood, man, an' if d'spirit o' God prevent me mak' joke wit' yo' me is reasonable, but does vex. Have me got tek it? Allow me tell yo', man, nothin' else me has to do wit' yo', man, outside o' business. When me walk wit' a man me got be happy wit' he. Yo' not superior

facing, above: THE ISLANDED NATURE OF THE MAZARUNI AND POTARO RIVERS
below: HAULING A BOAT OVER WHITE WATER ON THE ESSEQUIBO RIVER

O

to flesh, man, an' when yo' mak' rough jokes wit' I, me has unguarded moments, man, and me vex. An' yo' wan' d'whores too much, man, an' yo' no drink nuff, man. Why yo' value yo' life so immeasurably? When yo' yo'self, man, me give yo' a hearing, but I will give yo' no answer.'

We spent the night at a small village and made a start soon after dawn next morning. We were now reaching the first areas of the fields, and here and there on the bank were scrawled wooden notices of claims. Every mile or two the boat would put in at a landing and a bag of flour or rice would be handed to some starveling pork-knocker who had probably walked that day from his working deep in the forest. These ragged men always greeted the boat passengers with great civility; one old man gave the company in general a graceful bow as the boat approached, and cried out, 'Gentlemen, well, how-how-how?' and the men aboard answered, 'Well-well-well.'

At two places on the river we saw men preparing to dive for diamonds, in the headgear of a deep-sea diver. It was a new method of prospecting which had been successfully introduced in Brazil.

The long day went by, torrential rain alternating with passages of sun; I finished Boswell and moved on to Gibbon. It was a pleasant study in contrast to turn now and then from Gibbon's sleek, sly paragraphs on the Empress Theodora, to the green wall, the black water, to hear the gay chatter of Creolese and feel the tropical sun beating through the tarpaulin.

Dark and heavy rain was falling on the Mazaruni when we rounded a point to see a distant cluster of dark wooden shacks on a green bluff. This was Tumereng, the gold and diamond city, where the pork-knockers came for their drink and women, where packets of diamonds were scrutinized under the lenses of men who never made a bad bargain. The boat tied up, and one of the two pork-knockers who had been abusing each other the day before went to the gunwale, raised his hand to the shacks in a declamatory gesture and cried out, 'Me is here, you big tiger, man, Tumereng, me is here. Me come, me see, me conquer.' And with Caesarean dash he sprang ashore and ran up the muddied path. With less dash I followed him, and as I approached the shacks huge waves of music greeted me. An amplifying machine, on its last legs, was playing a much-used record of a particularly loud calypso. As I got nearer the sound became almost unbearable — mad, frenzied, hideous. At the window of a shack the faces of three Negresses appeared; they laughed and pointed at me, called out to me things that I could not hear but which I guessed to be obscene. A man appeared at a side window and I shouted to him, 'Where is Mr Chang — Mr *Chang*? And for God's sake turn down that noise.' He pointed to a door leading into the wing of the shack where the women were. In the strange state produced in me by the noise I thought this was some ruse to get me to enter a brothel, but the man himself came to the doorway. I went in; I was in a room less than fourteen feet square, and it must have contained more than ten women, all of them drunk. Some were chanting to the music and swinging their hips. Others bore down on me and picked at me like harpies, one crying, 'You come wid me, white boy, eh?' — while another cried, 'You frightened o' me, eh, frightened o' me?' and with a shriek of laughter excavated in her blouse to produce a huge pendulous breast for my inspection.[1] It was as near hell as I have ever been or hope to be. I felt a cold sweat as I pushed my way through the women to a flight of stairs and climbed it. The stairs ended in a trapdoor and I banged heavily on it with my stick. A moment later it was raised and I looked up into a bland Chinese face. Once in this hideaway, with the trap lowered, I said, with a note of hysteria in my voice, 'Please, please, tell them to turn this terrible noise down. I can't hear myself speak.' Mr Chang went to a control knob and turned the volume down very slightly.

'This is Tumereng,' said Mr Chang. 'A very bad place, and it is Saturday night. They like noise, they like as much loud music as they can get while they get drunk. It keeps them happy. This is a very bad place.'

I sat down and recovered my nerves while I explained to Mr Chang that I would like to stay in Tumereng while I made my arrangements for going over the Merume mountains to Kamerang. I had been told that he would help me.

[1] The Tumereng prostitutes are usually known by appropriate nicknames; Abuya comes from an Indian word meaning 'smells like a hog'; 'Gang pot' was a girl who never refused anybody at any time. On the Coast I heard of a girl known as Dollar Chance, from her habit of going through the rum-parlours calling 'Dorra a chance! Dorra a chance!'

'Yes, I can help you,' he said. 'It would have been better if you had brought a letter from Mr Camoens. I run the saloons and the shops and buy the diamonds for Mr Camoens. Do you know him?'

'No,' I replied.

'He has a little house here. I think I can let you stay there for a few nights. He uses it when he comes up from Georgetown.'

I had heard much of Mr Camoens during the past few days. He was one of the richest men in Georgetown. As a young man he had prospected diamonds himself and done well. Now he dominates almost the entire length of the Mazaruni; he owns the river transport, nearly all the pork-knocker shops, an hotel in Bartica, and by these means there is hardly a diamond found in the area which does not find its way to him. If a strange diamond buyer arrives in the area and offers better prices, Mr Chang radio-telephones Mr Camoens, who charters an aeroplane to Tumereng and within a few hours has made his arrangements to make sure the intruder does not succeed in his deals. The Camoens' monopoly is almost absolute.

It was kind of Mr Chang to offer me Mr Camoens's house but I'm afraid I priggishly wanted only to get out of Tumereng as fast as I could. I thanked Mr Chang for his offer and told him that I thought I would, after all, stay at the police-post half a mile down-river. He shrugged his shoulders and we returned, walking through the saloon where now half a dozen pork-knockers were dancing with the whores to the music of a cracked piano.

Twenty minutes later I was in a bright clean room attached to the police-post, and I relaxed on the bed. Tumereng had been an experience.

When I learnt by radio-telephone that the Grumman could only fly me over the Merume mountains in a week I tried to find Indians who would drogh for me up to Kamerang — perhaps Akawaios on their way back to the reservation. All I could find were an Akawaio and his wife and child, and they were planning to fly back by the Grumman whenever it should make a flight to Kamerang. They were willing to pay for the flight by using up the entire profits from a load of tomatoes they had brought down to Tumereng, and I learnt that this was a usual custom. Akawaios, in particular, have an intense curiosity about all forms of experience. I was told of one who paddled for a month down to Bartica because a friend had told him of a prostitute there whose genitalia were of unique construction.

It was a quiet and pleasant week at Enachu. Ivy, the girl who looked after me, would bring me my breakfast and sit herself down for a morning chat, telling me her news in a soft, sing-song voice laced with giggles. 'A frog jumped on my bed this morning,' she would say, 'and my — was I afraid! But I gets a big stick and away he goes.' Or she would confide her life story; how she had been brought to the Interior by a policeman two years before — but the policeman had taken another woman. 'All I wants is to get back to d'coast but I just goes on staying on here cos I don't have d'energy to start once amore down dere. But one day I is goin' to have ma heart's desire. A Necchi sewin' machine, a refrigerator an' a washin' machine. An' den I shall be happy. Dat fellow Cheddi Jagan, when he was talkin' in d'streets before those 'lections, he promises us all sewin' machines and refrigerators. But till now we don't see one dam' thing.'

Sometimes talkative old Mr Obadiah Wilcox would walk over and tell me about pork-knocking in the old days, of the bonanza he blued in 1923 and the bad conditions of today. 'Sah,' he would say, 'me an' other fellows of my inclination o' thinkin' calls dis d' "dollar area", cos yo' can't get anythin' less than a dollar. Grapefruit juice twenty-eight cents in Georgetown, one dollar here, Worcester sauce d'same, an' pilchards an' rice an' every dam' thing. An' freight from Georgetown is only six cents a pound, so us reckons Mr Camoens him makes a profit of nearly three hundred per cent on all him brings up here. An' him has d'monopoly, sah, what Mr Camoens says is d'rule in dese parts. Him says that d'prices must be high cos when he grubstakes d'pork-knockers many turns into bad debts, but even takin' all dat into account, sah, d'prices is out of all commensuration.'

One evening I gave a party for a dozen or so local people, including two police sergeants, one of whom told fantastic stories of hunts for criminals in the forest, with jaguars and anacondas appearing at every turn. The stories did not convince me, and finally Sergeant Munchausen broke into full laughter and admitted that he had invented all for the amusement of the company. The other sergeant played the guitar and the evening was full of song — even Obadiah Wilcox in his quivering voice obliged with a Victorian drawing-room ballad. A song in which everyone joined was a work-song in which the accented 'Mind how' was the signal for some kind of rhythmic action:

> Georgetown got some worthless gals,
> *Mind how* you swing you' tail.
> Swing you' tail in a decent way,
> *Mind how* you swing you' tail.
> Swing you' tail but don't touch me,
> *Mind how* you swing you' tail.
> Georgetown gals don't fetch no price,
> *Mind how* you swing you' tail.
> Give dem a shillin' an' kiss dem twice,
> *Mind how* you swing you' tail.

With everybody merrily tight the party finally broke up in the early hours, with promises of an early repetition. I had enjoyed myself almost as much as my guests; I never tired of the direct beauty of their language, their power of vivid narration, their complete lack of inhibition. Above all, the simple Negro does not have it in him to be a bore.

In the cool late-afternoons I would go fishing, not so much for pleasure as to conserve my precious stores for the march to Roraima. We would let the boat drift in the shallows where the fish were plentiful and the bites frequent — although I would land one small fish for every dozen bites. The water was inviting for bathing, but after an encounter one afternoon with an electric eel the pleasures of swimming did not seem worth its dangers. I and the police boat hand were in the boat we used for fishing, when an eel surfaced its shining black body, some five feet long. It brushed lightly against the hull of our boat, submerged, and repeated its action twice before realizing that the boat was not a creature that would react to its charges of electricity. It was using on us the precise method by which it can kill a swimming man. It will brush gently against him, giving him a slight shock at each contact until finally he is paralysed and drowns. A few weeks before, on the lower

Mazaruni, a man who capsized his boat had been drowned in this way before he could reach the shore. The Latin Americans call these gymnoti *tembladores* or producers of trembling, which, I gather, describes the kind of paralysis they produce.

Humboldt, whose desire for scientific information could on occasions quite overcome his humanity, has a horrifying description of his using horses as bait to capture electric eels alive. Several horses were driven into a river at a point where it was known the eels would be submerged in the mud of the river-bottom. The disturbance of the hooves brought them to the surface where they repeatedly struck at the horses' bellies, while Indians ensured that the horses did not escape.

For a long interval [writes Humboldt], the eels seem likely to prove victorious. Several horses sink beneath the violence of the invisible strokes which they receive from all sides, in organs the most essential to life; and stunned by the force and frequency of the shocks, they disappear under the water. Others, panting, with mane erect and haggard eyes expressing anguish and dismay, raise themselves, and endeavour to flee from the storm by which they are overtaken . . . In less than five minutes two of our horses were drowned. The eel being five feet long, and pressing itself against the belly of the horses, makes a discharge along the whole extent of its electric organ. It attacks at once the heart, the intestines, and the caeliac fold of the abdominal nerves . . . The horses are probably not killed, but only stunned. They are drowned from the impossibility of rising amid the prolonged struggle between the other horses and the eels.

Eventually the exhausted eels, most of their galvanic charge now spent, were captured.

The most remarkable thing about the electric eel is that its electrical apparatus, occupying two-thirds of its body, does not give off its charge automatically; it is a matter of instinctive will. The charge may be localized at almost any point on the fish's body, and if two people touch it simultaneously one may receive a shock while the other feels nothing. The eel is in some way equipped to distinguish between two dangers and to react to the greater. On other occasions the entire body gives out an equal charge. From my one experience with this monstrous creature I could well understand the fear in which it is held by all the river people; it forms, with the pirai and the vampire bat, the evil triumvirate of these parts. The alligator does not approach their category. A Negro swore to me that he had seen an eel attack a young alligator and reduce it to complete impotence with a series of rapid charges.

In Mr Chang's hideaway at Tumereng was a battered radio-telephone with which he sent weather signals to Georgetown and learnt of the proposed arrival of the Grumman. As the day of the scheduled visit of the amphibian approached I asked Mr Chang to get through to B.G. Airways in Georgetown to fix my flight over the mountain to Kamerang. I always enjoyed the radio-telephone; sometimes one would have to listen to other conversations for an hour or more before getting through. On this occasion we tuned in and I immediately recognized the voice of Tiny McTurk; he was in the middle of a long-distance consultation with a Georgetown doctor, and as we listened we realized that the subject of the consultation was a Makushi girl suffering from some stomach complaint. I could imagine the scene; the girl lying on the McTurk table while the doctor told Tiny what to do. The conversation went like this:

'Ask her if she vomits much, Tiny, will you?'

An exchange in Makushi, then, 'Yes, doctor, it comes up black four times a day.'

'Good. Now Tiny, I want you to press fairly hard about four inches to the left of her navel and tell me what you feel.'

'Nothing, doctor.'

'Now about six inches down — anything there?'

'Not a thing.'

'Now move over about another six inches to the right.'

'Just a nice firm belly.'

'Right. Now go down about another five inches. What do you feel there?'

At this point Mr Chang and I exchanged glances and his thin eyebrows rose very slightly as he waited for the reply. Finally it was decided that the girl did not have peritonitis and was fit enough to wait for the next visit of the doctor. If she had been seriously ill she would have been flown down to Georgetown for treatment — if she or her family agreed. So many Indians have gone to the Georgetown hospital and later died that the Indians look upon it as a place from which there is little hope of return.

We were on the air after Tiny, and learnt from B.G. Airways that Harry Wendt would be flying the Grumman to Tumereng in two days, that if the weather was all right he would take me on to Kamerang. When the day came I heard the engine almost to the minute of the scheduled time, and took the police boat up to Tumereng. The Grumman was taxiing to the bank as we arrived, and I met Harry ascending the bluff to Mr Chang's saloon.

'You've seen that hunk of cloud that's blown up,' he said, looking towards the Merume mountains. 'I'm not sure I'll be able to take you over. I can't fly *over* the mountains — have to go through them. It's a tricky flight.'

I sighed. If I didn't go that day, Heaven knew when or how I would get into the high land. But Harry is an understanding, patient and kind-hearted man. He was prepared to wait most of the day at Tumereng in the hope that the weather would improve. In Mr Chang's room he produced his sandwiches and Thermos flask of tea, and we prepared to talk until the clouds lifted. In his quiet, humorous voice, with a slight Yankee drawl, he told me about his one and only crash during twenty years of constant flying in British Guiana. He was taking an Ireland amphibian up to the Rupununi when the engine failed over the forest. 'I looked around for a good sturdy tree crown,' he said, 'and I brought her down very gently on that. There were six of us aboard and we just got out of the crate into the branches and climbed down. I'd chosen a tree I knew would have good lianas down to the forest floor. Five of us didn't have a scratch, the other broke his leg climbing down. I'd sent our position to Georgetown before the crash and they sent a boat up, and that was that.'

I asked him about the employee at the Demerara Bauxite Company who had accepted Caesar Gorinsky's £1000 bet that he couldn't drive a jeep up the cattle trail to the Rupununi. As if such things were part of his everyday experience Harry said, 'Oh, he didn't make it. He got to Cannister Falls and was trying to take the jeep across by raft, but the river was in spate. Anyway, the trail was a soggy mass and he was digging himself out every hundred yards. He ran out of food. I flew up to Cannister Falls two days ago and dropped him some stores. He's abandoning the jeep and going on by foot to the Rupununi. Anybody wants a decent jeep there's one if he can get it out.'

By mid-afternoon a few summits of the mountains were clear of cloud and Harry said he was prepared to fly, though he warned me that he might have to turn back. My stores and baggage were loaded, I said goodbye to Mr Chang, the pork-knockers and the now sober prostitutes, and we took off. Ten minutes later we were moving down a valley with mountains on either side and a great wall of mountain some miles ahead. Cumulus whirled round us, but between the cumulus visibility was good. Then, in a moment, all visibility was blanketed by rain-laden cloud; minutes went by and the air did not clear. I remembered the wall of mountain and studied Harry's face to see how he felt. He was looking all round him for signs of a break, but his expression gave no indication at all of the state of his mind. Perhaps a quarter of an hour went by, and my body was tensed the entire time. Then, in a moment, we were in clear air, with blue sky above — the mountains were behind, and below us the Mazaruni wound through undulating forests on whose horizons were isolated mesas, part of the table-mountain system that culminated in Roraima. To the right I could see how the land fell abruptly for hundreds of feet to the lower level of the Mazaruni. The river at Tumereng was only a hundred feet or so above sea level; at Kamerang, I knew, it was eighteen hundred feet. It makes this sharp descent in a series of great and impassable falls.

The Grumman circled above the little settlement of Kamerang and made its landing on the smooth black water of the narrow Mazaruni. A crowd of Akawaio Indians had gathered to meet us at the landing point formed where the Kamerang River joins the Mazaruni. The women wore floral dresses and the men had trousers, but from the amount of blue tattoo marks on the faces of the older men and women, one knew how recently civilization had come to Kamerang Mouth.

While my stores were being landed, Harry told me how lucky I was not to be back at Tumereng. 'I'd have turned back in the ordinary way,' he said, 'but I took a chance for you. There wasn't much room to play about in, but I had to get as much altitude out of the bus as I could, to get above the damn' mountains. Anyway we've made it — and it looks better now. Hope to God it doesn't blow up again.'

The afternoon was going and he had to be back at Georgetown before dark. As soon as I had landed everything he raised his hand in salute from the controls and taxied midstream for the take-off. I watched the little aeroplane climbing steeply towards the mountains, its silver body glinting in the sunlight. The last of my aids on the road to Roraima was gone. From now on, apart from a day by river, I would journey by foot through the forest and across the savannah, the Gran Sabaña of Venezuela. Two hundred miles to do at twenty miles a day, through more or less uninhabited territory. The really exciting part of my journey was now before me.

To the Mother of the Rivers

AMERANG MOUTH is a government station, from which the District Officer, Mr William Seggars, administers the five thousand square miles of the Indian Reserve, and buys the fruit and vegetables which the Indians bring by woodskin from every quarter of the district. Bill Seggars and his wife live in a simple, pleasant bungalow on high ground, with a superb view across the Mazaruni and above the forest to the distant mesas. They are idealists who have chosen this most isolated of all the colony's districts out of a sense of vocation combined with a love of wild places. They were not at Kamerang when I arrived; but I had seen them both in Bartica, where Seggars had talked to me about his hopes and longings for his district and its Indians, how he was weaning them from the worst of their tribal ways, teaching them better forms of husbandry, and hoping one day to market their produce in Georgetown at a good profit, which he would use to construct a series of fish-ponds and to buy farming implements. He is the only District Officer or Commissioner in the colony's service who is an Englishman, and in him one could not help sensing a real passion for bettering the conditions of primitive peoples. In Seggars's case the Indians are at a stage when there is no alternative to paternalism, and he loves his Akawaios as a father loves his children.

He had been in Bartica for the preliminary trial of a young Akawaio at Kamerang who had murdered an old man. Twelve witnesses, including a chief called King George,[1] had been brought to Bartica for the hearing, and would go on to Georgetown for the trial. Seggars looked on the whole case as an excellent opportunity to demonstrate to the Indians that the white man does not tolerate murder and that its consequences may be drastic. At the same

[1] When, on one occasion, I asked an Indian what his name was, he replied, 'Sirmalcolmcampbell'.

time he recognized that the boy had acted according to tribal custom, and he hoped that he would be acquitted.[1] The murder itself was of some interest as a revelation of the workings of the Indian mind. The old man had, in the opinion of the boy, charged him too much for some gunpowder and the boy had objected, whereupon the old man had threatened to 'blow' on him and his family. The quarrel and the threats had continued until the boy, in fear that kenaima, in the shape of the old man, would strike, followed him when he went fishing and battered him to death with a club. When Seggars accused him of the killing he had made no denial, since in the morality of the tribe it had been an act of self-defence.

Most Indian murders are of a similar kind. Later in my journey, on the Ataro River, I saw the scene of the murder, some years ago, of the kenaima Moses. An Akawaio named Bagit, whose wife and daughter had been killed by Moses' blowing, called on the kenaima one day, chatted with him for an hour or two, and then shot him. A District Officer eventually heard of the crime and Bagit was brought to Georgetown for trial. The following translated passage of his evidence is, I think, of interest.

My son Shiawuk and I [he said], shot Moses in the late afternoon because he was a very evil man. He used to boast about killing other Indians in Kurupung, Mazaruni, Kako and Ataro, and said he would wipe others off the face of the earth. He boasted also of killing a lot of my family. Before the killing Moses came to my camp with the barrel of a gun in his hand, and assaulted my sister with his hand in the dark of the night. Moses also killed my eldest brother. That is why all we Indians hated Moses. I have come to go through the court and speak what I know about what Moses did because I would like to be finished with this matter.

At various points in this book I have mentioned kenaima, which is perhaps the most potent force in all Indian life. I never missed an opportunity to ask an Indian about it — or him — but almost always the replies to my questions were evasive. Some ethnologists believe kenaima to be an evil spirit, others that it is an actual man,

[1] He was, in fact, acquitted.

like Moses, who is motivated towards evil. Others equate it with
the werewolf legend of Europe and the idea of jaguars changing
into men found in Mexico and Central America. My own feeling is
that it is, so to speak, a collective noun which embodies that side of
the principle of evil which ends in unnatural death — in the primitive
state this means almost all forms of death other than from old age;
thus kenaima can be applied both to the disembodied spirit and to
the local incarnations of that spirit.

During my first conversation with Vincent Roth in Georgetown
he had made my flesh creep by a description of the methods of the
embodied kenaima. This possessed man will follow his victim for
weeks or months, waiting for an opportunity to kill, and since he
only attacks someone who is alone, any man guilty of an act for
which he expects revenge will see to it that he never walks alone.
When the moment comes, the kenaima clubs his victim unconscious
and pierces his tongue with a poisoned wood splinter or a snake
fang; the purpose of this is to swell the tongue so that the man is
incapable of speech. The kenaima must never actually kill, but
simply provide the conditions for a lingering death. He may now
dislocate the victim's bones one by one and lubricate his body with a
poison that enters the pores; or he will draw out the guts *per rectum*,
pierce them with a wood splinter and replace them. The victim may
be able to crawl to his village, where eventually he dies, still unable
to name his murderer, since he cannot speak. In some cases the
kenaima may be the man who desires revenge himself, or his close
relation, or a hired assassin. In every case the murder will always
have been done in accordance with the sacred laws of vengeance and
retaliation.

I asked Mr Roth if these examples of kenaima killings had come
within his experience, and he admitted that they had not, but that
he had heard of such killings during his years in the Interior. In
remote parts of the colony killings like this still probably take place
without anyone knowing, but I am inclined to think that such
elaborate acts belong to an earlier period. All the same the theory
of kenaima is still very much alive among the Indians as the source
of death and evil. The two recent murders among the Akawaios (a
tribe celebrated for kenaima power) were the direct result of the
belief. Probably both Moses and the old man of Kamerang had

terrorized their murderers' families by blowing and by threats of using kenaima powers against them. According to the Indian law of retaliation the victims may then avenge themselves. In so doing, they in their turn presumably become kenaimas, although Bagit and the Kamerang boy both seemed to act from a sense of moral purpose — 'he was a very evil man', said Bagit of Moses. The fact that both avenger and avenged become in turn kenaimas suggests how innocent the Indian is of the civilized conception of good and evil — or how confused the two conceptions are in his mind. The confusion has spread to the minds of most people who have written on the subject, and I certainly do not claim that in these paragraphs I have done anything to lessen the confusion. I prefer to think that kenaima is for the Indian a word of a thousand uses and subtle connotations, a symbol-word as elusive in its meaning as Ibsen's wild duck. I will end my remarks on this grisly subject with a gruesome quotation from Richard Schomburgk's experiences of kenaima:

To discover . . . in which district the kenaima lives, the Indians practise an abominable custom which, as witness of it, gave me an awful shudder. To the accompaniment of an awe-inspiring, monotonous song, the corpse [of the kenaima's victim] was carried to an open space where . . . the father cut off the thumb and fingers from each hand, the large and small toes from each foot, and a piece from each heel and threw the bits into a new pot filled with water. In the meantime a fire had been lighted near the corpse and the vessel placed on it. The water commenced to boil, and according to the side over the edge of which the boiling and bubbling water first threw the mortal remnants as they started bobbing up and down indicated the direction where the kenaima was hiding. There was something gruesome, something devilish about it to see these copper-coloured individuals during the singing of the song of sorrow staring with steadfast gaze upon the prancing pieces to catch the very moment for the first one to be slithered over with the bubbles. Directly this occurrence took place it was notified by a yell that pierced one's very marrow. One of the fingers had fallen over the brim on the western side of the pot, in the very direction whence the Indians had come. After long consultation they seemed to be of the opinion that the kenaima must be living in their own village.

I was far from alone in the fading light of the evening of my arrival at Kamerang. The balcony of the wooden rest-house where I was staying was filled with silent staring figures who observed my every movement, old old women with facial tattoos that marked their various proficiencies like Girl Guides' badges, old men with white shirts and fewer marks of proficiency, squat girls with shining black hair held tightly back, and round mongoloid faces, slimmer boys and young men — all satisfying the innate curiosity of the Indian. At last I knew something of what it was like to be a plate-mouthed Ubangi savage on view in some circus sideshow. I returned the staring with a little of my own. Physically these were the purest Indians I had yet seen — there was no sign of the survival of carelessly sown European genes. Yet in one or two of the faces I thought I saw slight negroid characteristics, and later I learnt that some Indians had once brought to Kamerang a Negro baby girl whom they had found over the mountain. She had been brought up as an Akawaio.

When I had finished my meal, still watched by the inanimate faces, weirder still in the feeble light, I asked one young man who spoke English if his people would sing for me. He called up three young men of his own age, and they stood in front of me like bashful choirboys in a row. Then together they produced one of the strangest series of sounds I have ever heard — not for its barbarousness but for its combination of primitive atonalism and a harmonic scheme reminiscent of Baptist chapels and the Salvation Army. The words themselves I recognized after a while to be basically English, though it was difficult to believe it was not some primitive language.

> By and by we see the Lord
> By and by we see the Lord

they sang and when it was over I asked Joe Mitchell, the man who spoke English, where they had learnt the hymn. 'At our mission up-river,' he replied proudly. 'We Seven Day Adventist and know plenty songs. People down here Kamerang side not Adventist they no know the true story of the Lord who is coming.'

facing, above: THE GRUMMAN AMPHIBIAN LANDING AT KAMERANG MOUTH
below: AKAWAIO HALLELUJAH INDIANS DANCING TO HALLELUJAH CHANTS

He talked on, smug in his religion and rather contemptuous of the people of Kamerang. I looked round at the exponents of 'Hallelujah' and told Joe to ask them to sing. 'They no know new songs only old,' he said, and I told him that I preferred old ones. He interpreted my request, and without a change of expression one old woman closed her eyes and began a repetitious but strangely moving chant, a kind of murmuring wail, with a chorus in which the others joined:

Bazigo, bazigo, wobuleima Papai yebu
Bazigo, bazigo, maimubai Papai yebu
Hallelujah, hallelujah.

Hallelujah came into all the chants they sang, and the words Papai and Mamai Meili. When I learnt more about this strange religion I found that Papai was a kind of God or Christ figure, and Mamai Meili was a corruption of Mother Mary. The lines quoted above would be translated as,

Sisters, sisters, we must pray, our Father is coming,
Sisters, sisters, we must find words, our Father is coming,
Hallelujah, hallelujah.

After some questioning I found a Hallelujah man who could speak a little English, and from him I learnt enough about the religion to make me realize that I had come across something unique in British Guiana, an autochthonous version of Christianity — a religion that existed almost entirely without benefit of missionary teaching. In other parts of the colony I had found this imposed and regimented Christianity a dull façade; here, on the contrary, was a living and passionately held religion which, if its dogma would not have been quite acceptable at the Vatican, was Christian in principle. The few answers which my informant gave me made me determined to know more.

I asked him who had brought his people their religion, and he said it had been brought to them by someone called Abel from the Rupununi savannahs. I asked him what he thought about Christ, and he said, 'Which one — Jesus or Christ the bad man who then was good?' 'Jesus,' I said. 'Oh,' he said, 'me know nothing about

facing, above: FIRST STAGE IN THE MAKING OF A 'WOODSKIN' CANOE
below: AKAWAIO HALLELUJAH INDIANS AT PRAYER AT IMBAIMADAI

P

he.' 'Who is Mamai Meili?' I asked. 'She our Big Sister.' He told me that they made pilgrimages to the village of Amokokopai where Abel had lived and built his *chochi*, and that their day of prayer and worship was a day called *Zundaga*. I asked him if the white men had ever come to his people to tell him about Jesus and Christianity, and he said none had ever come. Hallelujah had come to them direct from God, had nothing to do with the white people.

The origin of Hallelujah, as far as I can make out, goes back nearly a century. A Makushi Indian called Bichiwung came down to Georgetown and worked as a servant in the house of a clergyman there. He was taught the rudiments of Christianity, and eventually, with a collection of useful European objects, returned to the Rupununi, where, with his descriptions of the good life of Christians and the demonstration of the objects he had brought with him, he convinced his fellows that Christianity had its advantages. He preached his version of the gospel and was heard by the Akawaio, Abel, who was travelling in the savannahs. During this period all Indians who had come into contact with the white people seemed to have had an obsessive desire to change the colour of their skins,[1] associating the luxurious living of the whites with their pigmentation. One of Bichiwung's promises was that converts to Christianity would lose their copper skins, and a tenet of the Hallelujah religion which Abel based on Bichiwung's teaching was a change of skin — converts would become *Palanagula*, or pale-faces. Queen Victoria had her place in the heavenly hierarchy as Kwin, the daughter of Papai, or God. Abel's teaching seems to have had the basic concepts of Christianity; he taught the virtues of hospitality and good husbandry, that *magoi*, or sin, was to be rejected and kindness and goodness to be pursued. He created a network of *ebulus*, or religious leaders, who were distinct from the piaimen. There was immense enthusiasm for Abel's teaching among the Akawaios, and although he died about forty-five years ago his name is still venerated and his teaching accepted. I was told that his youngest daughter, born in his old age, was still living at Amokokopai.

Missionary societies operating in every part of the world could study the case of Hallelujah with profit. It seems to me that the effects of a conversion from a primitive state of animism to the

---

[1] The desire still exists, but it is far less obsessive.

metaphysical subtleties of Christianity are likely to produce chaos in minds incapable of so sudden a change in belief and morality. I know that in fact the process is slow, and lip service to Christianity covers an adherence to tribal ways. But if men like Bichiwung and Abel grew up as a natural growth, their odd teaching would form the necessary bridge between primitive thought and Christian or 'civilized' concepts. I say all this on the presumption that the integration of the Indian into the colony's life will be pursued in all seriousness — and that Christianity will play its part in the civilizing process.

Joe Mitchell took me hunting next morning. The forest had been cleared for a mile or more around the village, and as we made our way across the burnt earth between the great buttressed stumps of moras I felt the beautiful, unviolent heat of the mid-morning sun. The sky, unlike the usually glowering skies of the lower areas of the colony, was a vault of blue, the air cool and without humidity; it seemed to be a different world from any I had yet known in these parts, protected by mountains and precipices from the blanketing drift of cloud from the Atlantic. On the Mazaruni at Tumereng, hardly an hour had passed without a burst of rain, but Joe told me there had been no rain at Kamerang for two weeks. With these climatic differences I expected to find a different kind of forest, but to my untrained eye it was all as I had known it. I recognized new bird sounds — the rushed call of the pompadour chatterer and the distant billing of birds for whom Joe had names I have forgotten.

There was little opportunity for me to contemplate the scenery or listen to the forest murmurs; my questions to Joe had convinced him that I was a man of power and substance in the colony, with a vital interest in his problems. He had learnt his English and the ways of civilization partly as a launchman on the Mazaruni, and in so doing he had lost the aloofness of the Indian and the reluctance to talk to any but his own people. Joe never stopped talking. He was, he said, not an Akawaio but an Arekuna, and had been born in the village of Sant' Elena in the Venezuelan Gran Sabaña, where his uncle had been chief. An American Seventh Day Adventist had come to the village when he was a boy, and he and his family had been converted to Adventism. 'But the Catholics,' he said, 'they no want Adventism and they plan kill American and later my uncle the chief hear they going kill him as well so he take me and my brother and we come over border here to British Guiana and settle up-river at Paruima where there is Adventist mission. The years go by and my uncle go back to Sant' Elena but leave we in Paruima, and soon we hear uncle he dead. Perhaps die natural perhaps killed by Catholics. We never know.'

It is difficult for an Indian to enter into the life of a village other than his own, even if he can claim tribal kinship. In Joe's case he was from another tribe, speaking a variant of the 'true' Carib spoken by the Akawaios. His life would almost certainly have been that of an outsider, and although he did not say so I imagine the American missionary and his wife, who were living at Paruima at the time of his arrival, would have taken a special interest in him. The circumstances of his life had produced immense ambition in him — a concept I had imagined impossible to the fatalistic Indian mind — a longing for self-realization, and an obsession with money as the means to that end. His attitudes and values were in a way parallel to those of the crazy mixed-up kid of the Western world. He told me that Bill Seggars had offered him the job as storeman at Kamerang. 'But if me take that,' he said, 'me will have position to keep up, and fifty dollars a month not enough for keeping up position. Why Government no wish help a man who wishes develop he character?' He repeated this last question frequently during the morning. I sympathized with his difficulties and admired his ambition to improve himself, but their corollary was a certain priggishness. He laughed at and scorned the Hallelujahs — a common thing among the Adventists who count themselves in every way superior; he looked down on Indians who were satisfied with their life as it was; he told me he had not yet, at twenty-six, found a girl fit to marry, and he doubted if he ever would. Even this I could have taken, but in the end there was no doubt about it: Joe Mitchell was a crashing bore, and if I had not let him know firmly that I had heard enough, I doubt if we should have bagged the excellent Dokorra partridge which I had for dinner that night.

I was glad Joe did not volunteer as a drogher for my march to Roraima, although he was going to captain the corial that was to take us up the Kamerang to Paruima. The chief drogher was a man of about forty — Austin Vierra, who spoke a little English, could cook, and, so Seggars had assured me, was a man of charming, equable temperament. His younger brother Peter was coming, and two of his friends, also in their late teens, made up the party. All four came to my terrace that afternoon and sat at my table, contemplating me endlessly, smoking my cigarettes and turning to each other occasionally to make what I hoped were appreciative remarks about me. To pass the time I produced the very vague map of the area which I had brought with me, to show them the route we should be taking. I knew that maps would be entirely meaningless to them, and expected only the usual aloof curiosity of the Indian. Instead they crowded excitedly round the table and looked with intense interest at the pattern of contours and rivers. This was not, as I thought at the time, an interest in a map *qua* map, but part of the fascination which all written or drawn things have for the primitive Indian. Pieces of written or printed paper will be kept and cherished for years as charms or amulets. It is perhaps thought to be part of the magical power by which the white man has won his power and advantage. One day, in the forest, when we had made camp, I saw Austin show Peter the inside of a cigarette packet which I had thrown away, and Peter burst into uncontrollable laughter, which was later shared by the others until all four were in absolute fits. I asked to see whatever it was had caused the joke and, with much reluctance, Austin handed me the cigarette paper on which in pencil he had drawn the sort of representation of a man which a child of three will make. I looked for some phallic attribute or pornographic meaning but I could see none. The joke had evidently been the achievement of a drawing at all — the achievement, in fact, of some of the magical power of the white man. But why this should have produced laughter I do not know. However, that first day, encouraged by their interest, I traced our route and asked Austin's advice over various problems.

I was approaching Roraima from an unusual direction. Robert Schomburgk, who discovered the mountain in 1838, came to it from the Rupununi, which lies to the south. Carl Appun in 1864, Barrington Brown in 1869, and Michael McTurk and Boddam-Whetham in 1878, had all approached its eastern mural face through the forest, experiencing the extraordinary scene of the great red mesa rearing up out of the forest. Not wanting the boredom of returning the way I had come, I was planning to move in a circle from Kamerang to Kamerang, with Roraima as the climax. If we approached the eastern face we could get there in about a week, but that would be followed by a two weeks' march across the Gran Sabaña with our backs to Roraima. I preferred to miss the sight of the mountain from the forest and have the long, expectant savannah journey first, with Roraima appearing now and then between the mountains or below the clouds. I am sure this is psychologically the most satisfying way of going to the mountain.

We set out from Kamerang Mouth at seven o'clock, in a twenty-foot wooden dugout with an outboard engine. The river was narrow, tacoubas blessedly few, and giant bullet trees reared up on either side. It is one of the most beautiful rivers in the colony, but by now I was becoming blasé about the beauties of tropical rivers and spent most of the day reading. At midday we stopped for some cassava bread at a village, from the highest point of which I could see the distant mesas half encircling the horizon, stepping stones to Roraima itself. An hour or two before sunset we reached falls which are impassable at most seasons of the year. The water rushed white and furious for a hundred yards, and beyond the river point lay the heavy rocks that formed the falls proper. It was clearly impassable and we tied up at the landing to make the long portage to calmer water. We had brought two extra boat hands so that, by each man taking the utmost he was able to carry, there was no need to make two journeys.

At the upper landing we fortunately found a corial large enough to take us and our baggage, and with the Indians' usual communism about such things Joe did not think twice about screwing the engine into position. Huts on the river bank now became more frequent, and as we approached each one we would slow down and Austin would hail the owner of the hut. In three cases a colloquy followed and then we would proceed; at the end of the fourth exchange the young Indian on the bank went into his hut and we remained stationary. Three minutes later the Indian reappeared with a girl, loaded with a packed warishi. They got into their woodskin and paddled towards us; when they were alongside they held on to the gunwale of the corial, our engine started and we both proceeded up-river to Paruima. Austin was sitting behind me and I turned to ask him why the Indians were coming with us. 'Me no know trail Roraima, sir,' he said. 'This man William come that country, he know trail.'

The girl, one of the prettiest Indian girls I had yet seen, was his wife Cecilia. He had brought her because he had nobody else to bring, said Austin. An Indian from one village will never travel with people from another village unless he brings a companion from his own. It is part of the necessary protection against kenaima.

It was dark when we reached Paruima, but our approaching halloos had brought a cluster of figures to the landing to receive us with lantern light. They stood silent and almost motionless on the bank above us as we landed in the squelching mud, their faces red and malevolent in the light thrown upwards by their lanterns. They led us up the path to a clearing where a large wooden hut stood on stilts in the coastal fashion. It was the chief's hut, I was told, and to my questions the Indians answered that Mr Black, the Negro missionary from Georgetown, was still down on the coast. The chief's hut was filled with people, swinging in their hammocks and talking. Although there had been a lantern or two at the landing, here the only light came from the low and slimly crescent moon. I tripped over protruding legs, smashed my knee against a bench, and was pleased finally to relax in my hammock while Austin coaxed some embers into flame and prepared me something to eat.

My main memory of that strange night is of an incident which happened an hour later, when the hut was silent except for the heavy breathing of sleepers. I, too, was almost asleep when I realized that I was no longer alone in the little room that had been given me. I looked up through my mosquito netting to see the face of a young Indian girl smiling down at me like some protoplasmic materialization. In a dazed second I sorted out the various possibilities of the visit; curiosity, a generous thought on the part of the chief that I might wish to have the favours of his prettiest daughter, or an illicit idea of the girl herself. I closed my eyes, and looked again: she was still there, smiling. Asininely I said, 'Do you want something?' and then, with a giggle that proved she was no chimera, she had retreated into the shadows, while I lay awake for a long time, wondering and a little disturbed. The incident had stirred thoughts that had lain dormant for a long time. But I did not pursue the vision.

Paruima lies in what is probably the most fertile part of British Guiana; there are ample vegetables and fruit here at all seasons of the year, and cassava grows long and thick in the root. I asked the chief for as much food as we could carry, and the boys festooned their warishis with great hands of plantains and bananas, pineapples, limes and grapefruit; crisp cassava cakes, two feet in diameter, were broken and wedged between the laces. For all this I gave the chief half a pound of gunpowder, some shot, a hundred fish-hooks and some small apron beads for his women. He was clearly pleased.

Before starting out that morning I had a talk with William, our guide. He spoke no English, but had learnt some Spanish during his early years in the Venezuelan savannah, where he was born. As my Spanish was as limited and fractured as his own we could make some sort of rudimentary conversation. He had never been to Roraima, he told me, but he knew where it lay. He knew an old woman in Paruima who would be able to give him further details of the route. We found the old woman at work outside her hut and she gave William what was apparently a detailed account of the route. When I asked him how long ago the old woman had gone to the mountain he told me that she had never been there — she remembered the description of the journey given by a man from Paruima who had been to the mountain when she was a girl. The women form a repository of tribal information; like spinning, weaving and cooking, it is their duty to train their memories to hold all details which are of practical use — in lieu of any other way of recording them. The women thus share in the incessant talk which takes place in the huts at night, when their men go over each detail of the day, reliving their experiences in speech, just as simple — and not so simple — people do the whole world over. In other respects an Indian's memory can be remarkable — he will do a job of work for a European and disappear without payment: years later he will turn up at the same place and casually ask for the money or kind due to him.

Joe Mitchell and the two boat boys returned to Kamerang that morning and I, Austin, Peter, Antonio, Samson, William and Cecilia took the corial up-river. Within an hour we had come to another stretch of impassable rapids. The Kamerang was navigable no longer. To the right the forest spread up a steep hillside, the first of the hills we should have to surmount as we gradually moved from Kamerang's 1800 feet to Roraima's 9000 feet. We landed on a sandbank, the droghers rearranged their burdens, adjusted the warishi straps to their shoulders and foreheads, and without a glance at me moved off into the bush, Cecilia taking a seventy-pound load with the rest. From now on the journey would be on foot.

We were climbing or descending all that day, the land rising in a series of steep ridges in whose clefts broad creeks ran down to the Kamerang. Where the slopes were best exposed to the sun the Indians had made large clearings and planted their plantains that now formed a fantastic forest of thirty-foot trees, composed, it seemed, entirely of the great tattered leaves, moving in the breeze like the ears of shaggy elephants. And where the forest was un-touched we moved through large stands of Brazil nut trees, the trail strewn with the nuts in their carapace, now like sodden cricket balls. There were no tree-trunks laid across the creeks; each had to be forded and I gave up all hope of dry feet that day. Even on the steepest slopes, where I needed to conserve all my breath, the boys kept up their ceaseless monotone of chatter as they marched behind me. At one point Antonio slipped on the smooth mud and the rest roared with laughter; I felt a point of contact through this primitive urge to laugh at the mishaps of others.

At midday we crossed the Kamerang, picking our way from stone to stone across the torrential water. An Indian family from the savannahs was resting on the other bank and we joined them for twenty minutes. Quietly Cecilia took the small child that one of the women was carrying and fed it at her own breast. William told me that she had recently lost a child. We must have been gaining height all day, for by late afternoon we were in a region high enough to hear the bell-bird.[1] Suddenly, in the absolute silence, it seemed as if a delicate silver gong had been struck — dor-o-o-o-ng — and then a moment or two later the curt answer, kong-kay. I stood still to give all my attention to the repeated call; I was listening to one

---

[1] *Casmoryhnchus carunculatus.*

of the most beautiful natural sounds I had ever heard, more haunting even than the call of the necklaced jungle wren, pure and effortless, almost ventriloquial in its effect. I went on, and the higher I climbed the more it seemed that all around me the bell-birds were making a fugue of their two calls. Sometimes the dor-o-o-o-ng would come from above, and the kong-kay from twenty yards away — the distances gave a beautiful perspective to the sounds. I sat down and listened, while I waited for the others to catch me up.

'I want to see a bell-bird, Austin,' I said. 'Can you find one for me?'

'*Parandorai*, sir?' he replied, and moved off into the bush silently, with me following.

A few minutes later he stopped beneath a mora and pointed up into its crown. After searching with my eyes I could just see a small white patch, the singing male bird, but without field-glasses it was impossible to make out any details. Not until long afterwards did I learn that this pure white bird is a little larger than a dove and that a wattle, or caruncle, an inch long, protrudes from its forehead, hanging loose during its periods of silence but inflating like some children's party blower when the calls begin.

I shall always be grateful to the bell-bird; during all the long hard days that I spent in the higher altitudes of the forest it gave me, by the beauty of its notes, a kind of encouragement — something to fix my mind on in order to forget the hardness of the way. That first day I was in no need of such help; I was fresh and delighted to be moving through the forest once again. Even so, when the bell-birds had stopped calling, I found my mind wandering away from the things of the forest, pursuing strange irrational trails of its own. I was beginning to long for the light and air of the savannah.

An hour or two before sunset we came to a battered benab by a creek, where we decided to camp. The benab was triangular in shape and just large enough to sleep one man; the structure was strong but the leaves needed replacing. I rested in my hammock while the boys busied themselves with unpacking and bringing water from the creek. It had not rained all day and, foolishly, rain was now far from my mind. Suddenly a few heavy drops fell on my head and thirty seconds later the rain had come. My hammock was swung between two trees and was well wetted by the time it was slung beneath the leaking benab. The deluge went on and on, turning the site to mud, water running in streams towards the creek. Darkness came and the rain showed no sign of diminishing. We fixed a groundsheet to keep some of the rain out of the benab, and I lay in the cold damp hammock, knowing that water was coursing down its scale lines. The boys sat under a tree, drenched but resigned. The rain eased slightly and they went out to find the saplings and the leaves to build themselves a benab. In a corner of mine Austin made a small fire and heated a tin of meat for me, which I ate, utterly dispirited. Later in the night the rain was spent and the fireflies played through the forest all around us. I had never seen fireflies so large or so powerful, moving heavily like swinging lanterns rather than in the elusive leaps of their Mediterranean cousins.

I was glad to be up and to find a patch of sun to warm myself before we broke camp. All morning we climbed with no descent, and the path took the slope without the easy zigzag of European paths. The Indian goes by the shortest route even if it is the hardest. I was expecting to reach the savannah in another day or two, and when at midday I saw bright light shining through the forest in front of us I imagined we had come to a large clearing. Then, to my delight and amazement I moved in a few steps from the full, undiminished forest to find a panorama of green rolling savannahs descending gently to the valley of the Ouchi, with the flat-topped Warimatepu beyond to the left. It was a wonderful moment of liberation, and in my excitement I did not fully realize the phenomenon of this sudden change. To left and right behind me ran the perimeter of the forest, giant trees and vegetation abutting directly on to the open savannah like the edge of an English wood; no gradual lessening of growth, but a firm line of demarcation. These forests behind me that stretched uninterrupted to within a few miles of the coast, west to the Orinoco and east to the Amazon, had ended like this, with a bang not a whimper. From now on savannah dominated the land, with forest merely veining the courses of rivers.

The air was dry and cool, the sun not too strong and pleasantly occluded by passing clouds. I sang my way through an area of trees burnt years ago, their remains standing far apart, white,

ghostly stumps. We came to the Ouchi river, a mile or two above
its great falls, where the water, though still violent in its course, is
passable. It was about sixty yards broad and I realized how
treacherous it was when Austin made a reconnaissance crossing,
picking his way with care across the slimy stones, using a long stick
to test the stones and the depths of the water. The boys carried their
packs across, linking to each other three at a time, for the strength
of the water was much greater than it looked, so that when my turn
came I had to lean into it up to my thighs in order not to be thrown
backwards. If a foothold were lost and one were carried away by
the current into deeper water I doubt if there would be much
chance of getting to the bank. One would be carried downstream
to the eight-hundred-foot falls and hurled into the gorge.

On the farther bank we rested and had a meal, before climbing
for half an hour through the riverside bush. We found a reward
at the top, a large area of flat savannah, sweeping finally down in all
directions to give a view of blue-hazed mesas that made a panorama
taking up half the circumference of the horizon. To the left
Wakaoyeng, flat and descending in three long terraces, its final
escarpment descending into dark forest; then Warimatepu and
Wararantepu, both thrusting up from the forest; and in between
the Kumbiata savannah, folded and expansive, patterned with
ribbons of bush, intensely green and unmodified by any human
hand.

'Tepu', Austin told me, meant 'mountain', and the etymology
seemed familiar. Variants of tepec in many Mexican languages mean
hill or mountain (Tehuantepec, Hill of the Jaguars; Popocatepetl,
Smoking Mountain) and I presumed there must be a language link
here. It was months later, when reading Humboldt, that I was able
to take the link still further. Humboldt had noticed the similarity
between *tepetl*, the Carib *tebou*, and the Tamanac *tepu*, stone.[1] He
traces the word back to the Tartar root — *tep*, stone. If his etymology
is sound this must form one of the few language links between
Eastern Asiatic peoples and the Indians of the New World.

With the sun at four o'clock (I was not using my watch) we
climbed a small hill on whose flat summit we had seen two round
adobe houses with cone-shaped roofs. Though they were in good

[1] The Tamanac word for mountain is *tepu-iri*, place of stones.

repair they had apparently been abandoned by their owners, and contained no signs of possession other than a black water-gourd and a few pots. William had led us to the place, saying that he remembered it as an inhabited farm in his childhood. I asked him about his own home in the Gran Sabaña, and he pointed beyond the mountain of Ubutepu and said, '*Dos dias más, señor* — two more days.' He added that he did not know how much of his parents' house would still be standing, or even if there would be any trace of it at all. But he wanted to show Cecilia his own true land — she had never left the forest all her life. William, in fact, was the only one of our party who had travelled in the savannahs. Austin knew only the small savannahs not far from Kamerang. I had expected to see signs of wonder that such country as we were in should exist, but the Indian is the most unemotional creature alive.

Next morning the trail was a long descent, with Ubutepu gradually changing as we skirted it, the strange funnel protruding from its centre broadening into a turret. We came to the Kamerang once more, now a creek of rushing water, but an easy crossing. It was here that I learnt not to enjoy the approach to creeks, however cold and clear their water: minute kaboura flies rose in clouds as we forded, attacking all exposed skin. Within a few days I was covered with the specks of congealed blood which their bites leave behind. Insect repellents were no good — they were washed away by sweat as soon as applied.

A solitary round hut appeared on the horizon and I could make out naked figures of women at work in the compound. When we were sighted the women rushed into the hut and emerged on our arrival wearing tattered cotton frocks. A man stood with a long stick which he was smoothing with a knife — an occupation which had no practical purpose, merely a form of whittling popular with the savannah Arekunas. As we were leaving, a five-year-old girl, naked except for a blue queyu apron, approached the hut from the near-by woods; she carried a small warishi on her back filled with firewood and corncobs. She put down her burden, and regarded us with a worldly frown.

We went into the bush along the track she had used, and soon were cutting our way through strong secondary vegetation — until William decided that we had come in the wrong direction. We retraced our steps. Once we had found the track the going was easier, but the sun could penetrate these low trees so that the forest floor was far more luxuriant and overgrown than the true tropical forest. I was lacerated with sword grass, and sometimes for ten minutes at a time we would crawl along tunnels in the vegetation less than three feet high. Nature was struggling everywhere to make the greatest use of this abundance of sunlight: trunks were festooned with epiphytes, and lianas writhed more fantastically than I had ever seen them.

Savannah once more, and new round hills formed graceful curves; green, green, as far as one could see: green relieved, as we walked, by scores of small enchanting flowers — sturdy flowers, as they must be to exist in this green desert of sterile earth, where cattle cannot live on the un-nutritious grass and few plants will grow.

By mid-afternoon we were looking down a long rocky slope at the derelict houses standing on a bluff beyond a creek. William pointed to them and with some emotion said, '*Esta la casa de mi papa*', and he and Cecilia walked quickly ahead. The roofs had largely fallen away to reveal the complicated skeleton structure on which the thatching was laid; there were gaps in the adobe walls, but the husks of a melonlike fruit containing eatable beans showed that it had been used within the past month by nomadic Arekunas. It was charming to watch William talking to Cecilia, pointing to the near-by mountain as he perhaps told her some exploit of his child-hood, or sweeping his arm through the points of the compass to indicate that all this vast area of land was his, theirs. Then he found the hollowed-out trunk of a tree, which his mother had probably used as a washtub; when the sun had gone beyond the red mountain, and the kabouras were no longer active, I went down to bathe and found William and Cecilia washing their clothes in the tub. It was as if they were making some symbolic domestic act on his own land.

I went to sleep looking up to the wide ridge of land that obscured all the country lying beyond, except for one pointing finger of a mountain. Perhaps tomorrow we should have our first sight of Roraima.

Reluctantly, sadly, William led us next morning up to the ridge, beyond which was a paradise of wild flowers among the rocks. We

escended slowly through some passages of difficult bush. In the
pen country some sixty miles away a snakelike sliver of flat moun-
ain showed beyond the eastern ridge of Kutepu, and as the light
hanged and clouds dispersed its pink surface and fissures became
pparent. My heart rose with excitement — we had sighted the
vestern face of Roraima. The clouds descended once more and all
vas vanished.

We camped in the bush by a creek — it was the only place where
ve could sling hammocks — and I was driven mad by kabouras
ntil sunset came and I went slowly off to sleep, thinking that each
ay was like some serial story, ending with an exciting promise for
he morrow. From now on Roraima might appear from the clouds
t any time. The morning was disappointing; grey, cloudy with
he threat of rain, so that when we reached the summit of a high
idge the vast panorama of the Venezuelan savannah lay in mist,
nd even Kutepu was now invisible. It was evidently a rainy area,
or we had to walk for an hour across a bog, sinking up to our
alves at each step. A long rocky slope occupied us for the next
our, and this gave on to rolling moorland, now dark and miserable
s the landscape of Wuthering Heights. I calculated from the known
eight of the mountains that we had reached an altitude of some
ve thousand feet. No wonder this savannah was so different from
hat of the Rupununi, which lies at four hundred feet. Driving
ain from the north-east followed for some hours. All day a dark
lue curtain of cloud obscured that part of the landscape I wanted
nost to see. We camped, wet and miserable, at a bush oasis in this
noorland desert.

Sunday came, and the hardest day of all, though the most
nagnificent yet. In the gloomy morning we started across the
ogged savannah with the whole range of mountains still in blue
loud. Then Ualkar, the Monkey Mountain, began to be visible;
s the morning went by the mountains cleared, and it was hot in
he sun as we climbed an immense spur to receive another panoramic
iew. The descent on the other side was through a sort of Dead
Man's Gulch fissured with volcanic cracks. Then up again to see
he valley of the Iruani, blue and sparkling far below, twisting off
nto Venezuela, with green, palm and bush-covered hillsides — a
velcome lushness after the desolation of the last two days.

William said we must make the two-thousand-foot descent to the valley and climb another two thousand feet on the other side to the Arekuna village on the top of the ridge. We would need a boat to get across the river, he added, and to give the Arekunas warning must send a smoke signal. With delight Austin and Peter put matches to the grass at three places. When the smoke was billowing we began the descent, and before long an answering signal told us that men were coming down to the river to ferry us across. By midday we had reached the river, and as there were no kabouras we bathed while we waited for the boat. As I emerged from the river I looked to where I had presumed Roraima to be and there for a few minutes she lay unclouded, her pink sandstone walls glistening in the sun till the clouds returned.

In my excitement I had not noticed the arrival of a long dugout paddled by two young Arekunas with shy manners and broad Brazilian straw hats, guns, cutlasses and blowpipes. They were the first people we had seen for four days and I was curious about the village high above us where we were to spend the night. It was a precarious crossing with heavy loads and a strong current in midstream. Then came a very long climb, up an almost vertical path through slopes of Ité palms which gave first into bush and then into an unending series of steep ridges, on each of which I prayed we should find the village. After two hours my breath came like a groan, and when at last we reached the final ridge I lay quite exhausted.

When I was able to take in my surroundings once more, I gasped at the splendour of the great valley, the slopes we had descended that morning and the series of mountains that formed their backcloth beyond, all counterpaned by sunlight and cloud-shadow. We were on the highest land we had yet reached, dominating the raised landscape like some impregnable fortress. Roraima came through as we walked towards the twelve round huts forming the village; the late sun struck her walls till they sparkled, and only a few wisps of cloud clung to the ramparts.

The village of Uraianda was more civilized than I had expected; the men wore trousers and shirts, the women floral dresses; cows were pastured near the houses and fowls pecked in the grass. Fowl are kept by the Indians neither for their flesh nor eggs, but as pets who pleasantly herald the dawn. Two seven-colour parrots flew around the strangers' hut where we camped and I traded both birds, with bananas, plantains and cassava bread, for shot, gunpowder, beads and salt, with boiled sweets for the children. The red queyu beads which I offered the women were, as at Paruima, politely refused, and I could find no women during my journey who would accept them. I don't know whether they had some magical significance or whether they rejected them on entirely aesthetic grounds; I myself thought them too bright in colour and unpleasantly shiny — but there hadn't been a wide variety to choose from.

I was woken next morning by the concert of howler monkeys from the near-by bush and by the scraping of cassava, with which, long before dawn, the women begin their day. It had been cold and windy all night and I went for a smart walk round the mesa, hoping to see Roraima in her early morning aspect; but all was in thick cloud. It seemed a pity, as we started the long descent from Uraianda, — the parrots, Polly and Macheath, perched on two of the boys' warishis — to lose so much height again, knowing that somewhere we must ascend another three thousand feet to reach the lower slopes of Roraima. We were no longer in open savannah country; around us was a series of hills divided by watercourses and bush. At one point in the bush the track came to an end in thick secondary growth, and William guiltily admitted that we had taken a wrong route an hour before. Wearily we returned to the open hillside and climbed once more to the point where another trail moved faintly off along the ridge of the hill. William took every opportunity during the next days to show me his contrition for having led us astray. By now the character of all the boys and Cecilia had become plain, even though I was able to talk only to Austin and William. Austin, calm, humorous, given to fits of quiet giggles at my various eccentricities, a dependable man who looked after me like a perfect valet — Sir Walter Raleigh had found his Carib an ideal personal servant. Peter, Austin's young brother, smiling and helpful as a good Boy Scout, playing his jaguar-bone flute at night round the camp fire; Antonio and Samson irritated me, I found, the first with his too knowing manner and swaggering walk, the second with his incessant giggling and his habit of imitating my voice in his own language — it had amused me at first, but the joke went on too long. William and Cecilia I felt most attached to; William treated his shy, almost silent wife with undemonstrative love, and when we camped he would sling their hammock some distance from the others and sheath it with sewn-together rice-bags. As soon as we had eaten they would retire into their carapace, murmuring affectionately together until they fell asleep.

In the mid-afternoon of that day, with Roraima no longer visible, rain came again, hard driving rain that soaked us in a minute. Lightning lit up the rolling purple clouds and the thunder reverberated from hill to hill. By camping time we arrived at a benab — or *rancho* as William called them — on the top of a hill. I looked towards the mass of cloud where Roraima lay; in the foreground two hills intersected to form part of an enormous inverted triangle. The rain passed westwards and I could almost see the sun clearing the mists, until the red walls of Roraima, luminous in golden sun, stretched across from hill to hill to form the third side of the triangle. I stayed watching this beautiful sight until the sun set and the vision was gone.

The rain kept off but wind rushed through the benab all night, which I countered with frequent swigs from my brandy flask. Again I was pleased to be up and away to an early start. All morning we made the steep climb of Kaimaritepu,[1] where green and wooded slopes were always just before us, so that we did not glimpse Roraima all morning. At last we came to the flat top of Kaimaritepu, strewn with erratic boulders and lumps of iron ore, and behind us we could see all the pale green hills and savannah of our last three days' march. After ten minutes' walking the country that lay beyond the hill came into full view; below us the Kukenaam trickled along its valley from its source in Mount Kukenaam, which was divided from Roraima itself by a dark cloud-filled cleft. White billowing clouds clung to the mile-long ramparts of Roraima, and at this distance her fissured mural face, rising a sheer fifteen hundred feet from the bush-covered upper slopes, seemed almost toylike. Below the deep fringe of forest the grass-covered slopes swept steeply down for three thousand feet or more, strewn with rocks and patterned in places by dead, branchless, silver-white trees stuck on like

[1] Kamaiwawong on the official map.

cocktail sticks; streams turned in their course and gleamed in the sun.

We descended into the valley of the Kukenaam during the heavy afternoon rain which came each day at the same time. The river was in full spate, and we took some time to find a safe crossing and still longer to pick our way across. It was time to camp and we slung our hammocks in the small area of bush near the river. It was ridden with flying insects of every size and I retreated beneath my mosquito net while insects like giant cockroaches beat angrily against the netting.

'Austin,' I said, while he was cooking my curry and rice, 'round here — wasn't this Bekeranta, the place where all your people long ago had a battle?'

'Yes, sir,' he answered. 'This Bekeranta, the white people's land, place where bad man Awakaipu he come long time ago.'

The amazing story of Awakaipu is well documented. He was an Arekuna Indian who had lived for some time in Georgetown and learnt English. The Schomburgks recognized his usefulness and employed him on their expeditions. Richard Schomburgk speaks in admiration of the way he behaved when attacked by pirai — 'biting his lips with the raging agony he rolled about in the sand; yet no tears flowed from his eyes, no cry passed his lips'. From the tone of Schomburgk's remarks about him he seems to have kept his true nature from his employers. After the Schomburgks had left the colony, Awakaipu, still only twenty-five, was seized by a *folie de grandeur* and wished to make himself chief of all the Indian tribes of British Guiana. He sent messengers throughout the Indian country saying that all who wished to see wonderful happenings, and to know the way to become as rich and powerful as the white men, should meet at the beginning of the dry season in the valley of the Kukenaam at the foot of Mount Roraima. All who came, he said, must forget their quarrels and bring presents, for which they would receive magical presents in return. A thousand Indians from every tribe gathered at the foot of the mountain and gave Awakaipu knives, powder, shot and fish-hooks. In return he gave them pages from *The Times*, which he said would act as charms — I have already mentioned the Indian's reverence for print or drawings. These copies of *The Times* had been used by Richard Schomburgk for pressing his wild flowers.[1]

Awakaipu named his settlement Bekeranta, which is an Indian form of a Dutch-Creole word meaning Land of the Whites. He built a two-storeyed hut, living on the upper floor himself and installing a harem of chosen girls in the floor below. He enhanced his mystery by rarely mixing with the gathered Indians, and when he addressed them he swathed himself in magical ritual garments so that only his eyes were seen through the folds. On these occasions he threatened death to anyone who did not obey him implicitly. He encouraged cassiri drinking-bouts and dancing, hoping that this would induce a state of mind in which all would accept his leadership. Later he decided that he would have to kill all untrustworthy elements so that the others would follow him. On the night of a general orgy he appeared and announced through the folds of his gown that he had just been received in audience by the great spirit Makunaima, who had told him that the Indians must never be driven out of their own land by the white people. They must become greater and more powerful than the whites; they must have white women as wives, and themselves have white skins. Makunaima, he went on, had told him that all gathered at Bekeranta could have white skins. They would have to kill each other and their souls would rise to the summit of Roraima, where they would be reborn and return to the valley of Kukenaam in two days; their skins would be white and they would have all the knowledge of the white people. And they would be the rulers of all the Indians.

Awakaipu had touched the deep-rooted and still surviving skin envy of the Indian; they heard him with terror. Awakaipu seized a war-club, attacked a man and smashed his head open so that the blood spurted into a gourd of cassiri, which he then drank. The drunken Indians now began to fight each other and submerged hatreds erupted once again. It is said that four hundred men, women and children were killed during that night of massacre, and the survivors waited day after day to see the resurrected come down from Roraima. When two weeks had passed there were murmur-

---

[1] 'With nature still lying in perfect peace, and not a breath of air stirring, I would busily take advantage of these clear and quiet moments to dry my damp drying-paper, which consisted of copies of *The Times* that I had bought in London as waste-paper.' *Travels in British Guiana*, vol. II, p. 191.

ings against Awakaipu, who seems to have had sufficient belief in his intimations from Makunaima not to leave the valley. Food was now running out and there was hunger in the camp. Eventually it was realized that there would be no resurrection and a party of Indians went to the two-storeyed hut of Awakaipu and beat him to death with their clubs.

It is a strange, inconclusive story, with no indication of the real state of Awakaipu's mind. I have no doubt of the substantial truth of the incident. Decades later, travellers in the region who knew nothing of the massacre found small portions of *The Times* in Indian huts, being used as amulets — much as Christians might treasure a splinter from the True Cross. (In Appendix F I refer to two parallel incidents.)

When we set out next morning not only the mural face of Roraima was wrapped in cloud, but the whole mass of land that was more than a thousand feet above us. Below this level the air was clear, lit by the early sun that had not yet penetrated the immense night-gathering of clouds around the mountain. We spent two hours wandering in search of the track up the mountain, and at last William found a faint disturbance of the grass that to Indian eyes — not to mine — meant a track.

By this time, high above us and still distant, the lower part of the rock face was visible. It stretched, a vast pink ribbon of sandstone, for a mile on either side of us, ending on the left in the dark gateway between Kukenaam and Roraima. I was never to see that gateway without heavy cloud pouring from it like expressed smoke; it was like some volcanic Avernus. No one has ever explored this strange chasm between the two mountains; as in our case food stocks always begin to dwindle and it is impossible to live off the land in the savannahs, without going on long hunting expeditions, or living, like the Indians, on cassava and plantains. The perpetual saturation of the vegetation and the sunlessness of the place must have produced a unique flora.

At last only thin cumulus streaked along the summit, and I thanked the genius of the place for our good luck in seeing so much of the mountain revealed each day. Often for weeks on end the mass is swathed in unshifting cloud, and I might have made the journey without having seen the mountain at all. One of the Indian names for it is the 'Night Mountain'. The weather conditions we found, though not ideal during the actual climb, were far better than I had expected.

The pale mist dispersed and the definition of the precipice became almost perfect; I could see what appeared to be vertical streaks of white rock running down the pink sandstone, but as we climbed I realized with joy that in spite of it being the dry season these were the cascades of Roraima, 'the ever fertile mother of the rivers'. Six cascades fell in the forest, and another from Kukenaam, the main source of the river below. Roraima's water from this, the south-western face, flows into the Kukenaam as well. The Kukenaam joins the Yuruani to form the Caroni, a tributary of the Orinoco; from the two and a half mile long eastern face cascades become streams that finally link with the Mazaruni and the Essequibo. The quadrangle formed by Roraima, Kukenaam, Ayang-katsibang and Marima is the watershed of the three great river areas of Guiana: the Orinoco, the Essequibo and the Amazon. These cascades are famous among the Indians of Guiana from the Orinoco to the Amazon. Raleigh, at the junction of the Orinoco and the Caroni, was told of Roraima, though he does not mention it by name:

> There falleth over it a mightie river which toucheth no part of the side of the mountaine, but rusheth over the top of it, and falleth to the ground with a terrible noyse and clamor, as if 1000 great belles were knockt one against another. I think there is not in the worlde so straunge an ouerfall, nor so wonderful to beholde; *Berreo* told me that it hath Diamondes and other precious stones on it, and that they shined from very farre off: but what it hath I know not, neyther durst he or any of his men ascende to the toppe of the saide mountaine, those people adioyning being his enemies and the way to it so impassible.

The overfalls were not as magnificent as Raleigh's imagination had them, but they were beautiful to see, though they made me think, as they descended from the ramparts of this great fortress, of the streams of boiling oil poured from the machicolations of some medieval castle. The closer we came to the walls the more insistent became the analogy of a fortress; turrets and, at points, bastion towers appeared, and still the scale of the scene was beyond my grasp. I could not conceive that these walls rose fifteen hundred feet[1] from the forest, the highest mural face in the world, and stood five thousand feet above the surrounding tableland. The vastness of it all only comes to me now in memory; when I was there, all was reduced by the human mind that cannot conceive on these Antaean terms.

We saw two signs of animal life during the morning, the first we had seen on the entire savannahs, apart from the fowls and cows at Uraianda; a three-foot whip-snake, almost invisible in the grass, flashed past us with lightning movements, and in the distance one of the few surviving savannah deer leapt off as it became aware of us. After some two hours of climbing we stood in the shadow of the rock face, the Kukenaam four thousand feet below; and Kaimaritepu, dominating the land yesterday, now was not even apparent in the pattern of land below us. Uraianda and all the series of hills we had sweated up now joined the general flatness of the scene below us, purple and green as the sun broke through the clouds.

We found a dilapidated benab in the area where we wished to camp, and the three boys (Samson and Antonio had remained at the Kukenaam camp) began to repair it as best they could. Peter disappeared to return with what few leaves he could find to make a roof, and, when these were used up, my groundsheet more or less completed the roofing. Cecilia looked quietly up at the mountain. I imagined that for her as well as for the others the arrival at the sacred mountain was a special day; to mark it she had plastered her cheeks with the bright red dye with which the more primitive Indians decorate themselves.

I spent the next hours looking at the wall of rock we were besieging, at last overcome by the size and solemnity of it, seeing the light always changing, quartz and felspar glistening in sunlight at one moment and clouded over the next. No moment was the same. I picked the beautiful wild flowers that have made Roraima famous among botanists for its unique and various species. I saw the Roraima Emerald, a small glittering green bird, and heard the call of the tityra perched in isolation on a small tree not far from the

[1] St Paul's is 365 feet high.

bush. I looked at the long steep cornice, covered with forest for half its length, by which we would reach the summit. From this distance it looked like a narrow shelf with a sheer fall for most of the way. I could understand why it had taken so long for a route up Roraima to be found.

Robert Schomburgk was the first European to see Roraima, approaching it from the Rupununi in 1838. He realized that the eastern face was unclimbable and chose the cornice by the Kukenaam gateway for his assault. But weather, the condition of his stores and his Indians' fear of the mountain forced him to turn back. With his brother he returned in 1842, when Richard's botanical collections were the only solace for failure to reach the summit. Carl Appun's expedition of 1864 again failed, likewise Barrington Brown's in 1869 and C. A. Eddington's in 1877. A year later J. W. Boddam-Whetham and Michael McTurk, Tiny's father, made a thorough reconnaissance, but they turned back, largely, as Boddam-Whetham put it, 'through a desire for something to eat'. The first ascent was made in 1885 by Everard Im Thurn, then curator of the George-town Museum, and H. I. Perkins, a Crown Surveyor. With ample stores they were able to survey the cornice for a month, and with the help of a party of Arekunas who providentially arrived they cut a trail through the bush on the cornice. It is substantially this trail which we followed next day, though it is now much overgrown.

I slept fitfully that night, kept awake by my excitement, the cold and the rain that found leaves and groundsheet no great barrier. With a kind thought the people of Uraianda had lit a bonfire on their hill, knowing we would see it from the slopes. I was asleep when dawn came and awoke in full sunlight to see one of the most beautiful sights I have ever seen. A few hundred feet below, and stretching all round to the horizon, were the great crowns of cumulus clouds, moving and billowing, with an intense blue unclouded sky above. Roraima, whose long shadow was cast on the cloud, was miraculously clear, the ramparts knife-edged against the blue, the pink now a golden red; while Kukenaam's cliffs rose sheer from white cloud like a raging sea, waves suspended in their motion as they gathered against the cliff foot. But still the chasm was filled with cloud.

Austin, Peter and I were to make the ascent, returning the same

day and carrying only one small load. We walked down a slope
lateral to the rock face, crossed a creek and made a short steep climb
through soggy fern-bush, bright with violet utricularias, only a
little taller than ourselves. This bush gave on to a heavy high bush
that formed the weirdest natural scene I have known. Lying always
in the shadow of the mountain, saturated with moisture at every
season, forms have evolved here which are unique. It was a wilderness of dark, bamboolike turubanas, towering ferns, plants with
flapping flag-fronds and small drooping orchids; lianas writhed
in every direction like endless snakes, and every possible surface
was covered with cankerous growths of sponge mosses or hung
with a sinister long greenish hair gorged with ice-cold water, which
would stream from it as I gripped a turubana stem to help me up the
path. The path was composed of mud, moss and low fern, and
for long stretches it was overgrown with slippery lianas and roots
which we had to clamber over, our feet sometimes slipping through
the interstices to the earth some yard or two below. Everything
was ice-cold and wet, and we too, before long, were saturated with
cold moisture. Only an occasional blue butterfly would give some
lightness to the curious scene. On every side were delicate flowers,
pink, pale purple and white, pitcher-plants that in spite of their
prettiness shared the evil character of the place, enticing insects to
suck at their stamens and then enclosing them in their sepals. Sometimes I would, strangely, come across a bush of large ripe blackberries,
but their taste was bitter. All was muffled by these dark green
growths, and when I spoke in the absolute silence — for I heard no
bird all day — my voice seemed muffled too, absorbed by all these
slimy, spongelike surfaces. This was indeed the perilous and
stagnant garden which I, like some Perseus-Prince, had to traverse
before attaining the enchanted castle of the *Princesse lointaine*. I
had dreamt in the night of a tall beautiful girl standing far above me,
whom I was about to ravish. The dream had strengthened my
conviction that mountain climbing is a form of sexual deviation.

We crossed three rushing watercourses formed by the cascades,
climbed again and then, without warning, came out of a tunnel to
find ourselves at the point where the rock face and the slope met.
Almost trembling with emotion I looked up the smooth surface and
realized that the face slightly overhung the slope, as if the rock had

expanded as it burst into the air from the earth. We walked along the base of the wall until we came to a corner from which we looked down sheer into a bath of mist made by the large Katiaba cascade as it struck the earth. We had taken a wrong turning, and retraced our steps until Austin signed that he had found the right trail.

It was a hard and very steep descent to the Katiaba stream. As we approached it seemed to be raining, but in fact we were receiving the outer vapour of the cascade which, when Schomburgk first saw it, was seventy yards across. Soon the mild rain became a deluge, and as we rushed across the loose scree it seemed as if we were receiving the full force of the cascade, although in fact the water, as it falls off the ledge two thousand feet above, has dispersed into heavy rain before it reaches the ground. Beyond there was no more vegetation, only heavy scree that needed energy rather than skill to climb. We climbed for two hours, most of the time in swirling mist that would clear for a minute so that we could see, still mistily, the savannah five thousand feet below. We were now in those infuriating clouds that for the past five days had been clinging to the summit.

The summit came with extraordinary suddenness. Not knowing how much farther it would be, I put my foot up to a boulder and pulled myself over to find I could climb no higher. The roof of Roraima lay about us. During those first astonished moments of arrival it seemed to me that the monsters of the Lost World had been turned into black frigid monoliths; swirled in constantly moving mist and rising from an irregular surface of rock were gigantic forms carved by the elements from the sandstone and blackened by chemical action to resemble basalt; pinnacles with rudimentary limbs, ragged-edged pyramids and twenty-foot hourglass shapes, with waists so fragile that it seemed as if the heavy wind must bring the upper dolmen thundering to the ground. Nature, it seemed, had placed and carved these stones as the scene for a primitive rite; a Stonehenge disorganized, stones turned to the shapes of a mad fantasy.[1]

---

[1] Here is Im Thurn's account of his moment of arrival on the summit: 'Up this part of the slope we made our way with comparative ease till we reached a point where one step more would bring our eyes on a level with the top — and we should see what had never been seen since the world began, and should see that of which, if it cannot be said the whole world has wondered, at least many people have long and earnestly wondered, should see that which all the few, white men or red, whose eyes had ever rested on the mountain had declared would never be seen while the world lasts — should learn what is on top of Roraima.'

We were, as far as I could tell, on a projecting bastion at the south-western corner of the plateau. When the mist eased I walked to within a few yards of the edge which, to my calculation, should look towards Kukenaam; but above and below was uniform cloud, and I could see nothing of the gorge or of Kukenaam, which stood invisible before me. To the east the clouds suddenly revealed a twenty-foot ridge of rock, running from left to right; then mist obscured it. Its face, serrated like the monstrous figures, formed a series of irregular terraces. Nothing, in all that I could see, suggested that the landscape of Roraima was flat, and as we explored it we were to know its extraordinary complexity only too well. Pools of still brown water were everywhere, and from them grew plants like miniature trees, with small tough leaves and occasionally a purple flower, over which hovered large black butterflies. These sinister butterflies were the only sign of life we saw; the small rodents which are supposed to live on the summit never made an appearance. Although the water in the ponds appeared to be still, there was some slight flow along the runnels connecting the ponds; as the air-formed water came to rest on the rock at various levels, little waterfalls gave an Alpine rock-garden aspect to the scene.

It took us half an hour to wind our way across the two hundred yards that divided us from the ridge, which stood revealed every seven minutes or so as the cold breeze shifted the cloud mass. The going was like a maze which defeated the instincts of Austin and Peter. We would walk round ponds and patches of swamp and climb on to one of the stone figures only to find that the drop beyond was too great, and return to try another of the score of possible routes. At last we came to the ridge and climbed the terraces to its summit. Visibility there was less than twenty yards but I could see that the course of the water was more purposeful at this level; small tributary creeks conducted the water to a watercourse that had worn its way many feet into the sandstone, to make a wide crevasse that we could only just jump across. I followed this creek for as far as was wise and it seemed to me that it deepened as it approached the edge of the plateau. Since its course would have to remain downhill, this must mean that the cascades formed by a number of these creeks issue from the rock face some distance below the edge. From our camp they had appeared to flow directly from the summit.

I picked large utricularias and heliamphoras as I wandered about the plateau, forgetting time and the necessity to get back to the camp before nightfall. The climb had taken us five hours and I presumed that the descent would be less. I admit that I had not banished all thought of Conan Doyle even now that I was on the lost world that he had never seen; I thought of pterodactyls and brontosauri, and to my amazement at one point I came across the skull of a large animal with cowlike horns. I knew that there was no evidence of any animal larger than the rodent ever having lived in the plateau. I looked round for the skeleton but there was no sign. We began a systematic search for other bones. We found nothing. Could they have been crunched to powder by some other still larger animal? My excitement grew as I photographed the skull from every angle. Would they believe me in Georgetown when I told them of my wonderful discovery?

I lunched perched on one of the black Druidic rocks; it was a ritual meal brought specially for this day — the best pâté I could find in Georgetown, and a small pot of caviar, each spread on rather damp Norwegian flat bread. It seemed to be the ultimate luxury to be eating caviar on Roraima. I finished the meal with a slice of Dundee cake. The time came when we had to leave this strange place if we were not to be caught by darkness on the lower cornice. I left sadly, wishing that we had brought food, camping equipment and firewood for at least one night. It was a place to reward weeks of exploring, and I know that I shall always regret that we saw so small a part of the twelve square miles of the plateau.[1] In heavy cloud we started down the scree, and within a quarter of an hour I realized that the energy I had used on the ascent and in exploring the plateau had not been replaced. The effort of holding the body back against the force of gravity was perhaps greater than the effort of hoisting oneself up from stone to stone. By the time we came to the Katiaba cascade I could not run, and walked through the water not caring how wet it made me. During the rest of the descent I became more and more exhausted. We had come up the forest area on hands and knees, clinging to lianas; now we glissaded on our behinds with a momentum that often proved too much for the

[1] At a point on the northern end of the plateau, at 9094 feet above sea level, the frontiers of British Guiana, Brazil and Venezuela meet. Brazil and British Guiana share this northern end, and the rest, three quarters of the whole, is in Venezuelan territory.

plants that I grabbed as we descended. Sometimes I would slide for ten feet or so down the mud and leaves, until some obstruction could break the fall. Brandy and concentrated salt and sugar pills seemed to give me no extra energy, but it was perhaps through their help that I was able to reach the camp at all.

When, after these hard four hours, we moved up the slope of the savannah to the benab, strength seemed miraculously to return, and I posed, trousers gaping at the knee, with Austin and Peter, while William recorded the moment of return with my camera.

That night, though the wind was cold and the rain heavy, I slept with a glorious contentment. At last I had ravished Roraima.

The Way Back

THERE was no blue vault and white sea of cloud when we woke in the morning, only a thick mist that obscured both the country below and the summit of the mountain. William, Cecilia and Peter left early to collect the others at the base camp, while Austin and I started the descent an hour or so later, when the sun had eased some of the mist. As we walked, my passion for the mountain still obsessional, I would turn to look at it each hundred yards or so. It was sad that I had to turn, that I was in retreat, that from now on this conquered citadel would lie behind us.

On the lower slopes we decided to cut across country and pick up the trail to Arabopo village at a point two miles ahead, thus cutting out two sides of a triangle. It was exhausting going over rocky hillocks; and as there were no visible landmarks to keep our direction under control we found ourselves wandering, until Austin's experienced eye spotted a creek across which he knew the trail must pass. At last we found the trail and rested near the rapids until the others caught us up.

An hour later we saw a long spur lying a quarter of a mile away, silhouetted against the blue sky. Suddenly this skyline was broken by a figure coming up the trail from the other side, and then another and another, all moving antlike along the brow. It was a strange sensation, after having this great territory to ourselves for so long, to find that others were moving in it. I felt an intense curiosity to know who they were, to exchange some kind of news with them. I must admit, too, that my first reaction when they appeared was an instinctive one of caution; I had been living rough for long enough to share the Indian suspicion of all such encounters with strangers far from home.

The column of six Indians approached us. They were Akawaios from the forest village of Imbaimadai and all wore the red lap of the primitive Indian. Austin knew one of the men, but they exchanged

a few words without sign of friendliness. I told Austin to ask him
how the trail had been from the Ataro river, the trail we would be
taking next day.

'Him say trail very bad,' said Austin. 'Rain all day, much water
on ground. Very bad.'

I sighed. I was not looking forward to walking for a week
through the forest, even under good conditions. We started on our
way again, and twenty minutes later I looked to my left and realized
that we had rounded the south-western face of Roraima; the eastern
face was slowly coming into view, its huge length unfolding as we
walked. It was more than twice the length of the south-western face,
with no sign of a cornice — three miles of sheer mural surface. By
force of its vast scale it was more impressive than the south-western
face, but since I would never know it intimately and would never
stand beneath its bastions I looked upon it as a little characterless
in comparison with the face I had come to know so well.

We climbed a long hill, and two hours later stood facing the
mountain at right-angles. The hill, on its slope away from Roraima,
descended to a creek, beyond which stood six widely spaced round
houses. This was Arabopo, where we had been told we might get
food to augment our dwindling supplies. As we drew closer, the
blue unbroken water of the creek shone invitingly in the sun before
descending fifty feet to a lower level. I looked forward to a bathe
at sunset, when the kabouras were at rest, but to my surprise we
reached the creek — it was some sixty feet wide — to find no insects
of any kind in the air, although the sun was at mid-afternoon. I
shall never forget that bathe. The river bank puzzled me. It was
composed of flat red jasper which dropped in a perfect right-angle
into the water, as regular and exact as if it had been cut by a mason.
The entire bed of the river was at this point made up of a series of
absolutely flat pieces of jasper, which again seemed to have been
laid by human hand. The whole formed the most comfortable and
beautiful swimming pool I have ever swum in. Cecilia had gone up
to the village so I threw off my clothes and dived into the cool soft
water, wanting to sing with the glorious pleasure of it.

The others took off their clothes and went in single file down to
the bank, each with a puritanical right hand over his genitals.
It was now my turn to laugh, but I pretended I was laughing for joy.

After the bathe I washed, shaved and lay in the sun with my tired feet dangling in the water. This was paradise, paradise. Chateaubriand sighed for '*un désert, une bibliothèque et une demoiselle*', and if a good supply of food had been added to these three conditions I should have been happy to stay at this oasis for months. Only one small thing marred the joy of the bathe and the sun; when I examined my toes for jiggers I found a pearl-coloured sac containing a matured cup of eggs was protruding from under the nail of one of my big toes. For a moment I felt sick at the thought of the maggot that, unknown to me, had been burrowing into my flesh and laying its eggs. I showed my toe to Austin, who took a pin and with a quick stroke had removed the sac complete. It was the size of a pea and left behind a bloody crater in my toe which Austin wanted to stuff with burnt tobacco in the Indian manner. I preferred penicillin powder and a piece of Elastoplast.

We dressed and walked up to the silent village. A woman peered out from the dark interior of a hut, a child at her breast, and explained that all the men of the village were out hunting, but that the strangers' hut lay a hundred yards away, the one with the open sides. We slung our hammocks and started to prepare food, when another less timid woman came with a bowl of cassiri for us, which I sipped out of politeness, hoping that it had not been premasticated.

The next day was Saturday, and, as I expected, William came to me to say that he and Cecilia wished to remain at Arabopo that day. Saturday is the sabbath of the Seventh Day Adventists and William had been taught to prepare himself each sixth day for the possible advent on the morrow. The previous Saturday he had wanted us to spend the day in rest, but I had told him that he and Cecilia might remain behind while we continued. He had decided to come with us. Now he said that they would spend the day in rest and catch us up in the forest next day. I was doubtful whether they could overtake us with heavy loads, so I told the others to divide some of the loads between them, and told William and Cecilia I would pay them off in case they should be unable to reach us. I gave them two dollars for each day of marching, and added cloth, beads and salt for Cecilia, powder, shot and fish-hooks for William. We said farewell to them and the hospitable people of Arabopo and began our march across the savannah towards the forest.

facing, above: ON THE SUMMIT OF RORAIMA: AUSTIN IN FRONT, PETER BEHIND
below: THE AUTHOR APPROACHING THE MURAL FACE OF RORAIMA

The long ribbon of Roraima was vivid pink in the sun — I was glad she was visible and in full glory on the last day we should see her. The trail twisted up and down the hillsides and across a wide area of burnt grassland. Finally it began to descend towards the forest that stretched on to the horizon and began as suddenly as it had ended on the spurs above the Kamerang river. A point came on our descent where I turned to see the length of Roraima appearing along the summit of the hill; at each step the great cliffs descended with us until, like some special sunset, she had descended behind the hill; I should never again, I thought, see this unique and beautiful mountain that we had lived with for so long.

Half an hour later we plunged into the forest; the Gran Sabaña was over. The outer part of the forest was merciless secondary growth that had to be cut through, and soon all my exposed skin was stinging with the lacerations of razor grass. It was a hard, exhausting morning. On the savannah I had felt I could march for ever, but now my back ached with bending, I tripped on ground lianas and roots, and found that inclines which on the savannah would have been nothing now needed all my strength. All day my boots and socks were soaking, for in the cleft of each steep barranca was a creek to be forded, one of which twisted so violently that we had to cross it five times in an hour. By three o'clock I knew I could go on no longer and told Austin to make camp. They built me a small shelter against the night rain and I fell into my hammock. I did not write the usual pages of my journal: instead I made one or two shorthand notes that ended with, 'Bad day. Worst bush by far I've ever known. Think I am beginning to loathe the forest.'

That night I was woken by the sound of some heavy animal moving through the bush, and in the beam of my torch I saw the ungainly form of a tapir making an ugly progress past the camp. We woke at dawn to the cry of howlers and were on our way by seven, I refreshed and hoping the day would be easier. It started badly. We were going down a long slope when Austin, who was in front of me, suddenly began to run. I imagined he had spotted a maam or a powis and I stopped in my tracks to see what he was about to do. Half a minute later I cried out as I felt half a dozen stabs of pain in my legs, and looking down saw scores of giant ants making their way over my boots and up my stockinged legs. The path in front of

facing, top: EARLY MORNING VIEW OF KUKENAAM FROM RORAIMA
centre: AREKUNA INDIAN AND HIS WIFE
below: AREKUNA INDIANS OUTSIDE THEIR OPEN HUT

R

me was alive with them. I pulled them off my legs and ran along the path until it was clear. I hoped they were not the famous twenty-four-hour ants whose sting can be paralytic for a day and a night. I dabbed the bites with spirit and soon the pain had gone. It was not to be our last encounter with ants; ants and termites seem to enjoy the higher altitudes of the forest.

William and Cecilia, to my surprise, caught us up during the day, took their loads, and behaved without giving a sign that anything unfortunate had happened. When we camped Austin told me, as an item of news, that William had lost all the dollar bills I had given him, and Cecilia the material. 'How?' I asked. William explained. He had left the money in his warishi with the material, and while they were bathing a cow had entered the strangers' hut and eaten the money and most of the material. He showed me the chewed remnants of the stuff. 'It is the fault of the captain of the village,' he said. 'He owes me the money. I will claim it when I go to Arabopo next.' He seemed entirely unaffected by his loss.

The trail now went up and down a series of gradually diminishing sandstone hills, surfaced with a few feet of soil, on which inexplicably the great forest had managed to grow. The trees, unable to secure themselves deep in the earth, had spread their leg-thick roots in every direction, intertwining in the hope of giving each other support, and at the same time heaving the trunks above them high towards the sun and air. With many of the trees it would have been possible for me to crawl beneath the trunk itself, between an archway of roots and vast buttresses. I had seen nothing like it before, and it was a fantastic sight; the forest seemed composed of a vast army of monsters on raised legs, their necks thrusting so high that their heads were invisible. Not all were immovable; there was a weird sound which, as the days went by, I was to hear often. It was like some plaintive animal crying for help, insistent, repeated, but unchanging. It was the sound of a weakened tree rubbing its trunk against another before gracefully giving up the ghost and roaring down to its death.

It was the path of roots and lianas that made me hate the forest. The roots agonized my feet — unfortunately the soles of my feet do not have that beautiful concavity which I admire in others. I tripped and stumbled along the path, never taking my eyes off its crazily corrugated surface, knowing that if I did so for one moment I would catch my feet and fall. During the morning of that second day I realized that I was becoming both mentally and physically exhausted by those accursed roots. Each step I took became more and more decisive, complete almost in itself yet necessitating an endless repetition. Looking back on it now I think the psychological effect of the roots accounted for most of my exhaustion, and when the heavy rains came there was nothing to do but attempt to benumb my mind and think of nothing. When the rain kept off, the wonderful call of the bell-bird was comforting, yet ironical in its expression of ease and leisure.

I went on for as long as I could and then we made camp. It was wonderful how my hammock, tea and food restored my spirits and strength. That night we were again attacked by ants. My hammock was enclosed in the bananalike sheath of mosquito netting which hung to the ground. Under the hammock I spread my plastic mackintosh to provide a clean floor. When I awoke with the first light I looked down at the mackintosh to find that the whole floor was composed of earth. Looking closer I saw hundreds of leaf-cutter or parasol ants trailing across the space holding semi-circles of the plastic tissue in their mandibles. Nearly half the mackintosh had been removed by the ants during the night, and was no doubt already providing new and luxuriant apartments in the ant colony. Fascinated I watched the regiment at its work, watched the regular columns and the workers sawing their way through the remnant of the plastic before raising the fragments like parasols and joining the retiring column.

I climbed quietly out of the hammock and followed the columns to the trunk of a fallen tree. They were moving along the trunk in ranks of four, but at one point the path on the bark narrowed and with perfect discipline the columns narrowed into single file, to resume the four ranks when the path broadened. I have been told that if there is congestion at these points the ants will widen the path with their own bodies so that the columns can move along a living causeway. In the same way they will span a wide space by composing a living bridge of clinging bodies across which the others may move. I was not lucky enough to see any soldier ants in action. They do not work on leaf-cutting, or organize transport.

Their heads, armed with spearpoints, make this impossible anyway. When the colony is being attacked the workers retreat and the soldiers rush to the weak spot. After assessing the danger they vibrate to call the assistance they need. If a soldier is killed others will circle him while others form flanks to protect the retreating workers. As the column of workers moves it is permanently protected by pickets of soldiers.

Two more miserable, back-breaking days went by and we came to the great and beautiful falls of Ukutuik, where the river falls over a thousand-foot escarpment to country three thousand feet above sea level. An Indian benab stood at the side of the gorge looking across to the misty falls whose water was lost after five hundred feet in a sea of cloud. The Indians were very primitive Akawaios of fine physique. The women wore fine queyu aprons, necklaces of jaguar teeth and tight bead circlets at the ankles and below the knees, whose purpose was less decoration than an attempt to develop — and thus beautify — the calf muscles. The men were in laps and, like the women, had their faces smeared with red dye. I noticed an old flintlock in the hut, but it was little used and I was told that most of the hunting was done with bow and arrow or blowpipe. No one understood a word of English; we were still on Brazilian territory. British Guiana was a morning's march away. The Indians were a smiling, friendly and utterly un-avaricious people. They gave us pineapples and poured us calabashes of pink cane-juice spirit, which I found smooth, excellent and extremely potent.

We slithered down the escarpment to find the forest at the lower level was a sea of mud corrugated by exposed roots. This made the way still harder and I began to curse aloud at the terrain as I dragged myself across it. I never wanted to see the forest again. I detested it as I had detested nothing in my life. Towards three o'clock we came to a cassava clearing which meant that a village was near, and ten minutes later we approached three large round huts with rounds of cassava bread gleaming on their roofs as if in some scene by Breughel. The people of the village were as primitive as those at Ukutuik, and nearly all had faces of uncommon beauty. The father of the family looked like some wise old mandarin as he leant on his bow and fingered his long wisp of beard. One of the children, a little girl of five, had a hauntingly beautiful face that I never tired

of looking at. I think the belle of the clan must have been hidden
away from me in case I should abuse hospitality. Later in the afternoon I peered through the half-open door of a hut to see the beautiful
face of a young girl looking curiously out at me from the shadows.
She retreated, and I never saw her again.

The sad event of the following day was the loss of Macheath.
I had enjoyed the company of the two parrots. In the savannah they
had perched contentedly on the boys' shoulders as they marched, but
in the forest they would answer the cries of other parrots and
macaws with their own, and were clearly distracted to find themselves
back in their natural habitat. The urges of the forest had returned
to them, and that day Macheath flew into the air and did not return.
He had known the forest only as a fledgling and had never foraged
for himself. Austin said it would be impossible for him to exist for
long alone in the forest. We looked everywhere for him but had
to continue without him. Austin cut one of Polly's tendons to
make sure that she would not follow her mate.

This, I had reckoned, would be the last day of the march. I would
give all the strength I had left to reach the landing on the Ataro
river, even if we went on till dusk. The landing is at the first point
where the Ataro, which we had crossed frequently after Ukutuik,
becomes navigable. We were counting on finding a woodskin there
and continuing by river. At midday I was resting while the others
went on ahead. Before I had finished my rest I saw Austin returning
down the trail. I cursed. I imagined that — as had happened twice
already — we had taken the wrong trail and must retrace our steps
for an hour. But he said 'We reach Ataro landing, sir.'

I wanted to shout with joy as I jumped up. Within a quarter of
an hour we were standing on the muddy bank of a sinister river of
still stagnant-looking black water. I looked around for a woodskin,
but there was none.

'No woodskin,' I said to Austin. 'Does the trail go on to Kukui
Mouth? We'd get one at the village.'

'No trail, sir. No woodskin.'

He seemed to accept the situation with infuriating calm and I
raised my voice when I said we'd have to cut a trail.

'Me go find woodskin,' he replied.

The quest seemed absurd. We had not passed a hut since the

morning. Nevertheless the boys went off through the trees to comb the forest for a woodskin, while I sat on my biscuit tin and cursed our luck. To my amazement they returned in ten minutes with a rotting woodskin to which they had been drawn by some magical instinct. They put it in the river and water immediately flowed in through leaks in the bows and stern. These they caulked with mosses so that the flow would be small enough to be kept under control by baling. As there were no paddles, Antonio and Peter disappeared into the forest once more to find the small tree of hard wood from which paddles could be cut. These found, they hacked at them with their cutlasses and in a few minutes had shaped out excellent paddles. There was room for only three people in the woodskin after it had been piled with my gear and stores. Austin, Antonio and I, it was decided, should go down to Kukui Mouth, and Antonio would take the woodskin back later in the day for the others to come down next morning.

It was a weird journey down the Ataro, whose sinister aspect was emphasized when I saw a large alligator spring with an amazingly rapid motion from the mud flats into the shallows. I saw one more alligator and heard the heavy splash of another. Apart from the small cayman in the lake near Tiny McTurk's house these were the only alligators I had seen during all the days I had spent on the rivers of the colony. The Ataro's slow currents and luxuriantly muddy shallows suited alligators better than the swift waters of the big rivers.

We came to the Kukui, a larger, more affable river. A round hut stood high on a bank, and in the water at its landing lay a long corial piled with pineapples and other fruits. We landed and found the hut inhabited by some half dozen men and women in laps and queyus. They were on their way to Kamerang Mouth, they told Austin, with fruit to sell. I asked them if they would let us have their corial, but their leader refused. I said I would take what I could of their fruit to Kamerang and would send back the corial as soon as we arrived, that I would give him gunpowder, shot and beads. He was a little more interested, but alas my stock of barter goods was low, and what I showed him seemed pitiably small. I offered him money. It is difficult to deal with Indians over money at all times, but when they are unable to conceive its value stranger troubles arise.

Fashions in monetary units are liable to change. One week it is fashionable to receive — or to demand — five dollars for anything from a couple of pineapples to a finely made hammock. Next week a pound of fish or a feather head-dress may cost two, ten or twenty dollars. The fashion for that week was ten dollars. If I had refused to give ten dollars and had offered twenty dollars the man would probably have stubbornly insisted on ten dollars. I gave him a note and slept peacefully, lulled by the unceasing hum of conversation in the hut as I lay in my hammock under the trees.

I am glad I finished my river journeys in British Guiana with two such beautiful days as those we spent in the woodskins between Kukui Mouth and Kamerang Mouth. There was no outboard engine to scare the duckler, poised on tacoubas as they waited for fish, and as we moved with the slow stream of the Mazaruni I could hear the faintest call of the birds and watch the gambolling otters on the bank, oblivious to our silent presence. It is the only way to know the full beauty of a tropical river, to become part of its life rather than its disrupter.

When dusk was falling on the second day I asked Austin if we could reach Kamerang before midnight. 'Seven points to go, sir,' he replied, for we had reached a part of the river which he knew well. He was unable to translate a point into hours and minutes, and I already knew that an Indian's idea of a river point is not a European's. It seemed to me that we had rounded three points before Austin had conceded one. At last we came to a stretch of water at whose farther end lights were flickering high on the bank. We had made the full circle, Kamerang to Kamerang, and my journey seemed to be over. I did not bother to ask myself how I should get back to the Coast, whether there would be an aeroplane or whether I would have to continue by foot across the Merume mountains and down the Mazaruni to Bartica. I was thankful that we were back and that I should spend that night between sheets on an iron bedstead. The Seggars, I knew, were still away from Kamerang, and I was surprised to see a light in their bungalow. When we landed I groped my way up the muddy slope and climbed the stairs to their veranda. I knocked on the door and entered. Three white men I had never seen before were dining. One, a tall fair young man, rose with a startled look on his face and walked towards me. My hand went out.

'Swan,' I said.

'Attenborough,' said the young man. Each of us metaphorically clicked his heels. (It was not until next morning that we congratulated each other on not saying 'Dr Livingstone, I presume'.)

The greetings over, a plate of steak and kidney pie was ordered for me, and a tumbler of rum and ginger ale. David Attenborough was making his famous television films for the B.B.C. about wild life in British Guiana, and the expedition was using the Seggars's bungalow as its headquarters.

'We've been hearing about you here and there,' said Attenborough. 'Tiny McTurk said to us, "If you ever run across that fellow Swan and he tells you he shot a pirai with a bow and arrow, God damn it — it's the truth."'

I was delighted to know that I'd contributed one small story to Tiny's mythology.

'By the way,' Attenborough went on, 'you're in luck. The Grumman's coming tomorrow with the rest of our stores. You can go back to Georgetown on it — unless you want to stay on here?'

Next morning I paid off the Indians and divided the remainder of the stores and trade goods among them. When we heard the sound of the Grumman circling overhead I suddenly felt the pain of parting. Already I had forgiven the forest for that terrible stretch between the savannah and the Ataro, already those glorious days of the march towards Roraima were touched with a kind of mystic quality. It would be strange not to be woken with a mug of scalding cocoa, with the roof of leaves above my head; it would be strange to be without that daily target of twenty miles which we had set ourselves and departed from only in the last stretch of forest.

I climbed into the Grumman, and the last faces I saw as we taxied into midstream were the still emotionless faces of Austin, Peter, Antonio, Samson, William and Cecilia. Then we were off into the clouds.

At my hotel in Georgetown that afternoon, still in a dream, I telephoned a friend. 'Ah,' he said, 'so you're back, Colonel Fawcett. We hadn't heard a thing of you — thought you'd been eaten by a tiger. We're giving a party tonight — come along. And later there's one for the Aussie cricket team. You missed Cricket Week. Bad luck.'

During the party I kept remembering that twenty-four hours before I had been on the Mazaruni, listening to Austin's assurances that Kamerang was only three points away. My mind was still in the Indian country. I talked to Vincent Roth, who pricked up his ears when I told him about the animal's skull on Roraima. 'This is interesting,' he said as we went over to Jimmy Bamford to tell him about the discovery. He listened patiently to my account, and then he smiled mischievously.

'So it's taken twenty-four years to work,' he said. 'When I was on the Boundary Commission one of the Venezuelans took a cow's head up to the summit and planted it for a joke. Hoped some ass would fall for it one day and make a still bigger fool of himself. Well, at least I've saved you that one.'

We laughed.

Envoi

THE Falls of Kaieteur, the Old Man Falls, are the most famous sight in British Guiana, and my travels had not yet taken me to them. I had hoped to make an overland trip, and see the unforgettable view from the bottom of the Potaro Gorge, see the mass of water, four hundred feet across, thundering from seven hundred and forty-one feet above. But time would not allow, and instead I chartered the Grumman with three other people, to see it in a day.

Clouds were low and heavy when we set out, and the forest canopy an autumnal carpet of russet, yellow, gold and green, from which puffs of steam issued like hundreds of volcanic eruptions. We were forced to fly at four hundred feet, so that the details of the land below were plain. I could see the birds fly from the canopy as we passed. We followed the whole line of the Mazaruni between Bartica and Issano, and I realized for the first time the true nature of the fragmentation, the chaos of the islands and the confluence of currents at Paiarimap, Kaburi, Wara-wara, Pabracash and Anizet.

We turned westwards towards the Potaro and eventually entered the five-mile-long gorge, whose forest-covered slopes descended a thousand feet on either side. Kaieteur came into view at the far end — a mere trickle of water, it seemed, dwarfed by the immensity of the gorge. We gained height and landed on the Potaro, half a mile above the falls. We walked through the unique forest that surrounds Kaieteur, a forest whose character is made by the water permanently suspended in the air; the soil was spongy with sphagnum mosses and on either side giant bromeliads with thigh-thick stems drooped their huge leaves and flaunted their dense plumes. Shrubs related to the miniature trees of Roraima were everywhere, white flowers grew from the fissures of rocks, small scarlet flowers stood out against the greenness, and orchids hung from every tree. It was, indeed, a botanist's paradise.

At last the forest gave on to an open shelf of rock beyond which we could see the top of the falls as they broke from the innocent-looking waters of the river. The recent rains had been heavy and the falls were at their broadest. As we walked to the edge of the shelf the roar increased and our normal voices could not be heard. There is no more hypnotic sight than a great waterfall in full flood, and my eyes went up and down great white columns of water, as incapable of conceiving size as I had been before the mural faces of Roraima. I was not disappointed; I was as moved as I had been on the summit of Roraima. I turned to look along the gorge, where, far below, the Potaro tumbled like a twisted white ribbon, and the hills sent their buttresses hurtling down into the valley. The grandeur of it could hardly have been more extreme, and we stayed all afternoon, lying in the warm sun, looking from the water at our side, down into the gorge and up the slopes of the valley.

When we took off the Grumman taxied to a point a few hundred yards above the falls and then began a straight run down the river, leaving the water only at the point of the falls. It was a breathtaking sensation, a fitting way to take leave of what are probably the most beautiful falls in the world.

★

A few days later I was flying at a great height above the Orinoco towards the Caribbean. From Trinidad I flew to the small island of Tobago, for a rest at a copra plantation house which has been converted into an hotel. The days were idyllic, lying on the sand beach with a coconut palm grove behind and the white Caribbean breaking on the cove. One morning I went to the coral lagoon where Alexander Selkirk, Crusoe's antetype, was shipwrecked. A boat took us across a stretch of water which the big Negro boatman described as 'nylon water'. We swam over the coral reef, watching the beautiful darting gold, yellow, red and black fishes through goggles. Fascinated by what I saw and misled by the strange refraction of light under water, I did not realize that I had swum into the shallows; I stood up, and as I did so my feet caught in the crenellations of the coral; I fell over backwards with all my weight on to a coral antler. The boatman came over and fished me out. Two days later, in hospital, I learnt that a spicule of rib-bone had pierced my lung.

During the weeks I lay in hospital I would often think of the irony of the accident. I had made the journey from Bartica to Issano without incident, no jaguar or snake had attacked me in the forest. I had climbed Roraima without a fall and even managed not to succumb to the forest roots. Then, on this holiday island, Fate had, in its way, caught up with me.

At other times I would forget about ironies as I comforted my weakened spirit by reliving the days I had spent in the forest, on the rivers, or on the savannah. Already they were beginning to mean so much more than they had appeared to mean at the time. The pattern of one's travels emerges in the tranquillity that follows; what we have seen and done finally becomes real, a fraction more of the meaning of life on earth is understood. And that, in its absolute simplicity, is the point of it all. To move across strange contours of the earth's surface, to see stars never visible in European skies, to hear sounds that can only be heard in the high green canyons of tropical rivers, to have time given by the sun itself, and to discover the essential humanity of men who seem at first to be of a different species. Is the instinct to return to some primitive state caged away in all of us, even the most civilization-loving? It can become a dangerous little beast if given too great a freedom, leading one on a path too far from civilization, that civilization where lie the true glory as well as the full beastliness of Man. But once the primitive sources have been glimpsed rather than succumbed to, the glory can take on a new preciousness, and the memories from those strange and distant worlds can take their proper place, forming an uninsistent backcloth against which to set one's small, hopeful apprehension of Man's achievement.

APPENDICES

In Search of El Dorado

CONFUSION follows the fantasy which accompanies all myth-making, and in the palimpsest created by each generation the last thing one expects to find is evidence of the actual reasonable happening which inspired the long fantasy. Who would wish to know that the earthly Juno was a well-built fishergirl of Cos, or Hephaestus a celebrated blacksmith of Hiera? I was surprised, then, to find that there was an historical record of the annual ritual of El Dorado himself, a ceremony which died out in the town of Guatavita, on the shores of a lake near the modern city of Bogotá, forty years before the Spanish conquest. 'On the day appointed,' writes J. Acosta in his *Descubrimiento de la Nueva Grenada*, 'the chief smeared his body with turpentine, and then rolled in gold dust. Thus gilded and resplendent he entered his canoe, surrounded by his nobles, whilst an immense multitude of people, with music and songs, crowded round the shores of the lake. Having reached the centre, the chief deposited his offerings of gold, emeralds and other precious things, and then jumped in himself to bathe. At this moment the surrounding hills echoed with the applause of the people; and, when the religious ceremony concluded, the dancing, singing and drinking began.' Cochrane, in his *Travels*, describes how attempts were made in his day to drain this lake, and speaks of the diving operations which had reclaimed several gold ornaments from the slime.

This, clearly, was the *tabula rasa* on which the palimpsest began. Humboldt, who was apparently unaware of this record, assumed, with his extraordinary intuition, that Guatavita was the original place of the gilded king. When he travelled in these parts he saw the remains of a staircase hewn out of the rock forming the lake shore, and it had every sign of having been used in the ritual of ablution. The Spaniards included Guatavita among their many sites of El Dorado, and from the first days of the conquest the story was known. Oviedo y Baños, the historiographer, wrote an account to the ever curious Cardinal Bembo, saying that Gonzalo Pizarro 'sought . . . a great prince, noised in those countries, who was always covered with powdered gold, so that from head to foot he resembled an image of gold fashioned by the hand of a highly skilled goldsmith. The powdered gold is fixed on the body by means of an odoriferous resin, but, as this kind of garment would be uneasy to him while he slept, the prince washes himself every evening, and is gilded anew in the morning, which proves that the empire of El Dorado is infinitely rich in mines'.

It was natural for the Spanish *conquistadores* to think that the southern continent should contain more than the one great empire of the Incas. Men who had lazed in the scented halls of Montezuma and assaulted the stone palaces of the Inca Atahualpa imagined even finer riches to be had in the territory of the gilded king; but avarice did not enrich their imaginations with any great sense of the likelihood of things. They supposed that this empire of magnificent cities and abundant gold would have grown up in the space of a few decades. After the conquest of Peru, Manco-Inca, brother of Atahualpa, had escaped and was said to have established a new empire east of the cordilleras, in the land of El Dorado. It does not seem to be clear whether the Spaniards thought Manco-Inca had deposed the gilded king or that he was the gilded king himself. The Government in Spain, who had every reason to suppose that another empire was ready for their attentions, equipped an expedition led by two German *conquistadores*, Ambrosio de Alfinger and Bartolomé Sailler. They landed at Coro, on the Caribbean coast of Venezuela, in 1528, with — like Cortés — four hundred men and fifty horses. Alfinger set off a year or so later into the Interior in search of El Dorado. He contributed to the black legend of Spanish colonization, and his various cruelties were later read of in rage by Raleigh and Hawkins. For a year he and his men wandered in the tropical forests, starving and fever-ridden, dying by the score, finally to reach the freezing heights of the Andes. Then, when they had descended into the valley of Chinacota, they were constantly attacked by Indians. An arrow pierced Alfinger's neck and three days later he died. In 1532 the wretched remnants of his band, having accomplished a march in every way more hazardous than Cortés's marches to Tenochtitlán or Honduras, arrived back at Coro.

In 1534 another German, Georg von Speier, was given command of the mystical four hundred men, and set out for Coro and El Dorado. Speier marched south across the savannahs, but by avoiding mountain ranges was never closer to the Rupununi than some few hundred miles. He saw country no European had ever seen, and suffered for what he saw, his men decimated and killed by Indian attacks. They reached Coro in 1538, and two years later Speier, by all accounts a good man who treated the Indians well, died as Governor of Venezuela. He had brought with him one precious indication of an empire with which to fan growing interest in El Dorado. At an Indian village he had found a temple to the sun and a convent similar to those found in Peru. Had they been built during the eastward migration of Manco-Inca?

While Speier was marching back to Coro three other expeditions were on the move; Sebastián de Belalcazar from Quito, Nicholas Federmann from Venezuela, and Gonzalo Ximenes de Quesada from the Caribbean coast just east of the Isthmus of Panama. All three leaders were clearly agreed, unawares, that El Dorado must lie in the high Andes on the tableland of what is now Bogotá. Quesada reached this plateau in 1536 and found a reasonably civilized nation, the Chitchas, and the sack of their towns brought him an enormous haul of gold, silver and emeralds. It seemed as if El Dorado had been found. In 1538 Belalcazar reached the plateau and to his dismay found Quesada established. In 1539 Federmann arrived, and perhaps to comfort himself for Quesada's success told what he had heard of a truly magnificent empire lying to the east.

facing, above left: AREKUNA INDIAN WITH HIS GRANDCHILDREN
    right: AKAWAIO GIRL
    below: AUSTIN CAULKING THE WOODSKIN HE FOUND AT THE ATARO
       LANDING

The three parties, however, shortly made for the River Magdalena and descended it to Santa Martha, the town from which Quesada had set out.

Quesada's brother, Hernan, next continued the search and arrived back at Santa Martha a year later, after terrible hardships, with half his men. Meanwhile it was Venezuela's turn once more, and a larger expedition set out under the command of another German, Philip von Huten, who had been with Speier on the first expedition. Huten was determined to march in the general direction that Quesada had taken, but his calculations went astray; for a year this party travelled, often starving, and at one point reduced to eating a fruit which caused their hair, eyebrows and beards to fall out; then they discovered that they had travelled in a vast circle and were back where they had begun. Huten's determination did not vanish; with forty men he set out for the 'city' of Macatoa, which had been mentioned to him by an Indian. They reached this village of the Uaupes Indians, and there were told great news; southwards lay the land of the Omaguas, people with great cities and much gold and silver. These forty amazing men, weakened by starvation, set out with the intention of attacking the cities if need be. After five days they came within sight of a large township, with long straight streets, dominated by a large building which, so their guides told them, was filled with golden idols. This city, they added, was one of the lesser cities of the Omaguas and their king, Quarica. The Spaniards, imaginations aflame, charged the town but were forced back by the Indians, Huten being badly wounded. They returned to the main party, and marched on to Coro with their news, which caused a sensation throughout the world. The Bogotá plateau was relegated to an unimportant province of the empire; El Dorado proper now lay in the country of the Omaguas which Huten had glimpsed. Humboldt, who was interested in the geographical results of these remarkable expeditions, refers succinctly to the 'false reports' of Huten, and I think it is clear that the city with its temple became more and more magnificent in the imaginations of the *conquistadores* as they made the long march to Coro. But there is no reason to disbelieve that the Uaupes had told them of the great wealth of the Omaguas. Throughout the whole tale of the search for El Dorado one situation recurs; the enthusiasm of the *conquistadores* interpreting on a grand scale the half-understood stories of the Indians, who in their turn were only too glad to encourage the Spaniards to be on their way. Even today, as I have constantly found, the Indians will tell you anything they feel you would like to hear.

The next expedition in search of the El Dorado worth mentioning here came in 1560, and was captained by Pedro de Ursua, who as a young man in 1545 had been in charge of the Government at Bogotá. In 1555 the Marquis of Cañete had arrived in Peru as Viceroy to find the colony in disorder and on the verge of revolt. An expedition in search of El Dorado was psychologically just the thing to occupy men dissatisfied with the portions that Peru had brought them. Fray Pedro Simon[1] says:

[1] 'Sixth historical notice of the first part of the Conquest of Tierra Fierme in the Western Indies.' (Hakluyt Society, 1861.)

facing: THE KAIETEUR FALLS, WITH THE UPPER POTARO RIVER BEYOND

In these provinces [of the Omaguas] of which the Indians spoke when they reached Peru, dwelt the gilded man, at least this name was spread about in the land, taking its origin in the city of Quito. It so excited the minds of these restless spirits with whom Peru was full, and who were ever ready to credit these rumours, that the Viceroy thought it prudent to seek some way by which to give employment to so large a body of turbulent men.

Ursua was chosen as a reliable commander, but, as the months went by, it became clear that the adventure had not changed the nature of certain restless and turbulent spirits. Ursua set out south-eastwards from Lima. Soon a leader whom he had appointed was murdered by two jealous rivals, whom he sent back to be beheaded at Santa Cruz. Other, more natural, dissatisfaction arose from the fact that Ursua had brought with him the beautiful Doña Iñez de Atienza, whom he proposed one day to marry. A small troop of soldiers was sent to strengthen Ursua's hand but, says Fray Simon, they were so cruel to the Indians on their march 'so that at the mere mention of Spaniards the natives trembled'. The expedition moved slowly on across desert country, and certain elements began to speak against Ursua's leadership. His murder was planned, and a certain Fernando de Guzman was chosen to be his successor if all went well. The mutineers went to Ursua's house at night where they found him lying in his hammock, talking to his page, Lorca. 'What seek you here, caballeros, at this hour?' he asked, and they lunged at him with their swords. Unwounded, he was on his feet, sword in hand, but the next moment the other mutineers had entered, and in a few seconds he was lying bleeding on the floor. 'Confessio, confessio, miserere mei Deus . . .' he murmured, but could go no further before he died.

The new leader, Don Fernando, called a council, and a document was prepared giving reasons for the murder of Ursua, which all the mutineers signed. One of the murderers was named Lope de Aguirre, the maestro del campo, and when it was his turn to sign he wrote, 'Lope de Aguirre, the traitor'. He explained his action, laughing at the notion of such a document being accepted by the King. 'We have all been traitors,' he said, 'we have all been a party to this mutiny, and have agreed that the country (in search of which we are) shall be sought for, found, and settled. Now should it be ten times richer than Peru, and more populous than Mexico, and should the King draw more profit from it than all the Indies together, yet as soon as the first Bachelor of Arts or pettifogging little man comes with powers from His Majesty to take up his residence amongst us, and to take note of what has been done by us, I tell you it will cost us all our heads.' Aguirre's plan was to return to Peru and raise a general revolt against the Crown. It was decided, however, to continue the pursuit of El Dorado.

Aguirre from now on dominates the scene. He murders Captain del Arze because he was a friend of Ursua's. He intimidates Don Fernando into uneasy friendship and murders the captain of the guard, Bandera, who was now the rival of another captain, Salduendo, for the attractions of Doña Iñez; Salduendo gave false witness to Don Fernando that Bandera planned his murder, so that Iñez could be his alone. It was the 'tragedy of blood' of Kyd and Webster transplanted from the Cenci Palace or the Castle of Malfi to the cold deserts of the middle Andes. Environment had made no difference to Renaissance Mediterranean man. It is Doña Iñez's position which most fascinates me in this drama, but Fray Simon does little to satisfy our curiosity about her; I want to know how she travelled, whether she rode, or was borne, like Genghis Khan's princess crossing the Mongolian plains, in a swinging palanquin on a heap of cushions; how did the Indians receive this first white woman in their country? But the discreet Friar is silent.

Aguirre continues to flatter Don Fernando, and it was at his suggestion that he was elected Prince of Peru and referred to as 'His Excellency'. The royal acquisition and perhaps the high Andean air went to his head; he became proud and demanded that he should have a royal treasury and live in royal state. He dined alone and was served with ceremony. The rebels now planned to attack and subjugate Peru, and their conversation was a daydream of the spoils that would come to them. 'Then they would', writes Fray Simon, 'at their leisure divide its great riches amongst themselves; and they would then take away from its inhabitants their wives and daughters each naming which woman should be his, for they knew them all. Even the Negroes were not to be forgotten; and in this arrangement, should one say, "I wish to have Doña so and so," another should reply "I was thinking of taking the same, but as you have chosen her, there will not be wanting another for me." '

Their confidence did not last; they began to see the wild foolishness of Aguirre's scheme and to feel remorse for Ursua's murder. Would it not be wiser to return humbly and accept the punishment they deserved? This was Don Fernando's counsel, but his faction was outnumbered by Aguirre's. Don Fernando felt that Aguirre's murder would be justified in the sight of God, but he appeared to have been too frightened of the consequences to kill him. The expedition had been waiting three months at a village for the building of a fleet of brigantines to transport it down what was later to be called the Amazon. Now they were ready and the embarkation began. Salduendo wanted to take aboard a mattress for the further comfort of Doña Iñez, and no doubt for himself, but Aguirre refused to allow the mattress. Salduendo and Doña Iñez eased their anger with indiscreet remarks which were repeated to Aguirre, who went to Don Fernando's house, where he knew he would find Salduendo, and ran him through with his sword. Aguirre, in his fury, now gave his men orders to find Doña Iñez and kill her. This they did with all the sadistic barbarity of which the sixteenth-century Spaniard was capable, mangling her body with their swords. Her life, as Gibbon said of the Empress Theodora, 'cannot be applauded as the triumph of female virtue', but her death was the most disgusting of Aguirre's acts.

Aguirre had performed a *coup d'état* and power was virtually his. He and a party of his men paid another visit to Don Fernando's house where they first killed three of the Prince's men before emptying their arquebuses into the body of the short-reigned Prince himself. Aguirre now called himself General and gave his followers the name of *Los Marañones*, from the word *Maraña* which can mean a place made impassable by vegetation, or a confusion of intrigue.[1] The brigantines moved off down the river, Aguirre killed a further three soldiers (whose loyalty he distrusted) before embarking. The weeks went by and they reached the junction of the Amazon and the Rio Negro. At this point it is not clear whether they continued on to the mouth of the Amazon, or went up the Negro in search of the El Dorado of the Omaguas. The early historians, Simon, Acuña and Acosta believe they went up the Negro, but Humboldt, and Southey in his *History of Brazil*, argued that they made for the ocean and coasted up to the Indies. There is one clue in Simon's narrative which suggests to me that they took the Negro route. He talks about their coming across a savage Carib tribe called Arnaquinas. The orthography of indigenous words is notoriously as wild as the savages themselves, and I think Simon is referring to 'Arekunas'. I came across Arekunas in the eastern marches of the vast Venezuelan Gran Sabaña and heard that Arekunas lived for many miles to the west. The Rio Negro should have taken Aguirre and his remnants through the western region of the Arekuna country.

I will give a brief account of the rest of this amazing exploit, which is one of the best documented of all the early explorations of South America. Aguirre and his men seem to have made some kind of portage across from the Upper Negro to the Upper Orinoco and eventually to have made their way out to sea from the Great Mouth of the Orinoco (i.e. not from the *Bocas chicas* of the northern part of the delta). He landed at the Spanish island of Margarita, west of Trinidad, intimidated the inhabitants and the Governor whom he made prisoner, robbed the Treasury and planned to turn Caribbean pirate. A relieving party was seen approaching the island, to which Aguirre's answer was the murder of the Governor and his companions. The various Spanish settlements along the Caribbean coast of Venezuela prepared for Aguirre's assaults, and plans were made for his capture. The Spanish poet Ercilla, at Lima, set out to help in the overthrow of Aguirre. Aguirre sailed on to the town of Burburata, a hundred miles west of Caracas. Here he wrote the first of his mad letters, this to the Father Provincial, in which he says, 'The soldiers of your paternity call us traitors, but they should be chastised, they should not say so, because to attack Don Philip, King of Castille, is the work of grand and noble souls. . . .'

The second of these letters was a long letter to King Philip himself, a letter so disloyal that Fray Simon did not print it in his *Noticias*. Aguirre gives an account of his upbringing and youth, his service to the Crown in the New World, saying that he 'firmly believed' the King to be ungrateful and cruel to him for his service. 'We now know', he says, 'in this country, how cruel

---

[1] The Amazon was called the Marañon after the expedition of Aguirre until Orellana named it Amazonas. Part of the river is still called Marañon. This source of the name seems to me much more likely than the inevitable etymological pun which says that the first Spaniard to see the vast expanse of the river cried 'Hic mare an non?'

thou art, that thou art a breaker of thy faith and word; therefore, if we receive thy pardon we should give less credence to it than to the books of Martin Luther . . . I take it for certain that few kings go to hell, only because they are few in number; but that if there were many, none of them would go to Heaven. For I believe that you are all worse than Lucifer, and that you hunger and thirst after human blood; and further I think little of you, and despise you all, nor do I look on your Government as more than an air bubble.' He ends this letter with a final flourish of hate, '. . . because of thine ingratitude I am a rebel against thee unto death — Lope de Aguirre, the Wanderer!'

At last, at Barquesimeto, inland from Burburata, he was defeated by Spanish troops. Two shots from an arquebus entered him, and saying, 'That has done the business', he fell dead. His head was hacked off and exhibited for days after his body had been thrown into its pit. Humboldt says that when the will-o'-the-wisp rises from the marshes round Barquesimeto the people say it is the soul of the traitor Aguirre.

Thus ended the most fantastic and the least productive expedition to the golden land. 'We Spaniards', as Cortés said to Montezuma, 'suffer from a disease that only gold can cure.'

In his geographical account of El Dorado, Humboldt distinguishes between what he calls El Dorado de los Omaguas and El Dorado de la Parime. Through the decades of the sixteenth century the supposed site of the lake and city had been moving steadily eastwards. By the late 1580s it had reached the area of the Orinoco. Quesada's son-in-law made a transcontinental journey which eventually brought him to Trinidad. In 1595 Berrio organized an expedition of two thousand men to seek the empire of the gilded king. The direction of this expedition was influenced by the stories of a Spaniard, Juan Martinez, who had years before been captured by Caribs and gone native in the Essequibo-Rupununi region. On his return to civilization he gave embellished accounts of the Empire and placed it not far from the country he knew.

In spite of its size and equipment Berrio's expedition had no success. Caribs attacked it on the whole course, killing many men. Others died of starvation and disease, and out of the two thousand men only thirty made their way back to the post of San Thomé, at the junction of the Orinoco and the Caroni. Berrio survived, and continued to Trinidad, of which he was governor. Meanwhile Sir Walter Raleigh was cruising in Caribbean waters, letting it be thought that he was on his way to the colony of Virginia, but in fact awaiting an opportunity to penetrate the southern continent and discover the empire of El Dorado. Raleigh made a landing on Trinidad, and although he does not specifically say so, his object was the capture of Berrio, from whom he wished to learn all that was known of the Empire of Guiana, as El Dorado was now called.

Raleigh's romantic nature longed to perform some exploit as magnificent as the conquests of Mexico or Peru, to conquer as he puts it 'more than was ever done in Mexico by Cortez, or in Peru by Pacaro [Pizarro]'. He succeeded in capturing Berrio who, having given up the search for the empire himself, filled Raleigh with information. Raleigh gives the following account of what he learnt:

> The Empyre of *Guiana* is directly east from *Peru* towards the sea, and lieth vnder the Equinoctial line, and it hath more abundance of Golde then any part of *Peru*, and as many or more great Cities than euer *Peru* had when it flourished most; it is gouerned by the same lawes and the Emperour and people observe the same religion, and the same forme and pollicies in gouernment as was vsed in *Peru*, not differing in any part: and as I have been assured by such of the Spanyardes as haue seen *Manoa* the emperiall Citie of *Guiana*, which the Spanyardes call *El Dorado*, that for the greatnes, for the riches, and for the excellent seate, it farre exceedeth any of the world, at least such of the world as is knowen to the Spanish nation: it is founded vpon a lake of salt water of 200 leagues long like vnto *mare caspiu*.

Raleigh sailed up the Orinoco by way of the *bocas chicas*, in small boats, as instructed by Berrio; I have already referred to the events of this voyage in the earlier part of this book. Raleigh's expedition was on a small scale and his penetration of the continent slight; its scale of achievement and the hardships endured cannot compare with the Spanish expeditions. But much was learnt; the empire, with its mines, was located south of the Orinoco. Raleigh returned to England determined to raise money for a full assault on the empire. He wrote his account of *The Discoverie of Guiana* in his superb springing poetic prose as part of his propaganda for his obsession. He flattered the Queen outrageously, he enticed financial backing with promises of infinite gold — 'the desire for gold will aunswere many objections', he said — and captured the imagination with tales of Amazon women and two-headed beings. He denied that he exaggerated. 'But', he wrote, 'it shall bee found a weak pollicie in me, eyther to betray my selfe, or my Country, with imaginations, neyther am I so farre in loue with that lodging, watching, care, perill, diseases, ill sauoures, bad fare, and many other mischiefes that accompany these voyages as to woo myself againe into any of them, were I not assured that the sunne coureth not so much riches in any part of the earth.'

On this first expedition Raleigh's brigantines reached the mouth of the Caroni, which descends to the Orinoco from the savannahs to the south. Raleigh looked on the river as the highway to what he called 'the golden partes of Guiana', but he found it in spate, the currents so strong that in an hour his barge of eight oars had advanced no more than a stone's throw. He decided to continue on foot, and at the same time search for a silver-mine which Berrio had mentioned. Indians encouraged him by saying that the Caroni descended from a great lake, on which lived three mighty nations — Lake Parima. The country which he saw and the series of falls on the Caroni inspired some of Raleigh's finest descriptions:

When we ronne to the tops of the first hils of the plaines adioyning to the river we beheld that wonderful breach of waters, which ran down *Caroli*: and might from that mountaine see the riuer how it ran in three parts, above twentie miles of each and there appeared some ten or twelue overfals in sight, euery one as high ouer the other as a Church tower, which fell with that fury, that the rebound of waters made it seeme as if it had beene all couered ouer with a great shower of rayne: and in some places we tooke it at the first for a smoke that had risen ouer some great towne. For mine owne part I was well persuaded from thence to have returned, being a very ill footeman but the rest were all so desirous to goe neere the said straunge thunder of waters, as they drew me on by little and little, till we came into the next valley, where we might better discern the same. I never sawe a more beautifull countroy, nor more lively prospects, hils so raised heere and there ouer the vallies, the river winding into divers braunches, the plaines adioyning without bush or stubble, all faire greene grass, the ground of hard sand easy to march on, eyther for horse or foote, the deare crossing in every path, the birds towards the euening singing on euery tree with a thousand seuerall tunes, cranes and herons of white, crimson, and carnation pearching on the rivers side, the ayre freshe with a gentle easterlie winde, and every stone we stooped to take vp, promised eyther golde or siluer by his complexion.

In spite of the sly copywriter's sales-point of the last phrases no one who has travelled across the Gran Sabaña and seen the smoke of waters rise from a gorge could fail to respond to the beauty and exactness of Raleigh's description. Yet still they found no great mine or even the tribes who were supposedly enemies of the Guianians, and whom Raleigh, clearly with Cortés and the Tlaxcalans in mind, hoped to make his allies for the assault on the Empire. Reconnaissances were made, and Raleigh was tireless in his questioning of every Indian they met on their way. It is remarkable that, considering the language difficulties, he should have learnt so much that was reasonably accurate and that his tribal and place names are recognizable today; in 'Arawagotos' we see 'Arawaks', in 'Barema', Barima; even in 'Europa' the River Guarguapo. If his romantic imagination made him over-credulous of the fantastic stories of wealth and fabulous creatures he made amends by his accurate contributions to geography, natural history and ethnology; he did find oysters that grew on trees and even if no Empire of Guiana lay south of the Orinoco it was finally proved to have its 'golden partes'.

El Dorado and the Empire of Guiana were the obsession of the remainder of Raleigh's life. They were the mainstay of his long years of unjust imprisonment, and appear like a Wagnerian *leitmotiv* throughout his *History*. He made assays of Guiana ore in the hen-house of his little garden in the Tower, and he was served there by the son of Topiawari, a Carib chief. Every year or so he sent a trading ship to Guiana to take his greetings to the Indians and to promise them he would return one day to deliver them from the Spaniards. In 1611 he made a bid to secure his release by offering to make another expedition to El Dorado. In his proposition to the Government he said that he was 'ready vpon a Mappe of the Country to make demonstracion [of the gold] if It please your Lordshipps to give me leave, but to the Kings Majesties wisdome and your Lordshipps I submitt myselfe. But that which your Lordshipps due promise is that halfe a Tunne of the former oare being brought home that then shall I have my Liberte. . . .'

It was not until 1617 that his offer was accepted. King James needed money; he also wished to remain on good terms with Spain — though, again, 'the desire of golde aunswered many obiections'. The outcome is famous; Raleigh, old and weakened, set out for the Orinoco, promising the King that he could reach the gold-mines without having to set foot on territory claimed by Spain. Gondomar, the machiavellian Spanish Ambassador, warned the settlement of San Thomé, at the mouth of the Caroni, of the approaching expedition. He planned to crush the man who had humiliated Spain at Cadiz. By the time they reached the Great Mouth of the Orinoco, Raleigh was too ill to make the journey up-river. Lawrence Keymis with a small force was detailed to find the mines, but not to fall foul of the Spaniards. Keymis found that San Thomé had been transplanted to another site, and now lay in his direct path to the mines. There was a clash in the forest, and finally Keymis made a successful assault on San Thomé, from which, however, he had to flee when it was besieged by the garrison. He arrived back at Trinidad to tell Raleigh of his failure, and that his son Wat had been killed in the fighting. Raleigh was horrified; he knew that all was lost, that he would return now to England without a sight of El Dorado, and return to his execution. Keymis killed himself in his cabin, and sadly the little fleet set sail eastwards.

Gondomar demanded that Spain should have Raleigh for execution, but the King did not allow this final injustice. Raleigh had not brought him gold; his death was necessary if friendship with Spain were to continue. So Raleigh was executed; Time had paid him with earth and dust. Among the contents list of his personal possessions left in the Tower are samples of Guiana gold and silver ores: a gold whistle set with diamonds, a seal of Neptune with Guiana ore tied to it, charts of Guiana and the Orinoco, and sixty-three gold buttons. One feels that even as he died he thought of the words he had written over twenty years before:

> *Guiana* is a countrey that hath yet her Maydenhead, never sackt, turned, nor wrought, the face of the earth hath not been torne, nor the vertue and salt of the soyle spent by manurance, the graves have not been opened for gold, the mines not broken with sledges, nor their images puld down out of their temples. It hath never been entred by any armie of strength, and never conquered or possessed by any Christian Prince . . . To speake more at this time, I fear would be but troublesome. I trust in God, this being true, will suffice, and that he which is the King of Kings and Lorde of Lordes, will put it into her hart which is the Lady of Ladies to possess it,

if not, I will iudge those men worthy to be kings thereof, that by her grace and leaue wil vndertake it of themselues.

But no Englishman ever set out again in search of El Dorado; only the poets dreamt as Raleigh had dreamt and acted on his dreams. Chapman wrote:

> Guiana, whose rich seat are mines of gold,
> Whose forehead knocks against the roof of stars,
> Stands on her tiptoes, at fair England looking,
> Kissing her hand, bowing her mighty breast,
> And every sigh of all submission making,
> To be her sister and her daughter both,
> Of our most sacred maid. . . .

And Milton, remembering the country that 'hath yet her Maydenhead', wrote of

> Rich Mexico, the seat of Montezume,
> And Cuzco in Peru, the richer seat
> Of Atabalifa, and yet unspoiled
> Guiana, whose great City Geryon's sons
> Call El Dorado.

APPENDIX B

The Caribs

I MADE my first contact with Carib-speaking people in British Honduras. Early one morning, during a trip by boat down the coast of the colony, I saw two long dugouts approaching us from the palm-fringed beach. The canoes were piled with pawpaws, pineapples and pink flat fish which were offered us for sale in an excited flow of language which I later gathered to be Carib — a language which, if one judged by sound alone, would seem to have nothing whatever to do with the soft monotony of Guiana Carib speech. The boatmen had all the physical characteristics of the Negroes of the colony, but they were members of a tribe who called themselves Caribs and lived a life quite separate from that of the African Creole. They were the descendants of African slaves who in the eighteenth century escaped from their plantations to an island where they married Carib women. Their children grew up to speak their mother's tongue, and the language of the Ashanti coast was forgotten, although the strong blood of Africa has won complete physical domination over that of the Caribbean. In 1795 the British Government suspected these Afro-Caribs (or Sambos) of alliances with the French and they were banished to the island of Ruatan, in the Gulf of Honduras, from where, when labour became short in British Honduras, they were transported to the coast of the southern part of the colony. It was here that I would hear their drums late at night, beating the Carib dance rhythms, and see them lying all day under the palms keeping each other amused with Carib tales.

They are not the only Caribs of the West Indian islands. A handful live on St Vincent and there is a Carib reserve on Dominica; but most of these so-called Caribs have Negro blood. In a small town on Trinidad I saw an ancient woman, African to the eyes, sitting in her armchair on the roadside to wave a greeting to Princess Margaret as she passed. She was, I was told, the Carib Queen, with her courtiers.[1] There are a few other pockets of Caribs in the Caribbean, but most are impure. There is, in all that great and beautiful sea, only a handful left of the race that filled Crusoe's heart with such fear, and who made fierce resistance against the invading *conquistadores*.

When the Marques had told me that the name for their tribe was Carinye, I suspected that Carib was an accepted corruption, for the early explorers of the New World confounded their mis-hearings of native words with an imaginative orthography. Raleigh, who had a poet's ear for the niceties of sound, refers to a tribe known as Carinepagotos (*pagotos*: people), but he talks of them as if they

[1] In 1831 there were 762 pure Indians on Trinidad, according to Robert Schomburgk.

were different from the 'Caribas' whom he refers to elsewhere. Columbus talks of the Caripunas on Haiti, and the French explorers of Galibis, but the first reference to Caribs comes in a letter of Peter Martyr in which he shows that Carib and cannibal had by now become synonymous: '*Edaces humanorum carnium novi helluones anthropophagi, Caribes alias Canibales appellati.*' The anthropophagy of the Caribs was one of the causes of their decimation; in 1504 Queen Isabella decided that such people could not expect Christian mercy and allowed her colonists to exterminate or take into slavery all who bore the name of Caribs. The Spaniards then discovered that the Carib race was far more extensive than had at first been supposed. The Spanish historians of the period say that Caribs could be found on all land between the Virgin Islands, near Puerto Rico, and the Amazon, that is between nineteen degrees of latitude. Peter Martyr says their source is the Punta Caribana in the Gulf of Darien, and others give maps with Caribana written along the whole Venezuelan coastline of the Caribbean. But the true Carib homeland[1] lies between the Orinoco and the southern mountains of the Guianas; the islands were Carib colonies won by conquest from the Arawaks and Ygneris who had originally settled them. Humboldt, with an uncustomary taste for the eccentric, believed that the Caribs moved southwards along the cordillera of islands from the peninsula of Florida, finally reaching the mainland of the southern continent. His argument is not convincing, and is mainly based on the findings of a Mr Brigstock, who uses the word Carib as if it were in use among the Indians, and were not a corruption. He believed that they were expelled from Florida by a stronger tribe, which is out of keeping with the Carib reputation for fierceness and prowess in battle.

From whichever direction they came, once their war canoes were established on the waters of the Caribbean, they dominated the smaller islands, making no attempt to invade the larger islands. They came, like Vikings, without their women, and as they settled they took Arawak women as their wives, who, retaining words of their original language, gradually evolved a new language for use among themselves, distinct from that spoken by the men. Some writers have misunderstood this disparity of language, thinking that the men produced a new language for discussing war and battle so that the secrets of a campaign would not be given away by their wives. This strikes me as an ingenious fancy.

During the time I was with the Guiana Caribs I gathered there were various meats, usually that of animals not indigenous, that were taboo. I did not ask them whether human flesh was on the proscribed list, but it seemed to me then how strange it was that a race from whom the word cannibal is derived should be so fastidious over comestible meats. Columbus was the first to report the anthropophagous habits of the Caribs, though his note has been preserved only indirectly by Bartolomé de las Casas, who says, 'Dice màs el Almirante que en las islas passadas estaban con gran temor de *carib*: y en algunas los llamaban *caniba*;

---

[1] I call this their homeland because it is in this area that they settled most securely in historical times. It is still not known what form the diffusion of the culture took. Some modern ethnologists believe that Guiana was the nexus from which the culture spread, but recent archaeological work has shown that the culture came into Guiana at a comparatively late date, from which direction no one knows.

pero en la Espa ola *carib* y son gente arriscada, pues andan por todas estas islas y comen la gente que pueden haber.'[1] The letters of Columbus have flights of fancy which show him to have been closer to the medieval cosmographers than to Renaissance man, but this testimony and the accounts of those who followed him cannot be ignored as inventions. All the same it puzzled me to find that there is only one story in the entire mythology of the Guiana Indians which refers to Carib cannibalism, and this is a myth of the despised Warraus which might be of recent date. In the sixteenth century the Spaniards excused their enslavement of the island Indians by convincing Europe that anthropophagy was the common custom there. Those nineteen degrees of latitude and the royal edict gave the colonizers liberty to do as they pleased with Indians who, without any doubt, were not cannibalistic. The area of Caribana conveniently covered the country of the supposed Empire of El Dorado. In a grave Latin tract the *cavaliere servente* of Lucrezia Borgia, Cardinal Bembo, gave full credence to the reports, saying, 'Some of the islands are inhabited by a cruel and savage race, called Cannibals, who eat the flesh of men and boys, and captives and slaves of the male sex, abstaining from the flesh of women.' With equal gravity the Spanish historian Herrera describes how the Caribs of a small island were converted from man-eating by sickness following a feast of roast Dominican friar. Père de la Borde, in the seventeenth century, wrote of the Caribs that 'They say that Christians would give them the stomach-ache, nevertheless not a year ago they ate the hearts of some Englishmen.' De la Borde, though a Frenchman, supported the Spaniards' divine justification for the rape of the Carib dominion. 'God,' he says, 'permits the whole of Europe to seize upon the country of this people, because they are so great a disgrace to their Creator, whom they will not recognize. Notwithstanding all that has been told them during the last twenty years they laugh at it, and the only hope of making them Christians would be first to civilize them and make them men.' Humboldt claims that cannibalism (on a smaller scale than supposed) only took place in the islands, and that the Caribs of Guiana held it in horror. Other continental tribes, however, he believed to be cannibals, though his evidence is hearsay, and I wonder if he was not the victim of Indian humour when a young mission Indian (and therefore a little sophisticated) told him that his people found that the tastiest part of a man was the palm of his hand. An apparently reliable old chief told him that three tribes in the Orinoco area ate their prisoners as a form of vengeance. The frequent absurdity of the early writers on cannibalism is best exemplified by a passage in Rochefort's *Histoire Naturelle des Antilles de l'Amérique* (1658) in which he says that Caribs had assured him the flesh of Frenchmen was considered most excellent by his people, and next that of the English; the Dutch were tasteless and the Spaniards too stringy and gristly.

All the evidence suggests that cannibalism did take place, by island and continental Caribs, but that it was far from being an orgiastic banquet, with the

---

[1] The Admiral says, moreover, that they had great fear of Caribs as they were passing the islands. 'Some call them Canibas, but in Spanish Carib — and they are a bold race, who travel about these islands and eat the people they can get.'

flesh eaten as food. An interesting passage in Richard Schomburgk's *Travels* shows the purpose of anthropophagy in an unaccustomed light.

Although [he says] the Caribs in the Colony are generally accused of cannibalism, especially by the Negroes, who still relate with horror what their parents told them about their eating the flesh of the fallen during the quelling of the Negro uprising in 1763, this was distinctly denied not only by my old chief but by all others from whom I made enquiry. The former told me the following about it. After a victory gained, their forefathers usually brought back to the settlement an arm or leg of the slaughtered enemy as a trophy, which would then be cooked so as to get the flesh more easily off the bone; a flute was made out of this to be used as an instrument on the next war expedition. One still frequently finds in the Carib camps such flutes made from human bones. At the big feasts which were celebrated immediately after their return in honour of the victory won, these trophies played an important role, and it was open to anyone to taste the cooked flesh. In order to increase their courage, however, and their contempt for death — a property that was ascribed to this measure — they cut out the victim's heart, dried it at the fire, pulverized it, and mixed the powder with their drink.

There is the stamp of truth about the old chief's explanation. Clearly the object of cannibalism was a kind of transubstantiation in reverse: the flesh or the powdered bone contains the living spirit of the dead. The Guiana Indians, like Christians, believe in the life everlasting of the spirit. Crevaux, in his *Voyage dans l'Amérique du Sud* (1883) talks of Cayenne medicine men going to the grave of a colleague and consulting him on certain matters. Each part of the body was supposed to be the residence of a separate spirit, and Theodor Koch-Grünberg, in *Zwei Jahren unter den Indianern* (1910) suggests that the bones were the final resting place of the spirits after the rest of the body was no more. This would explain the special concern with bones, which were drunk in powdered form or used — by the Island Caribs — for prophecy and witchcraft. The continental Caribs would dig up the body of a relation after a year and stack the bones in a neat basket which would be hung from the roof of the hut. This transference of spirit was, I feel sure, the real purpose of anthropophagy among the mainland and island tribes.

Whatever the cause, the Caribs were feared by all the islanders and soon were the dominant people in the Caribbean. They came to think of themselves as a master race; a sense of superiority even a century ago was apparent in their bearing and way of speaking. 'We alone are a nation,' went one of the proverbs, 'the rest of mankind are meant to serve us.' Humboldt says that he saw a Carib child, no more than ten years old, foam with rage because he was taken for a member of a tribe that had been nearly exterminated by his own people. One recognizes this pride of person only occasionally in Père de la Borde's character of his island Caribs — but he was clearly angry with them for their lack of interest in the religion he had come to proclaim.

'They have a sad temperament,' he says, 'and are dreamy and melancholic. They will sit silent for a whole day and care as little about the past as the future.' When he taunted them by calling them savages he seemed surprised that they should say that Christians seemed just as bad in their eyes, because they didn't live in Carib fashion. Tolerantly they would tell him that they had their ways of doing things and Christians theirs. When he preached to them about the delights of Paradise they did not beam with thoughts of future happiness, which the innocent Father took as a sign of their bestial nature. 'They are never willing', he says tetchily, 'to go and enjoy the delights which are above, because they must first die: and, as they have no other desire but those of the present life, they get angry when they are spoken to about going to Paradise. They are altogether unwilling to leave their present goods for future ones, quit what they possess for what is unknown to them.' It was clearly a congregation to have delighted Locke or Rousseau. He found them to have neither ambition nor anxiety; their conversation was confined to anecdotes about fishing, hunting and travelling, and in the intervals between conversation they would play on their flutes made from the small bones of Arawaks. The Caribs had a reputation for chastity, but as the friar succinctly and ingenuously puts it, 'I can affirm to the contrary.'

Père de la Borde is very interesting on the subject of couvade or *kenonimáno*, the tradition by which a Carib father takes to his hammock after the birth of a child, to be cared for by the mother as if he himself had gone through the pangs of birth. Like the cannibalism, this apparently ludicrous practice has been frequently misrepresented as an excuse for paternal indulgence, but in fact the period of couvade was[1] a period of penalty and restriction; the father, whose relationship to the child is greater than the mother's, inflicts suffering on himself for the child's benefit. De la Borde says that the fasting lasts for three months, and the man only leaves his hammock at night. If couvade is broken, and he eats the flesh of the proscribed animals, the child will not be brave and will have the physical characteristics of the animal whose flesh has been eaten. At the end of the fast the man is brought to a public place where, standing on two large circles of cassava bread, he is cut all over with agouti teeth, painted, and then ceremoniously fed by the women with bread. His child is rubbed with the blood produced from the cuts. After this the man returns to his hammock for two days' convalescence, and the couvade is over except for the proscription of certain animals for another six months. Richard Schomburgk says that the purpose of this cruelty was to transfer the father's courage, proved by demeanour during the ordeal, to his child. Schomburgk's passage on the subject is worth quoting:

> After the baby's birth, the father hangs his hammock near that of his wife, and keeps child-bed with her until the navel-string falls off. During this period the mother is regarded as unclean, and the father, before com-

[1] I came across no examples of couvade during my journeys, but the custom still exists among the more primitive Indians.

mencing his share in the ceremony, must, if he possesses no special house
for the reciprocal lying-in, separate his bed from hers by a palm-leaf parti-
tion. Neither the father nor mother may perform any work: the former can
only leave the house of an evening momentarily. The usual bath is forbidden him, and he dares not touch his weapons. The two of them may
only quench their thirst with luke-warm water and their hunger with pap
or cassava bread, which has to be prepared by one of the relatives. Still
more extraordinary is the prohibition not to scratch their body or head with
the finger-nails, for which purpose a piece of the leaf-rib of the cokerite
palm is hung close to the hammock. The neglect of these orders and pro-
hibitions will entail the death or life-long sickness of the infant.

Walter Roth found evidence that the Caribs' belief in the strength of the
father-child relationship was great enough for a myth of one-time male parturition to have arisen:

Uraima once had in his possession a bird's egg, which he kept in a
calabash; he took great care of it until it should hatch out. He met two
girls on the road: they saw the egg and asked him to let them have it. 'No,'
he said, 'I cannot.' They worried and even followed him, but he still refused. So they seized the egg, and in the course of the scuffle broke it.
Uraima then said to the women: 'Since you have done this, trouble will
follow you from now onward. Up to the present the egg has belonged to
man. For the future it will belong to woman and she will have to hatch it.'
It is only the female that lays eggs nowadays.

The tribal customs of primitive peoples reveal weird and fascinating aspects
of the human mind, but they are usually too distant for us to see in them even
the dimmest reflection of ourselves. On the other hand, their religions and
spiritual beliefs are produced at those primordial levels where the whole world
becomes kin. I was brought up to believe that there had been a revelation of
God to all men, and although, in my arrogant childhood, I decided that God
was a conception of Man rather than Man a conception of God, I had always
supposed that the conception of God was universal. From my conversations
with the Marques and other Christian Indians I realized that the idea of a supreme
God was something which had no interest for them — because the original
beliefs of their people were animistic and terrestrial. The early missionaries
found it difficult to understand that the tribes they were converting had no
God and no gods, but only the spirits of stones, rivers, trees and animals. Fray
Gumilla, in his *Historia Natural del Rio Orinoco* (1791), made great efforts to
discover Indian names for God, but he writes:

... no outward ceremony of divine worship or adoration has been observed. Nor are the terms which express God in the different languages so
particularized and indubitable as to convince us of their sure and certain

signification. The Caribs call God Quiyumucon i.e. Our Big Father, but it is not sufficiently clear whether they mean by this expression the First Cause or the most ancient of their ancestors.

The Jesuits Jean Guillet and François Béchamel (1698) managed to get the Caribs to acknowledge the existence of a God. 'But they do not worship him,' they wrote. 'They say he dwells in Heaven, without knowing whether he is a Spirit or no, but rather seem to believe he has a body.' The truth was that the Indians had not, and still have not, reached that stage of intellectual development when God or gods can be conceived. Even the animism which gives spirit to all inanimate objects does not allow for a being which has power over the object; the spirit is, to all intents and purposes, the thing itself. A study of the animism of the Guiana Indians can only convince one of the extremely slow evolutionary process which must be undergone by the divine revelation. Christianity has brought many civilized advantages to the Guiana Indians, but by short circuiting the evolutionary process, by attempting to turn animists overnight into believers in the Holy Trinity, it has produced a meaningless confusion in the Indian mind. I know that the Christian cannot accept (though he may believe) the idea of evolution in religious thought, but by not doing so he has made possible a remark to a missionary by an Amazonian cacique which is the *reductio ad absurdum* of the enforced conception of God: 'He [the cacique] told me he himself was God, and born of the sun, saying that his soul went every night into heaven to give orders for the next day, and to regulate the government of the universe.'

Although no traveller has ever come across that warlike tribe of women for whom the Amazon was named, I think the legend was supported by the known willingness of Carib women to fight beside their husbands when extra forces were necessary. Peter Martyr says, 'In the sanguinary opposition shown to the Spaniards the women, after their husbands had been killed, defended themselves with such daring and desperate courage that they were taken for Amazons,' and as late as 1823, during the slave insurrection in British Guiana, in which Caribs played a part, their women fought with them. However, it is certain that the Caribs themselves, as well as many other tribes, had traditions of a tribe of women who received men only once a year for purposes of parturition. Humboldt believed that the legend arose from the early travellers' desire to discover a survival of the life of the first age of the world, as described by ancient Greek historians, but if the legend was in existence in South America before the arrival of the Europeans this would not be a sufficient explanation. Orellana, making his magnificent descent of the river that was to be called the Amazon, was attacked by male and female warriors, and the origin of the idea has usually been attributed to him, though Columbus's account of his first voyage mentions an island of fighting women. Raleigh[1] clearly saw in the story of Amazons

[1] In his *Natural History of Guiana* (1769) Bancroft writes: 'The Caribbee Indians retain a tradition of an English chief who many years since landed amongst them, and

an opportunity to make a tribute to his Queen. He believed most of what he heard from Indians and Spanish prisoners, though not that they mutilated their bodies for the freer drawing of the bow: 'that they cut off the right dug of the brest I do not finde to be true'. By the time the missionary Father Acuña came to write his account of the Amazon the myth had had time to ripen, and his detailed account of the manner of life is clearly based on hearsay. Condamine, in the late eighteenth century, amazed the French Academy by declaring his belief in the Amazon women, and goes into the matter carefully in his *Amérique Méridionale* (1778). Robert and Richard Schomburgk found strong traces of the tradition on their travels, and were assured that the women lived at the head-waters of the Corentyne. From all the accounts I have read it seems that the tradition is only found among tribes who were in contact with the Caribs; all lines of inquiry lead to the Carib women as the Amazon originals. I should, however, mention the dampening paragraph in Wallace's *Travels* in which he attributes the myth to the long hair and breastplates worn by the natives of the River Uaupes. 'I am convinced,' he says, 'any person seeing them for the first time would conclude they were women.'

Wherever I travelled among the Guiana Indians I gathered that, for them, the natural state was one of happiness and contentment, and that all things evil in life were the work of spirits militating against the natural order. The Caribs have myths which suggest that the original sin was, as in Christian-Hebraic mythology, committed by Man himself, unaided by the spirits. A Carib told Walter Roth that in ancient times all were happy, no one ever died and you could fish by putting your calabash into the water, but that the Caribs themselves had put Yurokon, the Bush Spirit's baby, into the pepper-pot, and evil had come into the world as a result. Apart from the interesting reference to cannibalism this tale of original sin is typical of the strong, almost masochistic feelings of guilt which Carib mythology expresses. The other tribes are much less concerned with their own shortcomings. This, and the extraordinary beauty of much Carib pottery, suggests that in spite of their anthropophagous leanings they were a people at a higher state of intellectual evolution than the other tribes of the area. Their mythological imagination was more luxuriant, their sense of poetry more advanced.

The least attractive side to the Carib nature was their willingness to act as slave-traders for the European colonizers. The Dutch Governors of Guiana authorized post-holders at various points in the colony to barter European goods for slaves and, echoing the Royal Fifth of the Spanish Conquest, the Governor received every sixth slave as his personal property, without payment. For many years a proportion of the slaves on the plantations of the Corentyne, Essequibo and Pomeroon were Indians supplied by the Caribs. This tribe, favoured by the Dutch, was accordingly most hated by the Spanish Govern-

encouraged them to persevere in enmity to the Spaniards, promising to return and settle amongst them and afford them assistance, and it is said they still preserve an English Jack which he left them, that they might distinguish his countrymen.' This English chief must have been Raleigh or Laurence Keymis, who commanded the party which went up the Orinoco on the last ill-fated voyage.

T

ment and colonists north of the Orinoco. Caribs organized the contraband trade along the Spanish and Dutch coastlines and made cattle-raids on the Catholic missions; they tried to seduce Indians converted to Catholicism back into the true Carib way. The Spanish missionaries saw a sinister connection between these activities and the fact that the Caribs were in league with the Dutch. Humboldt, who had read everything that was then available on his subject, says that the works of the Spanish priests are 'filled with complaints of the *secta diabolica de Calvino y de Lutero*, and against the heretics of Dutch Guiana, who also think fit sometimes to go on missions, and spread the germs of social life among the savages'.

On one occasion, at least, the Caribs took advantage of the colonists' ignorance of the Interior. In 1810 the Carib chief, Maharnava, came down the Essequibo to Georgetown on a state visit to the Governor. He let it be known that his tribesmen could be counted in scores of thousands, all warriors thirsting for war and conquest. He does not appear to have directly threatened attack, but some sense had told him to play on the Europeans' known dread of his anthropophagous people. Maharnava told the Governor and the Court of Policy that he could keep his hordes under control — if given the means. His suggested tribute was handed over by the genuinely frightened colonists and he was invited to return the following year to receive the same amount of Danegeld. This he did, but his imagination now rioted to such an extent that the Governor decided to send a Commission to his country to discover the strength of his warrior force. This, the first English or Dutch expedition to penetrate the Interior of the colony, was led by a Georgetown physician, Dr Hancock, whose report revealed the extent of Maharnava's *fourberies*. He had no more than a few hundred scattered tribesmen. Hancock's *Observations on Guiana* (1835) was the first book to describe the Interior of British Guiana.

When slavery was abolished in British colonies the slavers dealt with the planters of Surinam, and in 1836 Robert Schomburgk met a party of Caribs on the Berbice river on their way to make a slave-raid on the Makushis of the Rupununi savannahs. The Dutch — and later the British — used the Caribs to recover Negro slaves who had run away into the bush. If, in the process, the Negroes were killed, the Caribs would barbecue a hand and take it to the postholder who, on seeing the proof, paid them so much for each hand. With the end of slavery these Indian allies of the colonists no longer had a practical use, and the long contact between them and the Europeans decreased, the Caribs moving farther inland where they tried to make the difficult return to their traditional ways of living. The British did little for Indian welfare, a betrayal that was on the conscience of Governor Light when, in 1838, he wrote of the Indians:

We used these people as auxiliaries — they were useful and faithful; we made them presents, often misapplied, too often baneful; their influence lost much larger numbers of Indians than at present are within our borders — it is evident, if some equally powerful motive were presented, they would again appear. We owe them a debt; let us endeavour to repay it in a useful way to ourselves, but let it be beneficial to a fallen race.

A vivid description of the conditions of the Caribs who had gone inland is given by William Hilhouse, who travelled among them in 1837. He found them 'lazy, drunken and faithless . . .' and says:

> . . . I found them . . . in a state of starvation . . . they were mere animated skeletons, and on enquiring the cause of all this squalid misery, I found it, strange to say, the result of the Protestant Mission established at the confluence of the Mazaruni with the Essequibo,[1] whose first essay at conversion had this melancholy effect. They had taught religion but not industrious habits, supplying the wants of the Indians without an equivalent return of labour, and, by the abolition of feasts and dances, abolishing also that provision of cultivation requisite for the supply of Piworry, their native drink, consumed enormously on such occasions, but the stock of cassava planted for which was always a security from famine.

When he reproached them for having planted so little cassava they said, 'We are Christians and God will feed both us and our children.' Hilhouse's wise words ring soundly today. The more intelligent missionaries realize the delicate nature of their task, that false emphases and thoughtless acts may produce in the Indians echoes of the neuroses found in civilization. I would often wonder, as I listened to my Caribs talking at night, what shape their thoughts took, exactly how their processes of mind differed from ours. Was there void at those levels where the civilized mind burns with its purest energy, was their unconscious as exciting a collection of repressions and sublimations, of censored egos and militant ids as a modern European's? It is the differences in the minds of all races on earth that is one of the most proper and fascinating studies of mankind. Yet it is a study which anthropology can only brush against; it inquires into the folk memories of primitive people, oral traditions that have been changed or modified down the centuries so that we can today only glimpse the ancient nature of these peoples in the contemporary accounts of often gullible travellers. How difficult it will always be to know what part the Carib has played, or is playing, in Pope's 'Vast Chain of Being'! Did Pope speak true when he wrote:

> Lo, the poor Indian! whose untutor'd mind
> Sees God in clouds, or hears him in the wind;
> His soul, proud Science never taught to stray
> Far as the Solar Walk, or Milky Way,
> Yet simple Nature to his hope has giv'n,
> Behind the cloud top't tower, an humbler heav'n . . .
> To Be, contents his natural desire,
> He asks no Angel's wing, no Seraph's fire;
> But thinks, admitted to that equal sky,
> His faithful dog shall bear him company.

[1] Now the site of Bartica.

APPENDIX C

A Note on the Carib Language

WITH the diffusion of Carib tribes from Guiana to the islands of the Caribbean the original language has obviously been modified in many directions, but since the Barama Caribs are agreed to be the True Caribs perhaps their speech may be taken to be the purest. I only made comparisons between Barama Carib and Akawaio, but in the following comparative word-list I have included words taken from a Carib-French dictionary made by Father Raymond Breton on the island of Dominica in the early eighteenth century. I have not changed Father Breton's gallicized spelling of Carib words.

	Barama Carib	Akawaio	Dominica Carib
1	anim		
2	oko		
3	awrua		
4	okobami		
5	onyeboni		
6	anin yoepmrepu		
7	oko yoepmrepu		
8	anrua yoepmrepu		
9	onyambatori		
10	onyambatori		
animal	tonomwi	wok	tikali
arrow	puliwa	perlayo	bouleova
alligator	takali	akale	acayouman
beads	sepuru	kasulu	
big	apoto	eke	oubutonti
bird	tonoro	torou	
black	topolu	ikurung	tibouloue
black man	meitolo	meicoro	
bow	urapa	urapa	ubaba
brother	kami	uyakon	iloi
bush-cow	mapuri	maipuri	
bush-monkey	tearacahi	iwaga	
bush-pig	pongio	poinko	backira (cf. peccary)
Carib	Carinye		Calinago
dance	wano	umaname	abinacani
falls	marari	marari	
fish	oato	morok	aoto

flower	epolihi	ipeli	illehue
girdle of beads	kasuru *or* kuyu	waiko	
girl	wuoli	manayakanepo	
gun	arakabusa	arakabusa	huelekia
house	owto	owte	toubonoco
hammock	nimianko	akwa	
hat	sumbederdu	arok	ichikatahi
head	yopopo	upai	boupou
howler monkey	arawata	araouta	
I	au	ure	
ill	anuku	inik	aneketi
jaguar	tikusi	kaikuse	malacaya
little	mimboko	aiko	raheu
love	yabokuru	takel	ibouinetobu
macaw	queari	wayara	
milk	pakamanatil	manakeuku	manatoui
nose	yena'taili	e'una	ichiri
orange	aranka		kemeti
parrot	culewako	kirikiri	
pawpaw	puku paiya	kapaya	
pineapple	nana	kaiwala	yayaoua
pot	tumaiyene	oine	bouteicha
rain	konopo	tuna	
rice	arishi	arichi	
	(*Sp.* arroz)		
shaman	piaiyen	piaichan	
shirt	nopma	upon	
shoes	sapatos		
snake	akoyu	akoi	aakoua
socks	sapatolaoawundich		
spirit	akuru	ankuru	nacali
trousers	puruku	puruku	
village	witopo	pata	aothebowocou
virgin	miandato	manayakau	abourakeiru
water	tona	tuna	tone
woman	wuoli	uelichau	ouel
woodskin	wepipyu	yeipipe	
yes	eheh (*nasal*)		hanhan

In Barama Carib there are no words for happy or unhappy, but 'happy' in Akawaio is *poli*. Barama Carib appears to differentiate verb meanings with more exactness than Akawaio. 'To live' is thus *yemaya*; and 'to die', *lomosa*; while the same words in Akawaio are *tu ko man ton pe* and *tu ma ta ton pe* (lit. 'to not live'). Nouns change their forms, in both languages, to express possession: thus 'my hammock' is *pweatich*, and 'your hammock' is *amoro patich*. Verbs, conjugations in both languages are often complicated, but appear to be logical in formation. Two typical verb structures are those of 'to want' and 'to love', given here in the present indicative.

	Barama Carib	*Akawaio*
I want	she ma	iche eyaik
you want	amolo she ma	iche me yan
he wants	mose she ma	iche man
we want	she katato	iche ene
they want	she mando	iche tok uchi
I love	yapokuru mema	uni nunga
you love	mose apokuru mema	ani nunga
he loves	mose ose na	ini nungaya
we love	na na ose na	ina nunga
they love	mongkain ose nandang	tok uchi nunga

Archaeology of British Guiana

THE most important archaeological survey of British Guiana for many years was made by Dr Betty Meggers and Dr Clifford Evans in 1952-53. In the *Handbook of South American Indians* (vol. III, 1948) it had been suggested that the Tropical Forest Culture had first developed in the Guianas and spread out from there into the huge tropical forest area. The Evans-Meggers expedition set out to test this theory by looking for archaeological signs that the Guianas had been occupied for many hundreds of years. Its other aim was to find evidence of any influences which had passed along the Guiana coast from Venezuela and then up the Amazon. Sites in the North-West District were examined in great detail, as this area was a known point of contact between various tribes.

The oldest phase discovered (Alaka Phase) revealed a swamp-dwelling, shellfishing people whose few pottery utensils were received in trade from a pottery-making agricultural tribe. The age of the shell fragments cannot be decided by the carbon test, but it was not believed that this phase was very old.

The Mabaruma Phase followed the Alaka Phase and fourteen village sites were examined. Pots were made by these people, often with incised decorations of a simple nature which linked them with the work of the tribes of Trinidad and the lower Orinoco. As this style appears fully formed in the North-West District it is probable that these people came to this area from Trinidad and the lower Orinoco when their culture was well developed. A detailed analysis will show exactly when this expansion occurred.

Next came the Koriabo Phase which produced pottery inferior to that of the Mabaruma people, whose work was popular as trade goods. No source could be determined for the Koriabo Phase, but it was a culture which came into this part of British Guiana from outside .

In the Demerara District a survey was made of the Abary River which suggested that the Abary Phase may have come from somewhere to the north-west, beyond the present frontiers of the colony.

In the Rupununi Savannahs no sites were found of any great antiquity, nor was there any possibility of dividing the north and south savannahs into separate ethnographic areas. The earliest site discovered appeared to date from well into historic times.

In the forest area of the Upper Essequibo thirty-four sites were visited. In the Taruma Phase the tribe producing the distinctive pottery found was wiped out by an epidemic in the early years of this century, and had probably lived in this area for only a few hundred years.

The Wai-Wai pottery came from occupied areas; the Wai-Wais have been gradually moving into the Upper Essequibo area from Brazil since the extinction of the Tarumas.

At the time of writing the full results of the Evans-Meggers expedition have not been published, but its interim report suggests that several important general conclusions may be made from what was learnt of the tropical forest cultures. The *Handbook of South American Indians* suggests that the Amazon was settled by people with a Caribbean type of culture, advanced in religion and tribal organization, who reached the Amazon along the Venezuelan and Guiana coasts. During this migration it degenerated into the simpler Tropical Forest culture. Evans and Meggers believed that such a migration would be easy to trace archaeologically. In 1948-49 they excavated Amazon sites and found traces of the Tropical Forest culture — but with affiliations with tribes to the west, up the river. They found similar evidence against this theory in British Guiana; although the Orinoco-Trinidad culture had penetrated slightly and at a late date into the North-West, there was no evidence of a strong cultural diffusion from this direction. They could find no evidence, either, that the immigration moved straight from the Caribbean-Trinidad-Orinoco area to the Amazon, by-passing the Guianas.

The *Handbook* said that 'because the Guianas have the greatest number of traits regarded as characteristic of the tropical Forests, they may be postulated as a centre of dispersal'. Evans and Meggers believed that if this were so archaeology would show this type of culture to be at its oldest in the Guianas. Their excavations proved the opposite. The earliest archaeological sites are in the North-West and the most recent in the central areas of the colony. In the Rupununi and, most probably, the Essequibo Phases, pottery-making cultures date only from post-Columbian times. Their report makes it clear that the tribes moved into the Guianas at a comparatively late date and the area was not a cultural source. This discovery has led Dr Meggers and Dr Evans to search in another direction for the original source of the Tropical Forest culture.

POT FROM THE NORTH-WEST DISTRICT

The Schomburgks in British Guiana

In 1834 Robert Schomburgk (born 1804, Freiburg), was commissioned by the Royal Geographical Society to make an exploration of what Humboldt had called the *terra incognita* of Guiana. Humboldt himself had made exploration of the geography of the area north of the Orinoco and wished to know the exact physical character of the land to the south, about which he had made suppositions. Robert Schomburgk, who was an unsuccessful tobacco planter in the West Indies, had surveyed the island of Anageda (B.W.I.) for the R.G.S. His first explorations lasted three years, cost £900 and employed twenty-two people. From this expedition he took three Indians back with him to England, who entertained Londoners with demonstrations of arrow shooting and blowpipe expertise at a gallery in Regent Street. In 1840 he was commissioned to make a survey of the colony's boundaries, and for part of this expedition he was accompanied by his brother Richard (born 1811) who had been commissioned by the Tsar of Russia to make scientific collections. Richard's travels occupied him for four years. Robert was knighted by the British Government and was made British Consul in Santo Domingo in 1852 — later being given a similar post in Siam. He died in Berlin in 1865. In 1847-48 Richard published his *Reisen in Britisch Guiana*, and in the same year as the publication of the second volume he came under a cloud for his support of the 1848 revolution. He emigrated to Australia and farmed for sixteen years before becoming Director of the Botanical Gardens at Adelaide, where he died.

Richard Schomburgk's *Reisen* is the most important single work on the Interior of British Guiana, but I am assured by competent authorities that he is not to be entirely relied on in other than botanical matters. His narrative is prolix, but the book has many memorable passages. Richard put all his knowledge of the country into this book. Robert Schomburgk, on the other hand, wrote no large work on the colony, but contributed frequent long articles to the *Journal of the Royal Geographical Society*. I have read most of these articles, and it seems to me that of the two brothers Robert was incomparably the more gifted writer and the finer mind. He was without Humboldt's genius, but he frequently reminds one of the man whose work he was continuing.

The following is the bibliography of the Schomburgks' works:

Richard Schomburgk

Reisen in Britisch Guiana (3 vols., Leipzig, 1847-48) translated and edited by Walter Roth, Georgetown, 1922.

Robert Schomburgk

'Diary of an ascent of the River Berbice', *Journal of the Royal Geographical Society*, vol. VII, 1837.

'Expedition to the lower parts of the Barima and Guiania rivers', ibid., XII, 1842.

'Excursion up the Barima and Aryuni rivers', ibid., XII, 1842.

'Diary of an ascent of the Corentyne', ibid., VII, 1837.

A Description of British Guiana (London, 1840).

'Journey to the sources of the Essequibo, etc.', *Journal of the Royal Geographical Society*, vol. X, 1841.

'Journey from Fort San Joaquin to Roraima', ibid., X, 1841.

'Report of an expedition into the Interior of British Guayana', ibid., VI, 1836.

'Journey from Esmeralda to San Carlos', ibid., X, 1841.

'Visit to the sources of the Takutu', ibid., XII, 1843.

APPENDIX F

THERE are two parallels to the Awakaipu story of the massacre at Roraima (see pp. 243-5). In 1845 an Indian travelled through the Interior saying that he was God and would give everybody fine lands and would make a whole field of cassava grow from a single stick. He apparently had a large following.

The Report of May 25th, 1838, from the Presidency at Flores, Venezuela, tells its own story.

It is now more than two years ago that a man by the Indian name of Joao Antonio, living at Pedra Bonita, which lies about twenty miles distant from this township, surrounded by forest and close to two huge crags, called the inhabitants together and told them that enclosed in these crags was an enchanted Kingdom of which he proposed to break the spell, and that as soon as this was done King Don Sebastian would appear at the head of a large army. He thereupon busied himself clearing up the spot until November of last year when, at the bidding of the missionary Francisco José Correa de Albuquerque he removed to the desert region of Suhamon, whence he despatched an individual Jono Pereira, who, on his arrival in Pedra Bonita proclaimed himself King, and filled the minds of the people with all kind of superstition. He told them that in order to restore the kingdom it was necessary to sacrifice a number of men, women and children who, in a few days' time, would rise again and remain immortal, that great riches would be distributed among all classes and that all those of a darker colour would become white like Europeans. He thus managed to obtain numerous adherents to carry out his evil orders and wicked doctrine, and there were not even wanting parents who delivered up their own children to the knife of the bloodthirsty monster. On the 4th of the present month the sacrifices commenced and in the course of two days not less than 42 people had been slaughtered at his hands. But he came to a very miserable end.

SELECTED BIBLIOGRAPHY

APPUN, C. F., *Unter den Tropen* (Jena, 1871).

BEEBE, WILLIAM and MARY, *Our Search for a Wilderness* (London, 1910).

BODDAM-WHETHAM, J. W., *Roraima and British Guiana* (London, 1879).

BRETT, W. H., *The Indian Tribes of Guiana* (London, 1868).

BROWN, C. B., *Canoe and Camp Life in British Guiana* (London, 1877).

HINGSTON, R. W. G., *A Naturalist in the Guiana Forest* (London, 1932).

HUMBOLDT, ALEXANDER VON, *Personal Narrative of travels to the Equinoctial regions of America* (3 vols., London, 1852-53).

IM THURN, EVERARD P., *Among the Indians of Guiana* (London, 1883). *Thoughts, Talks and Tramps* (London, 1934).

KOCH-GRÜNBERG, THEODOR VOM, *Roraima zum Orinoco* (Berlin, 1911).

RALEIGH, SIR WALTER, *The Discoverie of Guiana* (London, 1596).

ROTH, WALTER, *An Enquiry into the Animism and Folklore of the Guiana Indians* (Washington, 1913).

SCHOMBURGK, RICHARD and ROBERT, *see* Appendix E.

WATERTON, CHARLES, *Wanderings in South America.*

WAUGH, EVELYN, *Ninety-Two Days* (London, 1933).

INDEX

'ABEL' (native religious leader), 225-7
Acosta, J., 271, 276
Acuña, Father, 280, 289
Aguirre, Lope de, 276-7
Alfinger, Ambrosio de, 272
'Amazons' (women warriors), 288-9
Amuku, Lake, *see* Parima
Animism, 24, 97-8, 226-7
Antonio (native porter), 232, 241, 247, 262, 264
Ants, Giant, 257-8, 259-60
Appun, C. F., 229-30, 248, 299
Arabopo, 254-6, 258
Arakaka, 70-77
Arapaima fish, 174, 180-1
Archaeology, 295-6
Arrowroot, 36
Atahualpa, 272
Ataro, River, 261-2
Atienza, Doña Iñez de, 274-5
Attenborough, David, 264
'Awakaipu Massacre, The', 243-5, 298

BALATA TRADE, 120, 127, 174
Bamford, James, 117-21, 139, 140, 148, 159, 160-2, 171, 265
Bancroft's *Natural History of Guiana*, 288
Barama, River, 76, 94-101, 102-4
Barima, River, 56-79, 96
Bartica, 121, 140, 173, 191-7, 220-1, 263, 266, 268
Béchamel, François, 288
Belalcazar, Sebastian de, 272
Bembo, Cardinal, 271, 284
Berrio, 277-8
Birds:
 Bellbirds, 86, 233-4
 Bunyas, 86
 'Cock-of-the-rock', 145
 Duraquaras, 88
 Kiskadees, 104
 Maam, 66, 85, 88
 Macaws, 85-6
 Music-birds, 102, 104
 Pai-paio, 85
 Parakeets, 99
 Parrots, 86
 Powis, 85, 86, 88

Roraima emerald, 247
Tinamou, 183
Tityra, 247-8
Trogon, 85, 86
Troupiole, 172-83
Trumpet, 96
Woodhewer, 183
Bleakly (geologist), 30, 31, 32, 33, 39
Blunt, Wilfred Scawen, 83
Boddam-Whetham, J. W., 229-30, 248, 299
Bogotá, 271, 272, 273
Booker's (Sugar Estates), 30, 185
Boundary Commission (1930), 118-19, 140, 265
Brazil, Adolf, 140, 183
Brazil, Boundary disputes with, 118, 125, 130-1
Brenan, Gerald, 190
Breton, Father Raymond, 292-4
Brett, W. H., 96
British colonialism, 105-10, 142
British Guiana Airways, 76, 128, 216
Brown, C. Barrington, 20, 229-30, 248, 299
Brown (bow-man), 197-202
Brown, Henry, 67-69
'Brown, Old' (engineer), 58-9
Butterfly species, 86, 190

CAMOENS, MR, 212
Cañete, Marquis de, 273
Cannister Falls, 217-18
Carib-speaking peoples, 282-91, 292-4
Caroni, River, 278-9
Cassava, 87, 90
Cattle trade, 127-8
Cecilia (wife of Guide William), 231, 233, 237, 238, 241, 242, 247, 254, 255, 256, 258, 264
Chang, Mr, 211-12, 216-18
Chapman, 281
Chitchas, The, 272
Church Missionary Society, 193
Cleveland, President, 73
Cocaine, 145
Cochrane's *Travels*, 271
Coffy (camp manager), 76-8, 81, 103
Columbite workings, 203, 207

301

Condamine, 289
Corentyne, River, 22, 289
Coro, 272, 273
Cortés, 272, 277, 279
Cossou (District Commissioner), 123-4, 136, 139, 140, 148, 160, 168
Couvade, 286-7
Crevaux, 285
Curare, see Urari
Cyril' (Marques), 80-1, 84, 87, 88-92, 94-6, 101, 102-3, 282, 287

DE LA BORDE, PÈRE, 284, 285-6
Dialects, Analysis of, 184-5, 292-4
Diamond digging, 141
Discoverie of Guiana, The, 61
Douglas, Norman, 15
Doyle, A. Conan, 32, 189, 252
Dutch settlers, 22, 34, 61-2, 72, 73, 80, 192, 289-90

EDDINGTON, C. A., 248
Electric eels, 214-16
Elizabeth I, Queen, 278, 289
Emeria, Mountains of, 72
Essequibo, River, 72, 73, 121-2, 133, 137, 191, 193, 246
Evans, Dr Clifford, see Evans-Meggers Expedition
Evans-Meggers Expedition, 295-6
Everard, Mt, 64-5, 70, 105-6

FARINE (NATIVE FOOD), 152
Federmann, Nicholas, 272

GENGHIS KHAN, 275
Georgetown, 18-19, 23, 30-1, 38-9, 57, 65, 76, 78, 105-14, 125, 128, 157, 184, 191, 212, 220, 264-5
Gold-digging, 25, 57-8, 67-8, 72-4, 93-4, 133, 158-9, 171, 204
Gondomar, 280
Gorinsky, Caesar, 124, 127, 217
Gorinsky, Mrs, 124, 127
Grumman amphibian, 41, 76, 103-4, 191, 212, 216-19, 264, 266-7
Guatavita, 271
Guiana, Bishop of, 184
Guillet, Jean, 288
Gumilla, Father, 36, 287-8
Guzman, Fernando de, 274-5

HAMMOCK MAKING, 65
Hancock's Observations on Guiana, 290
Harrison, Sir John, 30

Harte, Ben, 124, 127, 129, 132-6
Hawkins, 272
Herrera, 284
Hilhouse, William, 291
Hill, Reggie, 191, 197, 199-200, 203-5
Holder, Capt., 194-7
Hortsmann, Nicholas, 137-8
Howler-monkeys, 66, 183, 241
Hume, David, 73

IMBARANG, 41-55
Im Thurn, Everard, 248, 250 n
Incas, The, 37, 271-2
Indian Tribes:
    Akawaios, 92, 212-3, 218, 220-1, 224, 226, 228, 254-6, 292-4
    Arawaks, 37, 38, 56, 61-3, 68, 279, 283
    Arekunas, 227, 240-1, 248, 276
    Baramas, 77, 92, 98, 101, 292-4
    Caribs, 37, 41, 61, 62-3, 68, 77, 96, 282-94
    Makushis, 120, 125, 134-6, 139-59, 160-1, 174, 175-7, 181-2
    Motilones, 32
    Omaguas, 273, 274, 276
    Uaupes, 273, 289
    Wai-wais, 296
    Wapishanas, 120, 125-6, 148-51, 153-4, 155, 156, 159, 160-71
    Warraus, 36, 37, 38, 56, 61-3, 70, 97-8, 284
    Ygneris, 283
Inquiry into the Animism and Folklore of the Guiana Indians, An, 24
Iramaikpang, Mt, 145, 146, 147
Issano, 193-4, 196, 205, 266, 268

JAGAN, DR CHEDDI, 18-19, 108, 110-14, 142, 213
Jagan, Mrs, 112-14
Jay (geologist), 77
Jesuit methods examined, 164-6, 181-2
Jones, Dr Cenydd, O.B.E., 120

KAIETEUR FALLS, 266-7
Kaimaritepu, 242, 247
Kamerang, 191, 211, 216, 217, 218, 220, 224-230, 232, 233, 262, 263, 265
Kamerang, River, 233, 237
Kanuku Mountains, 120, 129, 139, 144, 145, 149, 150, 157, 161, 172
Kenaima (evil spirit), 50-4, 221-4
Keymis, Lawrence, 137, 280, 289 n
Kijk-over-Al Fort, 192, 197
Kirke, Henry, 73
Koch-Grünberg, Theodor v., 285
Kukenaam, Mt, 242, 245, 248, 251

Kukenaam, River, 242-3, 246, 247
Kukui, River, 261, 262, 263

LAND RECLAMATION, 113-14
Languages, 292-4
Leal, Capt., 131
Legend of Kaieteur, The, 19
Lethem, 139 ff
Lethem, Sir Gordon, 128, 144
Lewis, Major, 67-8, 70, 72
Light, Governor, 290-1
Lima, 274
Lukanani fish, 175-6

MABARUMA, 35, 39, 56
McKenna, Father, 158, 162-6
Macleod (police officer), 148-50, 153
McTurk, Edward ('Tiny') and Mrs, 172-83,
   216, 217, 262, 264
McTurk, Michael, C.M.G., 173, 182-3, 229-
   230, 248
Maharnava (Carib chief), 290
Mahu, River, 137
Manco-Inca, 272
Manganese, 25, 57, 75
Manoa, 62-3, 137-8
Margarita Island, 276
Marques, The, see Cyril and 'Rod'
Martinez, Juan, 277
Martyr, Peter, 283, 288
'Massakruman, The', 78-9, 204
Mather, Father, 132, 143-6, 164
Matthew's Ridge, 74, 77-8
Maya civilization, 57, 90
Mazaruni, River, 72-3, 121, 189-219, 246,
   263, 265, 266
Medicine-men, 170, 175, 182
Meggers, Dr Betty, see Evans-Meggers
   Expedition
Melville, Anita, 141
Melville, Charley, 148-9, 156-9
Melville, Edwina, 156-9, 160
Melville, H. P. C., 124-9, 133, 134, 141, 178
Melville, John, 127, 161-2, 166, 168-71
Melville, Lally, 127, 139, 140
Melville, Nelly, see Gorinsky, Mrs
Melville, Olga, 169
Melville, Teddy, 127, 141
Merume Mountains, 212, 217, 263
Milton, 281
Missionaries, 91, 123, 125, 130-1, 158, 162-6,
   181-2, 226-7, 290, 291
Mitchell, Joe, 224-8, 230, 232
Montezuma, 272, 277
Morawhanna, 35, 37

More, Capt., 205

NAPOLEON III, 22

'OCEAN SHARK', 134-6, 182
Ojeda, Alonzo de, 61, 62 n
Orinoco, River, 35-6, 39, 63, 73-4, 235, 246,
   267, 276, 280, 297
Ouchi, River, 235, 236
Oviedo y Baños, 271

PAKARAIMA MOUNTAINS, 121, 156
Parima, Lake, 136-8
Paruima, 228, 231-2
Peberdy, P. Storer, 119
People's Progressive Party, The, 108, 110
Pequeno, Capt., 194-7
Perkins, H. I., 248
Peru, 272, 273, 274, 275, 277-8
Philip of Castile, King, 276
'Piaiman', see Medicine-men
Pirai (or piranha), 177-8, 243, 264
Pizarro, 271
Population, 185
Potaro Gorge, 266-7

QUARIAD (NATIVE FOOD), 156
Quarica, King, 273
Quesada, Gonzalo de, 272-3
Quesada, Hernan de, 273
Quito, 274

RALEIGH, SIR WALTER, 16, 31, 36, 61-3, 72,
   73, 137, 146, 147, 167, 241, 246, 272,
   277-81, 282, 288-9, 299
'Robert' (Barama Indian), 98-100, 102
'Rod' (Marques), 80-1, 84-5, 88-92, 94-6,
   101, 103, 282, 287
Rodway, James, 73
Roger (Indian boy), 60, 64, 67
Roosevelt, Theodore, 178
Roraima, Mt, 32-3, 118, 189-91, 229, 230,
   231, 232, 233, 239-53, 255, 257, 265,
   266, 267, 268
Roth, Vincent, 23-5, 136 n, 193, 222, 265
Roth, Walter, 24, 134, 287, 289, 299
Royal Commission on the West Indies
   (1938-39), 119-20
Rupununi Development Company, 126-7,
   152-3, 161, 166, 167
Rupununi, River, 122, 162, 181, 248, 272
Rupununi savannahs, 65-6, 120-38, 141, 144,
   151, 152, 157

SAILLER, BARTOLOMÉ, 272
Samson (native assistant), 232, 241-2, 247, 264
San Thomé, 280
Schomburgk, Richard, 20, 38 n, 62 n, 69, 77, 89-90, 96, 130-1, 146, 223-4, 243-4, 248, 250, 285, 286-7, 289
Schomburgk, Robert, 20, 62, 74, 77, 96, 130, 147, 229, 243, 248, 282, 289, 290, 297-8
Seggars, William, 220-1, 228-9, 263
Shabbi (native drink), 152
Simon, Fray Pedro, 273-4, 275, 276
Smith (vet), 103, 139
Solomon (Chinese trader), 57-9
Southey's History of Brazil, 276
Spanish invaders, 61-2, 72, 105, 271-7, 279-280, 283-4, 289-90
Sugar industry, 107, 109-13, 185
Sugrim, Capt., 196, 197, 198, 201, 202

TALBOT, DR, 38
Tasso (native dried meat), 152
Teresa, Sister, O.B.E., 56-7
Tobago, 267-8
Towakaima Falls, 76, 80, 94, 98, 104
Trinidad, 267, 277
Tumareng, 191, 205, 208-12
'Turkey, The Sultan of', 205-7
Turner (Rupununi Development Co. Manager), 166-7

UBUTEPU, 237
Ucucuamo ('Mountain of Gold, The'), 137
Ukutuik Falls, 260
Uraianda Village, 240-1
Urari, 145-8

Ursua, Pedro de, 273-5
U.S. Government, 73-4

VAMPIRE BATS, 200
Venezuela, 61-2, 74
Venezuela, British disputes with, 16-17, 73-74, 81-2, 118, 197
Victor (air pilot), 64
Vierra, Austin, 229, 231, 232, 234, 235, 236, 237, 240, 241, 248-9, 250, 251, 252, 253, 254, 255, 257, 258, 261, 262, 263, 264, 265
Vierra, Peter, 229, 232, 240, 241, 247, 248-9, 251, 252, 253, 254, 256, 262, 264
Von Humboldt, Alexander, 86 n, 137 n, 215, 236, 271, 273, 276, 277, 283, 284, 285, 290, 297
Von Huten, Philip, 273
Von Speier, Georg, 272
Von Tschudi, 69

WALLACE'S 'TRAVELS', 289
Warimatepu, 235, 236
Waterton's Wanderings, 146-7, 200, 299
Waugh, Evelyn, 120, 123, 134, 167, 299
Wendt, Harry, 127-9
Wichabai, 127, 161, 166
Wilcox, Obadiah, 213-14
'William' (boat-hand), 207
'William' (guide), 231, 232, 237, 238-9, 241, 242, 245, 254, 256, 258, 264
Wilson (anthropologist), 39-40, 41-55
Women, native treatment of, 151-2, 232

YOUD, MISSIONARY, 130-1